The Other Samuel Johnson

ALSO BY Peter N. Carroll:

Puritanism and the Wilderness: The Intellectual Significance of the New England Frontier

Religion and the Coming of the American Revolution (Editor)

The Restless Centuries: A History of the American People (Coauthor)

The Free and the Unfree (Coauthor)

The Other Samuel Johnson

A Psychohistory of Early New England

Peter N. Carroll

Rutherford • Madison • Teaneck
Fairleigh Dickinson University Press
London: Associated University Presses

Associated University Presses, Inc.
Cranbury, New Jersey 08512

Associated University Presses
Magdalen House
136–148 Tooley Street
London SE1 2TT, England

Library of Congress Cataloging in Publication Data

Carroll, Peter N.
The other Samuel Johnson.

Bibliography: p.
Includes index.
1. Johnson, Samuel, 1696–1772. 2. Church of England–Clergy–Biography. 3. Clergy–New England–Biography. 4. New England–Biography. I. Title.
BX5995.J59C37 283′.092′4 [B] 77–74413
ISBN 0–8386–2059–0

PRINTED IN THE UNITED STATES OF AMERICA

For my parents,
Bessie Nurko Carroll
and
Louis Carroll,
who introduced me to my first Oedipus complex

CONTENTS

PREFACE

The Samuel Johnson of this study—a distant relative of the more celebrated English lexicographer—lived and died in provincial New England far from the metropolitan exploits described by James Boswell. The two Samuel Johnsons never met. They moved in different circles and held different opinions about the contemporary world. The New Englander's rusticity contrasted markedly with the studied polish of his London namesake and where the American Samuel Johnson extolled the idealist philosophy of Bishop Berkeley, the Englishman, with a famous thrust of his foot, roundly dismissed the metaphysics of immaterialism. What the two Samuel Johnsons shared, however, was a lack of genius—an intellectual pedestrianism that kept their minds firmly grounded in the well-traveled byways of eighteenth-century thought. In their own ways they stand as representative figures of their times.

If the American Samuel Johnson lacked a Boswell to record his verbal agility, he nevertheless preserved a treasure of personal documents—sermons, diaries, essays, letters, and memoirs—that reveal the inner workings of his mind and his heart. From this wealth of material we may reconstruct an interaction between the man and his culture, a convergence between his personality and the wider contours of social activity. We may observe the formation of a mature personality and explore the subtle relationships between emotional, sometimes unconscious, feelings and more visible behavior. We may witness too the congruence of personality, role, and ideology. This broad level of analysis constitutes a "psycho-history," a historical methodology that strives to integrate the study of individuals and history.

Though scholars in many fields have adopted a psychohistorical approach, historians of colonial New England have been particularly attracted to this methodology. Within the past decade, they have studied such children of New England as Jonathan Edwards, Benjamin Franklin, James Otis, and the Salem witches. In part, these studies reflect a general interest in historical celebrities; they also represent the culmination of over four decades of rigorous scholarship.

Following the impressive work of Perry Miller, Samuel Eliot Morison, and Edmund S. Morgan, numerous historians have examined the complexities of Puritan thought. Of course, not everyone agrees about the conclusions of that scholarship. But to a remarkable degree, historians of early America share a general paradigm about the workings of the New England mind. And because of the prodigious research we know a great deal about Puritan ideas and values, the ideals that the settlers professed, and their attitude toward God, nature, and humanity.

During the past decade, moreover, several social historians, employing the insights of historical demography, have produced microcosmic studies of Puritan institutional life. Focusing upon scattered New England towns, the demographers have described the relationship between family organization and landholding, population trends and social structure. Their research has presented important information about the visible patterns of New England life, the behavioral norms, the institutional structure in which the Puritan ideology functioned. These studies, however, have generally ignored the questions raised by earlier intellectual historians. Though usually aware of the cultural implications of their findings, the demographers have said little about the relationship between family life and the value structure held by the Puritan colonists.

This sophisticated scholarship—from the perspective of both intellectual history and demography—provides an indispensable basis for psychohistorical investigation. The psychohistorian assumes that human beings shape, and are simultaneously shaped by, a larger culture. Such visible manifestations as ideology, beliefs, or overt behavior reflect a human cause; similarly, the created patterns of a culture influence the personalities of its members. These reciprocal relationships—and here it should be emphasized that the psychohistorical position is not monocausal—suggest a coherence of human existence, a linkage of cultural values, behavioral norms, and individual personalities. Thus psychohistory offers the possibility of bridging the scholarship of the demographers and the intellectual historians. If Puritan values and institutional patterns shaped the children of New England, these same children eventually became exponents of certain values and practiced specific behavioral forms. Chapter 2 constitutes a tentative exploration of the synthetic implications of a psychohistorical approach to colonial New England.

While psychohistory may offer new directions for historical research, it nevertheless retains important methodological limitations. The analysis of personality presumes the existence of sufficient documentary evidence. Yet few people are as prolific as Samuel Johnson and fewer still as concerned as he with preserving a historical record. Thus psychohistory remains an elitist discipline—at least for periods of widespread illiteracy or until scholars elucidate viable theories of generalization. Moreover, even people like Samuel Johnson become remarkably silent about the most ordinary—but perhaps most significant—aspects of their lives. Without adequate data, psychohistory easily reduces to mere speculation, what Sigmund Freud once condemned as "wild analysis."

In transcending these difficulties, the psychohistorian draws upon the fullness of his own life experience, both professional and personal. As in other disciplines, the interpretation of evidence requires a sensitivity to the subject, an awareness of persistent patterns as well as striking exceptions. Thus a significant slip of the pen followed by an unusually passionate letter provided valuable insights into Samuel Johnson's attitude toward the Great Awakening. Psychohistory also benefits by the researcher's ability to understand the subject by understanding himself. In analyzing the emotional patterns of one's own life—much as Freud first studied his own dreams—the psychohistorian develops a sensitivity to nuances that otherwise might escape him. Many of the insights of this book, particularly the notion of generational interaction, reflect not so much psychoanalytic theory as the personal experiences of the author. Such subjectivity inevitably affects all research. Psychohistorians merely attempt to control this situation by raising subjective feelings to the level of consciousness where they may be examined along with more traditional hypotheses.

Finally, a word about strategy. I have assumed that ordinary people can understand other ordinary people within the context of ordinary language. For this reason, I have avoided the esoteric phraseology of psychoanalysis and have transcribed most of the eighteenth-century quotations into modern English. For similar reasons, I have occasionally omitted interpretations that I believe to be true, but that, for want of hard evidence, might not be persuasive to most readers. For example, in listing his family genealogy, Samuel Johnson misplaced the birth of an aunt who had died long before he was born. The aunt bore the same name as two of Johnson's sisters, both of whom died prematurely. Did his error then constitute a fear of death? Or was it that the name was also that of his grandmother, the deceased wife of his beloved grandfather? The absence of further evidence makes virtually any interpretation plausible and I have consequently chosen to ignore the problem. Johnson's impact upon his descendants also deserves further attention, but that task probably requires another full-length volume. What is presented here, then, may be viewed as a case study of psychohistorical interpretation. And hopefully it speaks not so much about Samuel Johnson as about ourselves.

ACKNOWLEDGMENTS

In planning and writing this book, I have drawn freely on the counsel of many people—some close friends, some complete strangers—who have helped me in more ways than I could adequately acknowledge. During the research stage, Amy Carroll offered valuable guidance and assistance that greatly facilitated my efforts. Bob Ferry, my sometime research assistant on this project, maintained a healthy detachment throughout, reminding me frequently that one should render unto Caesar the things which are Caesar's while doing research. Joseph Ellis, whose book became available too late to be used in this study, generously shared his knowledge of the sources despite what could have become a nasty rivalry. Two of my former colleagues at the University of Minnesota, Bernard Bachrach and James Tracy, kindly translated Johnson's Latin, while David Freedman of Columbia University translated some of the Hebrew. Along the way, the staffs of the libraries mentioned in the bibliography provided efficient service, but special mention should be made of V. Nelle Bellamy of the Church Historical Society in Austin, Texas; Mildred B. Phillips, Town Clerk of Guilford, Connecticut; and Adeline Vitkowski and Virginia Moskowitz of St. Paul's Episcopal Church in Mt. Vernon, New York, who went beyond the call of duty. The research was partially supported by grants from the Graduate School and the Office of International Programs of the University of Minnesota as well as by a Younger Humanist Fellowship from the National Endowment for the Humanities. Several friends and colleagues read all or part of the manuscript. Judy Modell made numerous suggestions for improving the early drafts, as did Kinley Brauer, John Modell, and Peter Loewenberg. In the later stages, Jeannette Ferrary was an astute critic and a wonderful friend.

ABBREVIATIONS USED IN THE NOTES

HP	Francis L. Hawks and William Stevens Perry, eds., *Documentary History of the Protestant Episcopal Church in Connecticut*, 2 vols., facsimile ed. (Hartford, Conn., 1959).
HU	Miscellaneous MSS., Houghton Library, Harvard University
JCU	Samuel Johnson MSS., Columbia University
JHP	Samuel Johnson MSS., Hawks Papers, Church Historical Society, Austin, Texas (microfilm)
JYU	Johnson MSS., Yale University
MHS Colls.	*Collections of the Massachusetts Historical Society*
NEHGR	*New England Historical and Genealogical Register*
Pub. Recs. Conn.	J. Hammond Trumbull and Charles J. Hoadley, eds., *Public Records of the Colony of Connecticut*, 15 vols. (Hartford, Conn., 1850–90).
SJ	Samuel Johnson
SJ Papers	Herbert and Carol Schneider, eds., *Samuel Johnson: President of King's College: His Career and Writings,* 4 vols. (New York, 1929).
SPG	Society for the Propagation of the Gospel.
WSJ	William Samuel Johnson.
WSJ Mss.	William Samuel Johnson Mss., Connecticut Historical Society, Hartford.

Introduction

SOME THEORETICAL ASSUMPTIONS AND IMPLICATIONS OF PSYCHOHISTORY

The emergence of psychohistory as a field of inquiry is not unlike the story of Topsy, who grew. As a result, it has never developed a formal methodology nor established an orthodox procedure. Psychohistorians frequently disagree among themselves about the implications and direction of their discipline. Moreover, the term *psychohistory* has too often subsumed a multitude of intellectual omissions and scholarly sins. But an intellectual approach should not be assessed merely by its weakest expressions any more than the novel genre be judged by the racks at the corner drugstore. The following essay attempts to explain the theoretical assumptions that support this particular psychohistory. By implication, these assumptions could extend to other types of psychohistory as well. The essay also addresses questions that relate to other approaches to history, and attempts to suggest the value of psychohistory for all historians.

Historians have traditionally confined their analyses to the visible aspects of culture—social institutions, behavioral patterns, created artifacts, and articulated ideology. For colonial New England, we know a great deal about the conscious levels of life: what people did, what people said, and what people said they did. We may therefore describe Puritan life in terms of specific behavioral patterns (e.g., people attended the churches in declining numbers), an articulated ideology (e.g., only saints should be considered church members), and explicit evaluative statements (e.g., the failure of children to undergo conversion experiences signified the sinfulness of the society). From this perspective, the historian may depict changes in behavior or values and may speculate about the sources and significance of such changes. Thus an apparent disparity between professed values and actual behavior has led historians to infer the existence of mass insecurity and collective anxiety at the end of the seventeenth century.[1]

These studies generally ignore the inner lives of their subjects. In analyzing the visible layers of human society, historians assume that historical figures respond emotionally as they themselves would react to similar situations. The assessment of motivation therefore usually involves the application of a "common sense" psychology, heavily laden with the historians' own sense of "normal" responses.[2] Besides clouding our understanding of the unconscious life of individuals, this emphasis upon external activity precludes the possibility of exploring the unarticulated assumptions that bind social groups. All members of a society implicitly accept certain premises that, consciously or unconsciously, structure their lives and inform their self-conceptions. Thus, to understand the meaning of life for members of past culture, to extrapolate how historical participants evaluated themselves and their times, historians must penetrate to the unexplored world of the unconscious and semiconscious.[3]

This plea for the psychological investigation of historical subjects reflects more than a desire to examine the mental activity of historical celebrities, for the study of "great men" needs no additional justification; Martin Luther, Adolf Hitler, or Henry Ford invite further study of their lives, because historians already consider them important figures.[4] The careers of people of lesser stature, however, offer equally valuable lines of historical inquiry. All people live in cultures; all people inhabit specific societies and accept some notion of history. As products of time and place, individuals influence and are influenced by a wider cultural nexus. Examination of the external levels of culture reveals only part of the larger whole; a search for the emotional meaning that contemporaries ascribed to these visible relationships opens a second level of analysis. Moreover, the study of individuals controls the tendency of social scientists to transpose human attributes onto social groups. Many people may share ideas and emotions—indeed, an entire society may accept certain principles or express similar feelings; but in every case, these beliefs and feelings reside within the minds of individuals. To understand the subconscious layers of human activity, historians must base their interpretations on the life experiences of specific people. Only then can historians speak of the contemporaneous *significance* of particular aspects of culture.[5]

The discipline of history faces two formidable tasks. First, it must refine suitable concepts that explain the relationship between people and culture. Second, it must develop meaningful categories for generalization. Both problems require historians to seek analytic assistance from other disciplines. But in both cases history has much to offer in return. Besides extending the range of case studies necessary to confirm the hypotheses of other disciplines, history can explore these concepts *over time*. The notion of change—perhaps the most fundamental assumption of historical analysis—permits the historian to perform comparative investigation in changing temporal contexts. By focusing upon contemporaneous participants in different temporal cultures, historians may analyze the relationship between institutional change and value change, biological change and social change, cultural change and personality development. Such study should illuminate not only the direction and impact of change, but also the origins of change.

The present inquiry logically begins by examining the relationship between an individual and a culture, a process aptly characterized by Erik Erikson as a "psychosocial relativity."[6] The writings of such "ego psychologists" as Erikson, Anna Freud, and Heinz Hartmann have emphasized the fundamentally *social* basis of all stages of personality development.[7] As an individual passes from infancy to adulthood, he or she acts and reacts with a responding cultural milieu. The process of maturation involves increasing self-definition within the changing structure. Thus the newborn narcissistically views itself as the center of the cosmos, capable of ordering the world by demanding satisfaction. With biological maturity and growing self-awareness, the child becomes more sensitive to the *portions* of the world that it controls. The process of self-discovery–always measured within a social context–culminates at adulthood with an understanding and acceptance of a coherent personal "identity."[8] In the end, a person answers the question "who am I?" with reference to a perceived and perceiving environment. As Erikson has stated it,

> in psychological terms, identity formation employs a process of simultaneous reflection and observation, a process taking place on all levels of mental functioning, by which the individual judges himself in light of what he perceives to be the way in which others judge him in comparison to themselves and to a typology significant to them; while he judges their way of judging him in light of how he perceives himself in comparison to them and to types that have become relevant to him.[9]

This process of self-definition remains unconscious for the most part. Yet at all stages identity formation involves an outer world. First, an infant alters and reacts to a family environment; later, a child extends its domain beyond the immediate household to include an ever larger territory of experience. Consciously and unconsciously, a person recognizes what he is capable of doing and what he is not, what he may do and what he may not, and ultimately, who he is and who he is not. The resolution of such questions often entails great risks for the child and, depending upon the reality of one's initial self-image and the security of the environment, the growing child will emerge from this self-exploration with a clearer sense of himself. There is nothing inevitable about this developmental process, and each culture attempts to create a responding environment that will "socialize" a child into the dominant institutional and ideological patterns. Thus each culture endeavors to awaken psychological constellations in its offspring that will make the children sensitive to the dominant social sanctions.

The concept of identity–the categories by which an individual perceives himself in terms of others–provides a cultural basis for personality development. Moreover, the formation of an adult identity represents the outcome of a developmental process through which all children must pass. Each culture may define these stages of life in its own way, and there exist important variations among cultures. Thus recent studies suggest that the "adolescent stage" appears only in certain societies.[10] Yet *within* a culture, the stages of the life cycle remain fairly constant, presenting children with similar types of experience and offering them similar forms of expression. At each stage of life, the children of a culture confront specific problems relating to their biological growth and the demands of socialization. Obviously, individual members of a society react to these stages with considerable variation. But by defining patterns of self-expression, each culture creates a *finite range of acceptable alternatives.*[11] Thus, while personality development remains an individual problem, the cultural levels of that process suggest the possibility of generalization.

The developmental basis of personality presumes that specific life experiences influence the formation of an individual's identity–his understanding of his "psychosocial relativity." In social terms, each individual confronts particular opportunities that limit and define his place in the culture. Among these factors are structural locations–for example, a person's situation in terms of status, role, power, wealth, geography, and so on. Historians have employed these categories for a variety of interpretive purposes; thus, the increase of social and geographical mobility during the seventeenth century explains in part the growing discord in the New England towns. Equally important in creating personal boundaries is the individual's sense of his place in time. Consciously or unconsciously, all people locate themselves in history, as participants in a temporal epoch, as members of a generation.[12] Thus colonial New Englanders viewed themselves as sons, grandsons, or great-grandsons of the founding fathers. This historical lineage provided explicit boundaries for the members of the society and influenced, in fundamental ways, the identities of the children of New England.

The notion of a generation derives logically from biological and genealogical phenomena. Parents "generate" children who eventually "regenerate" themselves in the cycle of life. The concept also possesses important social dimensions. A person's biological and psychological age–his place in the life cycle–locates him in social and cultural terms as well. People born at the same time in the same culture frequently share similar experiences specific to themselves that affect their psychosocial development.

This sense of contemporaneity often gains reinforcement from a major historical event—a political crisis, an economic catastrophe, a scientific discovery—which serves to further define the generational group. In early America, for example, the transatlantic crossing or the intrusion of royal power represented significant generational events for colonials.[13] To be contemporaries, of course, does not necessarily mean that individuals *will* share common experiences (any more than all members of a class or status group necessarily experience the same things). Nevertheless, individuals often identify with temporal social groups and view their lives in generational terms. The concept thereby introduces the possibility of generalizing about some of the inner workings of a culture.

A social generation—measured not in chronological time, but in terms of the stages of life—encounters common experiences that affect the content and intensity of emotional relations; such a group participates in an inner community. Moreover, a generation shares distinct relationships with other contemporary (but not contemporaneous) generations. Each generation inherits a series of symbolic relationships from preceding generations which, positively or negatively, defines its place in the culture. Older generations seek symbolic regeneration in their progeny, while younger generations find spiritual continuity through their ancestors. "Parents lend children their experience and vicarious memory," remarked George Santayana; "children endow their parents with vicarious immortality."[14] The dialogue between generations thereby constitutes a basic level of historical interaction.

The simultaneous existence of several generations introduces various perspectives to the historical vista. Ortega y Gasset has noted that

> at every moment of history there exists not one generation but three: the young, the mature, the old. This means that every historical actuality, every "today" involves . . . three different actualities, three different "todays." Or to put it another way, the present is rich in three great vital dimensions which live in it together, linked to one another whether they like it or not, and, because they are different, essentially hostile to each other.

Each generation therefore responds not only to contemporary events, but also to the *responses* of the other contemporary generations to those same events. Children respond to their parents' responses, while the parents' reactions are influenced by those of their children. The existence of three contemporary generations further complicates the patterns. These interactions provide insight into the subtle process of historical change. For as the meaning of events alters between generations, so too does the cultural nexus.[15]

All cultural changes–in behavior, values, or self-image–begin in the life experiences of particular individuals and then, depending upon their general relevance, incorporate wider segments of the society.[16] Geographical isolation, cultural homogeneity, and environmental stability retard such change.[17] Yet, within cultures, the differing relationships that exist between subgroups create varying *perspectives* among members of the culture. Such structural differences prevent the simple repetition of cultural arrangements over time. Children do not react as their parents do because the *basis* of their experience is already distinct. Even without such amorphous concepts as "creative imagination," a structural explanation of change would exist. Moreover, for similar temporal reasons, a culture's relationship to its environment and to other cultures is never constant; the experience of younger generations also reflects the antecedent experience of its predecessors.[18]

The multiplicity of human experiences, the uniqueness of each person's relationship to the culture, the individuality of each "identity"–all diminish the possibility of creating a totally homogeneous culture. Each person's understanding of accepted behavioral norms and ideal values, though often shared with others, nevertheless reflects an individual perspective. Culture therefore in itself involves a process of shifting perspectives. These perceptual differences provide the basis for cultural change. People conceive or execute new things in the context of their perspective of the culture. Such innovations need not be regarded as deliberate or even as conscious.

Although the possibility of cultural change appears to be pervasive, most people cling to traditional forms, seeking security within familiar patterns of life. The persistence of cultural arrangements reflects not only human conservativism, but also a striking inability of people to perceive innovations. Members of a culture comprehend novelty from traditional perspectives and strive to interpret observed phenomena within the old frameworks. Even innovations that logically should threaten dominant values and practices are often defined and explained as adjuncts of the old order. *Recognition* of internal disparities requires a sense of detachment from the traditional patterns; positive *acceptance* of the innovations involves a radical shift in one's perspective.[19]

The members of a culture may embrace paradoxical values or even accept contradictions between their behavior and their values. Human societies reveal a remarkable ability to transcend such inconsistencies. For cultural change to occur, an alternative model of behavior or values must emerge. Innovative patterns may derive from individual creativity or, more commonly, from contact with an outside culture.[20] Such "intrusions" present members of the culture with an alternative configuration of values and norms. The "recipient" culture may reject the alternative, accept the new way, or attempt to synthesize the two (which is another type of cultural innovation). In any case, the interaction between the competing systems creates a crisis in the original culture, forcing individuals to reexamine their place in the world. In this sense a cultural crisis may be reduced to a series of "identity" crises, for external changes of this sort directly affect the "psychosocial relativity" by which individuals locate themselves in time and space.

These cultural contacts do not affect all individuals in the same way.[21] People who enjoy emotional satisfaction in their psychosocial position, who accept their "identities," would be least affected by the availability of alternative patterns of culture. People with less rigid or less-integrated identities (alienated, dissatisfied, or confused individuals) would be more susceptible to acceptance of the intruding alternative. Most important, children and young people, with only partially formed identities, would be less committed to the existing order and consequently would approach the competing alternatives directly. Their attitude toward the cultural crisis would be influenced not only by the visible choices at hand but also by the reactions of specific symbolic figures in the older generations.

The emergence of a cultural crisis places different types of burdens upon the various members of a society. As people in different status or economic groups enjoy particular advantages and suffer from specialized vulnerability, so too do individuals in different stages of the life cycle experience heightened strengths and weaknesses. Young infants, for example, are especially exposed to psychological impairments caused by irregular nutrition, while more mature people may particularly dread the possibility of sudden death. Such emotional patterns also affect a person's attitude toward more subtle changes. There is, of course, no inviolable connection between the stages of the life cycle and the response to cultural innovation. But it is observable that young people tend to embrace change, while older people—men and women with durable emotional commitments to the traditional order—tend to reject innovation. Indeed, conflicts between generations assume massive proportions in rapidly changing societies because of the intensity of these personal commitments. The elderly, in confronting cultural crises, defend the very meaning of their past lives, fearing that their children may deny them a symbolic immortality. The young who lack such symbolic commitments can afford to seek spiritual sustenance in new ways.

The presence of an alternative system forces individual people to reassess their lives. Those who reject the alternative model find security in the old way and seek to bolster the previously dominant system. They lament all historical innovations, which presumably corrupt the original purity of their society. Meanwhile, individuals who accept the new order seek to transform their lives in accordance with what they perceive to be a superior alternative. They attempt to imitate an articulated ideology, strive to create similar institutional arrangements, and crave more durable symbolic associations. Above all, they condemn the vestiges of the old way that interfere with acceptance of the new. Finally, a third group of people attempt to resolve the crisis by harmonizing the two patterns. These are the "synthesizers," who seek security and tranquillity in the present (rather than the past or the future) and who endeavor to transcend the contradictions involved in blending the rival movements. These alternative reactions, to be sure, need not be conscious; they are no less profound for that. For a crisis in a culture compels all people to confront what previously had been only assumed.

The dialogue between cultural alternatives often introduces a dialogue between the generations. In challenging the values of an existing culture, the external system threatens the symbolic sanctions that had served to socialize younger generations. The invading culture, by offering alternative symbols, denies the inviolability of the traditional order. This repudiation of the original system may liberate individuals from previously sacred social restraints. For specific people, it becomes possible to think the unthinkable, to choose the impossible.[22] Thus an innovator not only accepts new cultural patterns but also rejects the traditional patterns of older generations. In rapidly changing societies the generation gap becomes more pronounced and intergenerational conflict appears more pervasive.

The imperatives of the socializing process, however, can never be entirely obliterated. Early childhood experiences remain deeply ingrained in the unconscious of the maturing individual. The dialogue between the generations remains open on numerous symbolic levels.[23] The acceptance of one level does not necessarily destroy intense loyalties on another. Dutiful children, frustrated by changes in the external order, may endeavor to fulfill their own *past* by repudiating its visible forms. Such excursions, whether liberating or suppressive, reveal the subtle symbolic interplay within and between cultures. These inner lines of communication speak ultimately from the depths of the human life cycle.

The foregoing concepts help to explain the historical process in colonial New England. First-generation colonists, though usually adults at the time of their migration to the New World, established particular institutions and articulated a peculiar ideology. These external boundaries, together with the crucial role of geography, enabled these people to forge distinct identities as New Englanders.[24] Their children—the second generation—matured in a somewhat similar context. The ideology, the institutions, the mother country—all helped shape their psychosocial location. Yet, in addition, the children responded to the first generation, the symbolic patriarchs who built the first settlements in the wilderness. Third-generation New Englanders reacted to the ideology, the institutions, England, the founding fathers, the second generation, and the second generation's reactions to the first and third generations. The increased life span in seventeenth century New England, moreover, suggested that the first generation lived long enough to respond not only to their children but to their grandchildren as well.[25]

This multigenerational interaction structured both the inner and the outer worlds of the colonists of New England. As the settlers built more stable communities, as English politicians and businessmen intruded on the region, as parents begat children and buried the dead, the psychosocial relationships changed as well. The symbolic levels of that interchange remain to be found. In the life of one culture—Puritan New England—and in the life cycle of one man—Samuel Johnson—we commence that exploration.

NOTES

1. For citations regarding colonial New England, see the notes to chap. 2. The idea of collective anxiety appears in numerous works, most clearly in Clarence L. Ver Steeg, *The Formative Years* (New York, 1964), chap. 6.

2. Critics of the use of psychoanalytic approaches to history argue that the applicability of post-Freudian models is suspect since we cannot know for certain *how* people in past cultures thought. The same caveat could apply to *all* historical investigation. Historians assume that the thought processes of mankind are essentially constant and that their subjects remain psychologically and organically similar to themselves. To take a relativistic position about human nature logically forces the historian to reject *all* present-day mental activity—rational and irrational—as indicative of the thought patterns of past mankind. Very suggestive in this respect is Hans Meyerhoff, "On Psychoanalysis as History," *Psychoanalysis and the Psychoanalytic Review* 49 (1962): 3-20. A different approach to this problem is J. H. van den Berg, *The*

Changing Nature of Man: Introduction to a Historical Psychology (New York, 1964).

3. George M. Foster writes, "The members of every society share a common cognitive orientation which is, in effect, an unverbalized, implicit expression of their understanding of the 'rules of the game' of living imposed on them by their social, natural, and supernatural universes. A cognitive orientation provides the members of the society it characterizes with basic premises and sets of assumptions normally neither recognized nor questioned which structure and guide behavior in much the same way [that] grammatical rules unrecognized by most people structure and guide their linguistic forms. . . . The average man in any society cannot describe the underlying premises of which his behavior is a logical function." See "Peasant Society and the Image of Limited Good," *American Anthropologist* 67 (1965): 293–94.

4. The writing of psychobiography has become increasingly popular in recent years. For an early bibliography, see Bruce Mazlish, ed., *Psychoanalysis and History* (Englewood Cliffs, N.J., 1963), pp. 181–83. The classic study remains Erik H. Erikson, *Young Man Luther* (New York, 1958).

5. Abram Kardiner has warned that "to lose track of the sharp differentiation between individual and group, and of the fact that society is not an individual, is to abandon the chance for any precision in studying reciprocal relations empirically." See *The Individual and His Society* (New York, 1939), pp. 85–86. See also H. G. Barnett, *Innovation: The Basis of Cultural Change* (New York, 1953), p. 15.

6. Erik H. Erikson, *Identity: Youth and Crisis* (New York, 1968), p. 23.

7. For a discussion of some of this literature, see David Rappaport, "A Historical Survey of Psychoanalytic Ego Psychology," printed with Erik H. Erikson, "Identity and the Life Cycle," *Psychological Issues* 1 (New York, 1959): esp. p. 15.

8. Erikson has suggested the existence of eight stages of life, extending from birth until death; see "Identity and the Life Cycle." The process of self-definition continues throughout life, but for purposes of this discussion I have emphasized the formation of an adult identity.

9. Erikson, *Identity: Youth and Crisis,* pp. 22–23.

10. See, for example, John Demos and Virginia Demos, "Adolescence in Historical Perspective," *Journal of Marriage and the Family* 31 (1969): 632–38. In a provocative essay Kenneth Keniston points to the importance of further refining our categories of analysis within the stages of the life cycle; see "Psychological Development and Historical Change," *Journal of Interdisciplinary History* 2 (1971): 329–45.

11. Erikson has observed that "the historical era in which [an individual] lives offers only a limited number of socially meaningful models for workable combinations of identification fragments." See *Identity: Youth and Crisis,* pp. 53–54.

12. There is a vast literature dealing with the concept of generations. Most helpful in this respect were the following: Francois Mentré, *Les*

Générations sociales (Paris, 1920); Karl Mannheim, "The Problem of Generations," in *Essays on the Sociology of Knowledge,* ed. Paul Kecskemeti (London, 1952); Detler W. Schumann, "Cultural Age-Groups in German Thought," *Publications of the Modern Language Association* 51 (1936): 1180–1207; Yves Renouard, "La Notion de génération en histoire," *Revue historique* 209 (1953): 1–23.

13. Lewis S. Feuer observes that "often a generation's consciousness is shaped by the experience of what we might call the 'generational event.' . . ." See *The Conflict of Generations: The Character and Significance of Student Movements* (New York, 1969), pp. 25–26.

14. George Santayana, *The Life of Reason or the Phases of Human Progress* (New York, 1906), 2: 36.

15. See José Ortega y Gasset, *What Is Philosophy*?, trans. Mildred Adams (New York, 1960), esp. pp. 32–39.

16. Barnett, *Innovation,* p. 39.

17. Robert A. Nisbet, *Social Change and History: Aspects of the Western Theory of Development* (New York, 1969), p. 281.

18. Ortega has written: "In history it is important to distinguish between the state of being coeval and that of being contemporary. Lodged together in a single external and chronological fragment of time are three different and vital times. This is . . . history's essential anachronism. It is thanks to that internal lack of equilibrium that history moves, changes, wheels and flows. If all contemporaries were coevals, history would stop as if paralyzed, petrified in one definitive gesture, lacking all chance of any radical innovation." See *What Is Philosophy*?, p. 34.

19. Extremely insightful in this respect is Thomas S. Kuhn, *The Structure of Scientific Revolutions,* 2d ed. (Chicago, 1970).

20. See Nisbet, *Social Change,* pp. 281-82; Barnett, *Innovation*, p. 42; Allen Wheelis, *The Quest for Identity* (New York, 1958), p. 201; Karl Mannheim, *Ideology and Utopia* (London, 1936), p. 282. Mircea Eliade declares: "No such thing as an absolutely closed primitive society exists. We know of none that has not borrowed some cultural elements from outside; none that, as the result of these borrowings, has not changed at least some aspects of its institutions; none that, in short, has had no history." See *Rites and Symbols of Initiation* (New York, 1958), p. xi. For a different emphasis, see Robert Jay Lifton, *History and Human Survival* (New York, 1971), pp. 55–56.

21. See Lifton's essay "Images of Time," in *History and Human Survival,* chap. 2, and Kuhn's *Structure* passim. One scholar has observed that the overlap of generations means that "certain events and experiences will come to all of them. Yet each group will be affected differently because it will face any given event at a different stage in its development and will therefore assimilate it differently." See Harold S. Jantz, "The Factor of Generation in German Literary History," *Modern Language Notes* 52 (1937): 324–30.

22. For a provocative analysis of this problem, see Fred Weinstein

and Gerald M. Platt, *The Wish to be Free: Society, Psyche, and Value Change* (Berkeley, Calif., 1969).

23. See Erik H. Erikson, "Youth: Fidelity and Diversity," *The Challenge of Youth* (Garden City, N.Y., 1965), p. 23.

24. Though the Puritan founders continued to live in an international Protestant community, their exodus to New England affected their self-images in fundamental ways. Being in New England made them different from other people; they realized this situation and strove to transcend it.

25. For changes in mortality trends in New England, see Philip J. Greven, *Four Generations: Population, Land, and Family in Colonial Andover, Massachusetts* (Ithaca, N.Y. 1970), pp. 25, 136–37.

The Other Samuel Johnson

1

"THE TRUE DISCIPLE"

THE SMALLPOX crept stealthily into the town of Boston in the late spring of 1721 and began to claim its victims by the score. By June the disease had reached epidemic proportions. As family after family buried its dead, the contagion evoked horror throughout New England. Households and townships that remained uncontaminated adopted makeshift quarantines to preserve their purity. Meanwhile, men and women in more vulnerable places prayed and waited for the carnage to cease.

Viewed for centuries as an instrument of divine wrath, the smallpox sent New Englanders searching for an explanation of their plight. To most, it seemed obvious that the sins of the people had provoked this heavenly scourge. Violations of the Sabbath, a penchant for "worldliness"–more generally, corruptions of the heart–had called down the retribution of the Lord. To remove this judgment, the people had to purge their hearts of sin, seek repentance and reformation, and return their souls to God. Only then the Lord might consent to lift his avenging hand.

In 1721, however, strange notions entered New England to complicate this traditional diagnosis. As the smallpox spread through Boston, taking one life in ten until over a thousand had been buried, several ministers of the town, led by the celebrated Cotton Mather, proposed a new remedy for the crisis. Prayer, repentance, and faith, of course, remained essential to removing the unwanted affliction. Nevertheless, the ministers reported, a procedure borrowed from the Turks in which the smallpox infection was artificially implanted in the bodies of healthy people promised to weaken the natural virulence of the disease. Such inoculation, they maintained, provided immunity from the pox.

The proposal to inoculate uninfected people elicited strong opposition in Boston and launched a major intellectual controversy. Already terrified by the prospect of the plague, the laity of the town denounced their innovating clergymen and one irate citizen threw a bomb into Cotton Mather's house. The passionate debate over inoculation involved more than a struggle between new science and old religion. By proposing inoculation, the ministers, in effect, seemed to be suggesting that a divine judgment could and should be thwarted. Divine retribution, instead of being viewed as necessary justice, became a mere social problem to be overcome. Thus the smallpox epidemic and the debate over inoculation represented a larger cultural crisis. Ministers and people examined, not a scientific truth, but their relationship to God.[1]

As the controversy raged in Massachusetts, the smallpox slipped aboard the sloop of a Wethersfield merchant and silently entered the neighboring colony of Connecticut. In July the Governor and Council established quarantine procedures. But when the General Assembly of Connecticut convened at New Haven in October, it was necessary to repeat the Governor's orders and to restrict the movement of peddlers, hawkers, and "petty chapmen" who might inadvertently transport the pox along with their more visible wares. Basic as these preventive measures were, the Connecticut legislators recognized that they were treating symptoms rather than causes. If the smallpox signified God's displeasure with the sins of the people, it was also necessary to eliminate the offending practices. The General Assembly promptly approved an act designed to prevent the "Prophanation of the Lord's Day" and attempted to insure proper respect for "divine worship."[2] Such legislation would not in itself remove God's wrath, but it might cause some people to reconsider their wicked habits and lead them to seek spiritual regeneration. Then the Lord might hear their prayers.

Presiding over the General Assembly sat Governor Gurdon Saltonstall, undoubtedly the most prestigious man then living in Connecticut. As minister of the church at New London (1691–

1707), Saltonstall had forged an intimate friendship with his elder parishioner Fitz-John Winthrop, who, like Saltonstall, descended from a distinguished New England family. During Winthrop's tenure as Governor of Connecticut (1698–1707), Saltonstall served as his informal adviser, and when Winthrop died in office, the General Assembly took the unprecedented step of appointing a clergyman to succeed him. As Governor, Saltonstall had recommended the adoption of a presbyterial ecclesiastical polity, known in New England as the Saybrook Platform.

Above all, however, Saltonstall was renowned for his statesmanship, his learning, and his character. Loved dearly by his friends, Saltonstall's sudden death in 1724 shocked the colony and many people interpreted his departure as a further sign of God's controversy with New England. The Lord has frowned upon this colony by removing "him that sat at the helm of government and steered it with the greatest discretion and wisdom," preached Samuel Johnson, "the loss of whom justly calls for a universal gloom from the people." Nearly two years after the governor's death, another Connecticut minister described him as "a man of the brightest accomplishments" who stood "taller than his brethren by the head and shoulders," for the virtues "that in others exist separate, in him were conjoyned."[3]

Such accolades, no mere rhetoric for a departed leader, revealed the eminence that Saltonstall held in Connecticut society. His stature reflected his rare intelligence and personality. Yet his attainments, like those of his mentor, Fitz-John Winthrop, required a personal, and perhaps painful, accommodation to the provincial society of eighteenth-century Connecticut. Preaching the colony's election sermon in 1697, Saltonstall had emphasized New England's cultural and political dependence on the mother country, "the English Israel." "We are a little branch of that vine," he had remarked; "our civil life and liberty is bound up in theirs; we have felt the warmth of those benign influences, which have refreshed the wearied land of our forefathers sepulchres." As a remote outpost of the British Empire, New England offered limited advantages to its intellectual elite. Success in colonial America involved the acceptance of cultural isolation and the risk of provinciality, a high price for those who aspired to visible distinction.[4]

Saltonstall had lived with these limitations for years when, in October 1721, he invited the young pastor from nearby West Haven, Samuel Johnson, to deliver a sermon to the General Assembly. Although a full generation younger than Saltonstall, Johnson nevertheless faced the same critical questions regarding the meaning of his life. As a student at Yale College (class of 1714), Johnson had distinguished himself by his intellectual achievements and had, for a time, served admirably as a Yale tutor. Now firmly established in his pulpit at the age of twenty-five, Johnson continued his studies in the nearby college library and appeared ready to assume his place among the intellectual leaders of the province. His sermons had already made him popular among his parishioners and he had spoken to the legislature several times before.

In his sermon of October 22 Johnson chose his text from Corinthians, "the fashion of the world passeth away."[5] Following traditional Christian doctrine, he declared that the things of this world, the pleasures of the body and the rewards of society, soon disappear. Social eminence, especially in the constricted atmosphere of provincial New England, provided fleeting satisfactions. "None of the highest characters of human life," he maintained, "none of the most exalted stations in the world, have been able to preserve themselves from abasement and contempt. The glory of the greatest has frequently suffered and [been] eclipsed and many times been put under a total obscuration." Such alterations applied not only to social situations, but to humanity itself. "If every thing else which we converse with was durable and certain to be depended on," Johnson observed, "yet this alone is enough to make our state changeable, that we ourselves are so subject to change. . . . " By change, Johnson referred not merely to human nature, but to human life itself. "There is nothing more unsteady . . . than man is in his views," he asserted, because as we grow we adjust our interests, our desires, and our designs: "what we like today we shall dislike the next."

Johnson explained this mutability in terms of the stages of life: "Our infancy and childhood is entertained with gilded trifles; the bloom and spring of our youth condemns these foolish baubles, and is making ardent pursuit after the gayer pleasures and entertainments of the world; our riper years begin to reprove the folly and unthriftiness of our youth, and eagerly reaches after wealth and grandeur; our despairing and disappointed old age sits down and sighs over our hot youth's folly, and blames the other stages of life, disrelishes all the entertainment of it, and is dissatisfied with almost everything it meets with, fills with uneasy reflections upon what is past and out of its reach, and with anxious fears about what is to come." There were, then, four ages of man, organically connected and inexorably arranged. This developmental process assured that life would be "but a continued series of fluctuations and changes."

The changing stages of life produced an altered self-image: what satisfied the infant frustrated the adult. These alterations within an individual mirrored the changes occurring in the natural world, composed as it was of "empty, vain and perishing things." God alone seemed unchangeable amidst the transitory nature of life and only by trusting in the Lord could people hope to find solace on earth. Only then could they transcend the final alteration of death. "If we by our earnest addresses to God's grace, obtain his image instamped on our souls . . . , and become like him in a heavenly temper and disposition," Johnson assured the legislators, "we can't possibly be out of his favour, he cannot deny his own image and offspring, and will never abandon us nor forsake us." With such optimism, the young minister concluded his sermon and turned proudly to accept the generous thanks of Governor Saltonstall.

In December, two months later, Samuel Johnson resumed his search for spiritual security in a world of change.[6] Once again he emphasized the transitory nature of human affairs and the need for union with God. Worldly honor is both fleeting and insubstantial, asserted Johnson, for frequently "men of the greatest worth who disdain unworthy and sneaky popular arts are disregarded and laid aside and men of mean capacity preferred by means of little tricks." Society, continued Johnson, offers only "the uncertain puff of popular applause," and "he who is cried up" by the world one day "shall in a few days be as much cried down by the very same tongues." Humanity seemed hopelessly corrupted by envy and malice. Thus even respected people must be prepared to lose the favor of mankind, "and when disgrace comes it will be so much the more unsupportable, by how much greater the satisfaction" of popularity had been.

Here Johnson spoke autobiographically. At the stage of life when, in Johnson's words, men eagerly reach after wealth and grandeur, he had already attained a modicum of success. Men as respected as Gurdon Saltonstall had permitted him to address the colony legislature; parishioners crowded his church; the rector of Yale, Timothy Cutler, and the tutor of the college, Daniel Browne, were his closest friends. By all accounts, Johnson had won more than the "puff of popular applause." And yet something gnawing at his conscience forced him to examine his situation and moved him to prepare for the inevitable downfall. The very tongues that cried him up, he knew, would soon cry him down—swiftly and unmercifully.

Guided by the older Timothy Cutler, Samuel Johnson, together with Tutor Browne and several other young ministers, had acquired a reputation for learning among their neighbors. Meeting often either at the college or in their homes, the young men eagerly discussed knotty intellectual questions and ransacked the available libraries for new ideas. As their inquiry turned to questions of divinity and the status of the primitive church of Christ, the young intellectuals discovered, to their surprise, that the doctrinal verities that they had imbibed from childhood appeared to be wrong. Their conversations, "which used to be very delightful," became more "troublesome."

From their reading they discerned that the ecclesiastical system of New England, by eliminating the office of bishops, had departed from the Christian church of the Apostles. Without bishops to ordain ministers, the New England churches had interrupted the apostolic succession. To compound these doubts, the young scholars observed that the Church of England, from which their forefathers had fled into the wilderness nearly a century before, seemed to represent the purest form of Christianity then existing. Such conclusions, heretical as they appeared, confused and alarmed these young intellectuals. "They all loved their country, and were beloved by it," recalled Johnson many years later. "It was therefore very grievous to them to think of going into conclusions that they knew would be very distressing to their friends and very grievous to their country."[7] His sermons of the autumn of 1721 betrayed these anxieties. Still, Johnson and his friends knew that their spiritual peace depended not upon worldly fame and honor, but upon proper union with God. They therefore continued their studies, hoping desperately to resolve their doubts.[8]

Throughout the long New England winter and into the late spring, Johnson struggled with his conscience. To his diary he confessed the anxieties of his soul, the perils of his search. "O my soul awake out of thy stupidity," he cried; "let thy reason bear sway, be not a slave to thy passions, assert thy liberty. But alas, I have the same treacherous heart that I used to have." Beseeching the Lord to "communicate firmness and stability" to his soul, Johnson returned to the nagging doubts about the validity of his presbyterian ordination. I feel "that I am an usurper in the House of God, which . . . fills my mind with a great deal of perplexity," he wrote, "and I know not what to do. My case is very unhappy." He implored the Lord to reveal the truth and resolve his dilemma. "Do Thou, O my God, direct my steps, lead and guide me and my friends in thy way everlasting."[9]

Beset by confusion, Johnson traveled to Stratford in June 1722 to converse with George Pigot, a missionary of the Anglican Society for the Propagation of the Gospel and the only minister of the Church of England in the colony. After explaining his problem, Johnson arranged for Pigot to visit the college at New Haven and meet with his friends. Johnson later remembered that when the young men confronted the Anglican missionary, "they did no more than express their charity and veneration" for the Church of England. Pigot, however, saw beyond this façade and wrote enthusiastically to his superiors in London, predicting a "glorious revolution" in the churches of Connecticut. Several of the ordained ministers of the colony, he reported, were prepared to announce their conversion to the Church of England "as soon as they shall understand they will be supported at home."[10]

Pigot's enthusiasm may have been premature. Nevertheless, in publicizing his meeting at New Haven, he fed the fears of more orthodox people, who began to wonder at the activity of the doubting scholars. As early as the previous May, one worried parent had contemplated withdrawing his son from Yale lest the lad be corrupted by "Arminian books." Other people also became suspicious of the secret meetings. Rumors spread throughout the colony and many people journeyed to the Yale commencement in September "expecting strange things."[11] They would not be disappointed.

As the commencement approached, Samuel Johnson drafted a sermon that he entitled "The character of the true disciple of Jesus Christ."[12] Painfully aware of the unfolding crisis in his life, Johnson returned to his personal dilemma and reiterated themes that he had developed during the past year. The happiness and interest of mankind depends not upon satisfying the will of man, repeated Johnson, but rather upon resigning ourselves to the will of God. The corruptions of men blind them to the reality of Christ's spirit and, if we would be true disciples of the Lord, "we must be ready cheerfully to undergo whatever trials and afflictions" enter our paths "as we pass along in our Christian course." We must be prepared to suffer the same anguish and persecution that Christ endured to save humanity from its sins. There is always "a wicked generation of men," he declared, who because of their lusts or "their secular interests" condemn sincere Christians. Even now, asserted Johnson, "such is the corruption and depravity of mankind" that a conscientious believer "must expect at least a great deal of odium, and obloquy, spite and opposition from a wicked world."

Then, as if stunned by these thoughts, Johnson paused to allow his "treacherous heart" to speak. We must be certain that we suffer for the cause of God and not for the sake of self. If "we should lose our crown we must be sure that the cause we suffer for be good," whispered his conscience, "for we can't expect a reward for our folly or faction." How could one be sure, asked the voice? By committing ourselves only to the "necessary truths and laws" of the Gospel, replied Johnson. A true disciple must follow the "holy counsels, rules and institutions" of baptism, the Lord's supper, public worship, and the ministry—and no others. Then, seeking strength, Johnson concluded, "we have our . . . enemies. How ought we then to blush and be ashamed to think how unlike we are to our Lord whose disciples and followers we pretend to be?"

By the time Johnson presented these thoughts to his West Haven congregation, the Yale commencement had come and gone and with it the peace of the Connecticut churches. Ministers from all parts of the colony, including the Anglican George Pigot, had traveled to New Haven for the annual academic ceremony. They had heard rumors that impugned the orthodoxy of Rector Cutler and his younger friends and they hoped to have their fears allayed. Instead, they were struck cold when Cutler concluded his prayers with the distinctly Anglican words, "and let all the people say amen." Whatever his intent, Cutler had brought the intellectual crisis into the open.[13] Years of doubt, hesitation, and confusion now would have to be confronted once and for all.

As rumors raced through the town, the trustees of the college, hoping to "satisfy the dark apprehensions of the people," summoned the suspected ministers to the college library where each in turn, from the youngest to the eldest, was encouraged to speak his mind. Samuel Whittelsey, minister of Wallingford, nervously began. "I scruple the validity of my ordination," he stated; "I have endeavored to study the controversy between the Church of England, and the Dissenters, as impartially as I can, and my prevailing thoughts at present are, that Episcopal ordination is necessary" for the proper administration of the holy ordinances of God. Then, as though he had blurted out more than he had intended, Whittelsey hastily retreated: "But yet I am not so fully resolved, but that I can still go on to administer as formerly"; he desired "further light." John Hart of East Guilford, Jared Eliot of Killingworth, and James Wetmore of North Haven repeated Whittelsey's qualified sentiments. They could speak their doubts about presbyterian ordination, but could go no further. They too sought "further light."

Samuel Johnson, tall and serious, moved forward surely and began to speak. "Before I was ordained I did scruple whether those from whom I was to receive ordination, had power to ordain me," he admitted, "but I did so far get over my scruples as that I was ordained by them." Now, after impartial study, "I do think that Episcopal ordination is necessary in order to administer the ordinances; and therefore can proceed no further till I have further light, or further orders." Alarmed by this terse statement, the trustees sat ashen while Daniel Browne and Timothy Cutler concurred with Johnson; they too denied the validity of presbyterian ordination.[14]

Fearing a more general conspiracy and hoping to avert a panic, the trustees requested the dissident ministers to submit a written statement of their beliefs and begged them to reconsider their scruples. The seven men listened carefully to this appeal and then filed solemnly out of the library. With a General Assembly scheduled to convene in October, the trustees postponed any final decision and adjourned until that time.[15]

Meanwhile, word of the Yale apostasy passed through the land, alarming orthodox believers everywhere. "We are all amazed and filled with darkness," wrote Joseph Moss from Derby. Grief-stricken, two trustees of Yale lamented the corruption that had infiltrated the once-pure college. "How is the gold become dim! and the silver become dross, and the wine mixt with water." "It is a very dark day with us," stated another forlorn minister, "and we need pity, prayers, and counsel."[16]

The loss of seven divines to the satanic Church of England appeared sufficiently horrible. But what added to the terror of the Connecticut clergy was the fear that the infection might spread. George Pigot had earlier expressed hope that the Yale converts would lay the basis for a more "glorious revolution" within the New England churches. More orthodox people, while rejecting his sentiments, nevertheless shared his vision. "I apprehend the axe is hereby laid to the root of our civil and sacred enjoyments, and a doleful gap opened for trouble and confusion in our churches," asserted the worried minister of Fairfield. God only knows how many more ministers, influenced by the example of the converts, will "be encouraged to go off from us to them." Such apprehensions alarmed people in "all ranks," who feared a loss of their traditional civil and religious privileges. And some parishioners began to eye their pastors curiously, wondering whether these spiritual leaders might not be harboring theological secrets of their own.[17]

The consternation of the people reflected the bewilderment of their ministers. The Yale apostates had not only questioned the validity of presbyterian ordination, but also cited the participation of laymen in ordination services as proof that the New England churches had severed the apostolic succession. While orthodox clergymen felt that they could argue that "there is no difference between a bishop and a presbyter, jure divino," they themselves were perplexed by the use of lay ordination by their predecessors. "What led those eminent men, who first settled the country, to allow laymen to act in such an affair, is not for me to say," confessed one minister, who felt that such procedures would bring "more damage than all the arguments that can be brought for the necessity of Episcopal ordination." Equally mystifying for the Connecticut clergy was what advice to give to the congregations whose ministers had announced their doubts about presbyterian ordination. Technically, such ministers could not be dismissed without their consent; what were the churches to do if the apostates refused to abandon their pulpits?[18]

Appealing to their more learned colleagues in Massachusetts, several Connecticut ministers pleaded for moral and intellectual support. "I have not read much upon this controversy," confessed Derby's Joseph Moss in soliciting appropriate books. Yet we must now "put on our armour and fight," he declared, "or else the good old cause, for which our fathers came to this land [will] sink and be deserted." Meanwhile, as the Connecticut clergy awaited the wisdom of their neighbors, the laity grew restless and uneasy. One "Jethro Standfast" of "Nuhaven," grieving at the "hurle-burle amung us," criticized the silence of the ministers. "I think it is hi time for um to rite abute this Mattur," he asserted, "when all the Pepel are runnin Mad."[19]

Fortunately for the orthodox, the Massachusetts clergy immediately perceived the gravity of the situation. At a fast day in Boston, the aged Increase Mather "much bewailed the Connecticut apostasy" and his eminent son, Cotton Mather, defended the virture of the founding fathers. Only "a degenerate offspring," he asserted, could describe "these men of God . . . to be no true ministers of Christ." Writing to the ministers of Connecticut, Mather advised the congregations to sever their ties with the dissident clergymen lest their continued "pastoral relation" lead to further conversions. Nevertheless, he recommended that due caution be exercised and that church councils be summoned to effect the peaceful dismissal of the unwanted preachers.[20] Not everyone in Boston shared the hostility of the Mathers. "Silence Dogood," a sometime printer of the *New-England Courant,* who later achieved fame by his real name, Benjamin Franklin, proved more charitable to the apostates. Persuaded that the dissidents acted with "a seriousness becoming their order," the young Franklin merely advised the proselytes that "an indiscreet zeal for spreading an opinion, hurts the cause of the zealot."[21]

While the New England divines publicly betrayed their fears and doubts and scrutinized the motives of the apostate ministers, privately, but no less intensely, Samuel Johnson examined and questioned his theological position. Whatever the opinion of the orthodox, there appeared to him to be nothing irreversible about his public declaration in the college library. In presenting his "doubts" to the trustees, the young minister sincerely hoped to resolve his "scruples," and to remove the "intolerable uneasiness of mind." For the time being and "with great sorrow of heart," he suspended his sacramental duties. But the door had not been closed forever and Johnson again implored God for further guidance. Regretting that he had caused "so much uneasiness to my dear friends, my poor people, and indeed to the whole colony," Johnson prayed that he would not "be a stumbling block or occasion of fall to any soul." "Have mercy, Oh Lord," he continued, "have mercy on the souls of men and pity and enlighten those that are grieved at this accident. Lead into the way of truth all those that have erred and are deceived," he begged, "and if we in this affair are misled, I beseech thee show us our error before it be too late that we may repair the damage." A few weeks later, he reopened his inquiry, reevaluated his motives, and concluded, no doubt with satisfaction, that "upon the most deliberate consideration I cannot find that either the frowns or applauses, the pleasures or profits of the world have any prevailing influence in the affair."[22] Like the true disciple of Christ, Johnson prepared for the "spite and opposition" of the wicked world.

The General Assembly convened at New Haven on October 11, 1722. Gurdon Saltonstall, who "was very desirous to reclaim" the dissident ministers, proposed that the trustees meet with the converts "and argue the matter in a friendly manner before him." Moderating "very genteely," Saltonstall listened as the rival groups defended their positions. Johnson later admitted that the dissidents had a decided advantage, for they had studied the problems for years, while the orthodox ministers had never seriously examined their assumptions. Relying on "Scripture facts" and the writings of the early Christians, Johnson argued that episcopacy constituted the true form of church government, as pure in origins as the practice of infant baptism and the first-day Sabbath.

For a time this systematic assault on the New England way met only with stony opposition from the orthodox establishment. But at last "an old minister," disgusted by the rhetorical aplomb of the converts, stood up and interrupted Johnson's presentation. Furious at their self-righteousness, he "made a harangue against them in a declamatory way" and condemned their treachery. Before he had gone very far, however, Saltonstall intervened and stated that "he only designed a friendly argument." But the passionate outburst effectively ended the conference.[23]

The "harangue" of the old minister, while superficially unimportant, had immense symbolic significance.[24] By denouncing the apostates, he confronted them with the threat of permanent isolation from the community. He said, in effect, that if they questioned the validity of the colony's religious institutions and thereby impugned the sanctity of the communal fathers, they could expect no sympathy from the society. Such threats were overwhelming for some. John Hart, Jared Eliot, Samuel Whittelsey, and, for a brief time, James Wetmore abandoned the episcopal cause and returned to the fold. Their friends "were so very fierce and severe upon them that they could not stand it," Johnson later explained, "so they found some way or other to get over their scruples." The more stalwart proselytes–Johnson, Browne, and Cutler–had to endure still more "malice and rage." "I can scarce express the hardships they have undergone, and the indignities that have been put upon them," wrote a sympathetic Anglican of Rhode Island.[25]

The abortive conference at New Haven served a second symbolic function; it underscored the solidarity of the orthodox churches. In questioning the validity of presbyterian ordination, the episcopal converts had challenged the legitimacy of every minister in Connecticut and thereby launched a fundamental attack on the religious institutions of the colony. It was on these grounds that the Anglican Pigot had appeared so optimistic about a "glorious revolution" in the churches and it was for this reason that the orthodox ministers had initially been so confused by the declarations in the college library. Moreover, as Cotton Mather had instantly perceived, the apostates were questioning the wisdom, indeed the sanctity, of their spiritual fathers, the Puritan founders of New England. The old minister at New Haven realized that such fundamental assaults could not be repelled by "friendly argument." In raising "an odium," he forced his fellow ministers, and the genteel Saltonstall as well, to confront the Anglican threat for what it was.

If the meeting at New Haven stiffened the orthodoxy, it also steeled Johnson's nerves. He returned to his home at West Haven and on October 13, the day before his twenty-sixth birthday, sketched a final version of the alternatives before him.[26] Quickly he listed the arguments for conforming to the orthodox churches of New England: first, the possibility that presbyterian ordination might be valid; second, that he would break "the peace of the country in general and my own people in particular"; third, the "danger of stumbling weak brethren and the damage of precious and immortal souls, and grieving good men." These were weighty arguments, he concluded, and had to be balanced by sufficiently persuasive evidence.

Carefully and resolutely, Johnson proceeded to catalogue those arguments which supported episcopal ordination. Heading the list was the fact that the Scriptures "seem to me plainly to intimate that Episcopacy is of Apostolic appointment." If that was the case, Johnson reasoned that a "fear of breaking [the] peace should not shut up my mouth in a matter of so much consequence." After all, he observed, "peace without one of Christ's institutions is a false peace." While some might be "damnified by my doing my duty," many more souls might be lost "for want of Episcopal government in the country." Johnson paused and reread his draft. "These conclusions all laid together," he noted, "it seems to be my duty to venture myself in the arms of Almighty Providence, to cross the ocean for the sake of that excellent church, the Church of England, and God preserve me, and if I err, God forgive me."

The next day, Sunday, October 14, was his birthday. "Thus finished the 26 year of my life," he noted, "whereupon I conclude upon a voyage for England for Episcopal Orders. God prosper the design! undertaken for his glory and the good of his church."

"I commend myself to the protection of Thy Almighty Grace and Providence," he prayed, "especially in regard to the arduous undertaking which seems to lie before me. Oh Lord, prosper, protect, defend and bless me."[27]

One week later, almost exactly a year after he had preached to the General Assembly, Johnson bade farewell to his congregation at West Haven.[28] His departure from his people "was very tender," Johnson remembered, for "they loved him and he them." He offered to return to them if they would have him, but, he reported, "their prejudices were so great, that they could not think of that." He told them that the prayers and instructions that they had previously admired had been borrowed from the Church of England, but this had little effect. "How glad should I [be]," he preached on the morning of October 21, "if it was possible for you to see as I do . . . that I might yet continue in service to your souls. This would [be] my greatest joy." In the afternoon, preaching from Corinthians, he concluded by forgiving those who had slandered him. "I pray they forgive me as I forgive them," he stated, "and if I have injured any or all I ask your forgiveness. . . . Finally, Brethren Farewell."

By November 5 Samuel Johnson stood with Timothy Cutler and Daniel Browne at the rail of the *Mary* bound for Great Britain. Together they watched the New England landscape recede into the Atlantic mists and recalled the excitement of the past few months. They had come a long way, they knew. But they realized too that their intellectual odyssey had just begun.

As the *Mary* bobbed perilously across the Atlantic waves, the venerable Increase Mather, with practically his last breath, thanked God that the apostates had done so little damage in Zion. "I cannot but go away rejoycing," he exclaimed, "that the body of the sober people throughout the country, (so far as I understand) generally continue to discover a conspicuous aversion to the things" from which "their fathers fled into the wilderness." Nevertheless, he chided his people, there is "a too general decay of that real and vital godliness" which had once characterized the people of New England, and there remained the serious "danger of another generation arising, which will not know the Lord, nor the works done by Him, and for Him, among His people here."[29]

Six months later Eleazer Williams, preaching the annual Connecticut election sermon, returned to this theme. We are a sinful people, he intoned, and God has punished us with His wrath. During the past year, He has "threatened to pluck us up by the roots, and to destroy the school of the prophets."[30] Only repentance and reformation, he continued, would lead the Lord to restore His blessings on the land.

Thus the Yale apostasy, like the smallpox, became another divine scourge designed by the Almighty to wean the people from their sins. For the present, God had been content to threaten His people. But who could predict when He would withdraw His presence and unleash the fullness of His wrath? For two generations, New England ministers had repeated these warnings to little avail. But people who took such ideas seriously recognized that New England faced a crisis of major proportions. In a sense the personal crisis of Samuel Johnson constituted a microcosm of that larger problem.

NOTES

1. For a cogent analysis of the smallpox controversy of 1721, upon which this discussion is based, see Perry Miller, *The New England Mind: From Colony to Province* (Cambridge, Mass., 1953), chap. 21.

2. The proceedings of the General Assembly can be found in *Pub. Recs. Conn.,* 6: 264–78.

3. For a sketch of Saltonstall, see S. L. Blake, "Gurdon Saltonstall, Scholar, Preacher, Statesman," *Records and Papers of the New London County Historical Society*, 1, pt. 5 (1894): 3–28. SJ, Thanksgiving Sermon at West Haven, November 5, 1724, JYU; Phineas Fiske, *The Good Subjects' Wish, or, The Desireableness of the Divine Presence with Civil Rulers* (New London, Conn., 1726), pp. 31–32. For other contemporary accounts of Saltonstall, see Sarah Knight, *The Journal of Madame Knight* (New York, 1935), p. 29; Azariah Mather, *Good Rulers a Choice Blessing* (New London, Conn., 1725); Eliphalet Adams, *A Funeral Discourse Occasioned by the much Lamented Death of the Honourable Gurdon Saltonstall* (New London, Conn., 1724).

4. Gurdon Saltonstall, *A Sermon Preached Before the General Assembly* (Boston, 1697), p. 57. For an analysis of Fitz-John Winthrop's accommodation to provincial society, see Richard S. Dunn, *Puritans and Yankees: The Winthrop Dynasty of New England, 1630–1717* (Princeton, N.J., 1962), pt. 3. T. H. Breen, *The Character of the*

Good Ruler: A Study of Puritan Political Ideas in New England, 1630–1730 (New Haven, Conn., 1970), also links Saltonstall's development with that of Winthrop.

5. 1 Corinthians 7:31. Quotations are taken from SJ, Sermon before the General Assembly at New Haven, October 22, 1721, JCU.

6. Sermon on Hebrews 13:14, December 1721, JCU. The sermon was not delivered until the following March.

7. SJ, "Autobiography," printed in *SJ Papers,* 1: 12–13.

8. For the books read by Johnson at this time, see "Catalogue of Books," *SJ Papers,* 1: 497–500.

9. SJ, "Liber Dierum," *SJ Papers,* 1: 61–62.

10. SJ, "Autobiography," pp. 13–14; George Pigot to SPG, August 20, 1722, *HP,* 1: 56–57.

11. SJ, "Autobiography," p. 14; Joseph Morgan to Cotton Mather, May 28, 1722, printed in Franklin Bowditch Dexter, ed., *Documentary History of Yale University* (New Haven, Conn., 1916), p. 225.

12. The sermon, dated September 16, 1722, is in JCU. It was probably prepared prior to the Yale commencement.

13. There is some contemporary evidence that suggests that the Anglican leanings of the apostates were revealed prematurely; see "A Faithful Relation of a Late Occurrence in the Churches of New-England" [1722], *MHS Colls.,* 2d ser., 2 (1814): 137–38 and George Pigot to SPG, August 20, 1722, *HP,* 1: 56–57. For other descriptions of the commencement, see SJ, "Autobiography," p. 14; George Pigot to SPG, October 3, 1722, and John Davenport and Stephen Buckingham to Increase and Cotton Mather, September 25, 1722, both in *HP,* 1: 58, 69.

14. SJ, "Autobiography," p. 14; *Boston Gazette,* October 8–15, 1722.

15. SJ, "Autobiography," p. 14. Two historians of eighteenth-century Connecticut, citing oral tradition, suggest that Gurdon Saltonstall publicly disputed the points in question with Timothy Cutler. I have found no contemporary evidence to support that claim. See [Samuel Peters], *A General History of Connecticut* (London, 1781; New Haven, Conn., 1829), p. 397 and Benjamin Trumbull, *A Complete History of Connecticut, Civil and Ecclesiastical,* 2 vols. (New Haven, Conn., 1818), 2: 33.

16. Joseph Moss to Cotton Mather, October 2, 1722, *MHS Colls.,* 2d ser., 2:129; John Davenport and Stephen Buckingham to Increase and Cotton Mather, September 25, 1722, *HP,* 1:68; Joseph Webb to Cotton Mather, October 2, 1722, *MHS* Colls., 2d ser., 2: 131.

17. George Pigot to SPG, August 20, 1722, *HP,* 1: 56–57; Joseph Webb to Cotton Mather, October 2, 1722, *MHS Colls.,* 2d ser., 2: 131; [Samuel Browne to George Pigot?], September 21, 1722, *SJ Papers,* 1: 73–74; John Davenport and Stephen Buckingham to Increase and Cotton Mather, September 25, 1722, *HP,* 1: 70–71.

18. See the letters cited in n. 16.

19. Joseph Moss to Cotton Mather, October 2, 1722, *MHS Colls.,* 2d ser., 2: 130; *New-England Courant,* October 1–8, 1722.

20. Samuel Sewall, "Diary of Samuel Sewall," *MHS Colls.,* 5th ser., 7 (1882): 308; Cotton Mather to the Connecticut ministers [1722], *MHS Colls.,* 2d ser., 2: 133–36; see also the *Boston News-Letter,* October 8–15, 1722, which criticized Timothy Cutler.

21. *New-England Courant,* October 1–8, 1722.

22. SJ, "Catalogue of Books," p. 500; "Liber Dierum," pp. 62–63.

23. The only extant account of the meeting is SJ, "Autobiography," pp. 14–15. See also n. 15.

24. For a sociological approach to this question, see Harold Garfinkel, "Successful Degradation Ceremonies," *American Journal of Sociology* 61 (1956): 420–24.

25. SJ, "Autobiography," p. 15; James Orem to SPG, October 30, 1722, *HP,* 1: 79; E. Edwards Beardsley, *Life and Correspondence of Samuel Johnson, D.D.* (New York, 1874), p. 20. George Pigot suggested that Hart, Eliot, and Whittelsey would have converted to the Church of England had they been able to obtain episcopal orders without leaving New England; see Pigot to SPG, August 20, 1722, and October 3, 1722, both in *HP,* 1: 56–57, 59.

26. SJ, "Liber Dierum," pp. 63–64.

27. SJ, "Catalogue of Books," p. 500; "Liber Dierum," p. 64.

28. SJ, "Autobiography," pp. 15–16; Notes for "My Farewell Sermons at West Haven," October 21, 1722, JCU.

29. Increase Mather, "The Testimony Finished [November 10, 1722]," in *Elijah's Mantle: A Faithful Testimony to the Cause and Work of God in the Churches of New-England* (Boston, 1722), pp. 16–17.

30. Eleazer Williams, *An Essay to Prove, that When God Once enters upon a Controversie with his professing People: He will Manage and Issue it*–(New London, Conn., 1723), p. 37.

2

"AN INORDINATE VENERATION"

THE CONVERSION of Samuel Johnson and his friends in 1722 climaxed a period of profound personal anxiety. But, as the sermons of Increase Mather and Eleazer Williams revealed, few people in New England viewed the Yale apostasy simply as the result of individual perversity. However much orthodox New Englanders might harangue the proselytes for betraying communal values, they recognized that individuals were products of their times. The existence of an episcopal conspiracy indicted not only the apostates but also the society that had bred them. In this case it was the sins of the people that had brought down yet another divine scourge. The relationship between individuals and their culture, New Englanders believed, reflected the dimension of time as well as that of place. People not only inhabited "countries" like New England, but also lived in the history of their nation.

Like the biblical Israelites, with whom they identified, New Englanders measured their history by generations.[1] The sense of living in a new society in the American wilderness facilitated the adoption of this temporal device. All people knew the day of beginnings. The reduction of history to genealogy did not destroy the sense of time, for the planters of the family trees could be recalled as flesh and blood. When John Higginson, Increase Mather, or Fitz-John Winthrop saluted the first generation, they spoke not simply of imaginary founders, but referred more specifically to their ancestors, men like Francis Higginson, Richard Mather, and John Winthrop. The notion of successive generations forced New England to live in history. "As every season of a man's life carries its particular duties along with it," declared the preacher of the Massachusetts election sermon in 1676, "so doth every age of the world bring with it particular duties as the work of that generation."[2] On earth, people remained creatures of time; only hereafter could they expect anything eternal.

Despite this awareness of history, however, second- , third- , and fourth-generation New Englanders, by repeatedly glorifying the grandiose accomplishments of their ancestors, unconsciously transformed their patriarchs into archetypal figures.[3] In a paradoxical way human history became symbolic time and the great moments of the first generation assumed a timeless quality, a symbolic immortality, that ever after attracted the sons and grandsons of the founding fathers. So forceful was this image in the century after colonization that later generations of New Englanders continued to measure themselves against the standards that they imagined had been erected by the founders. By such archetypal criteria, however, the children of New England could not possibly prove worthy of their patriarchs. It was this search for historical continuity, nevertheless, that belied a cultural crisis in the early eighteenth century. In a world of history and time, men like Samuel Johnson sought the eternal and the immortal.

The fathers of New England, Puritan exiles in the wilderness, would have understood the dilemmas of their descendants, for they too had endeavored to escape from time. The Puritan movement that spawned the colonization of New England had historical roots in medieval Christianity and Protestant reform. More specifically, the Puritan colonists had been raised as English men and women and they were acutely aware of their place in Western history. Yet the Puritan fathers fervently believed that they could extricate people from history by establishing a timeless community of God on the rocky soil of New England.

At the peak of its vitality in the Middle Ages, the Catholic Church offered spiritual sanctuary to anguished souls throughout western Europe. In time, however, the mere repetition of forms and rituals gradually undermined the sincere piety that had characterized early Christianity. The ecclesiastical structure, heavily encrusted by tradition, also seemed inadequate to many pious Christians. Such anomalies as pluralism and absenteeism, which inevitably interrupted the regularity of divine worship, disturbed parishioners who worried about the future of their souls. This decline of the spiritual power of the Catholic Church provided the background for the Protestant Reformation of the sixteenth century. Searching for spiritual security amidst a world of change, men like Martin Luther defied the pope at Rome and sought to erect a reinvigorated church based on the holy faith of its membership.

In England these reformist trends found unwitting support from the domestic policies of the Tudor monarchs.[4] During the early sixteenth century, Henry VII and his son, Henry VIII, attempted to strengthen royal power by centralizing the government and by eliminating their dynastic rivals. These policies proved remarkably successful and by the third decade of the century, Tudor supremacy seemed secure. Only the ecclesiastical officers of the Roman Catholic Church acknowledged an authority higher than the king–and Henry VIII, early in his reign, hinted that he would have that homage as well. The issue climaxed over a simple family matter: the inability of Henry's wife, Catherine of Aragon, to bear a male heir. Determined to perpetuate the Tudor dynasty, the king appealed to the Pope to annul the marriage. When the Pope refused, Henry rebelled and summoned Parliament to sever England's ties with the Roman Catholic Church. In a series of statutes passed between 1532 and 1534, Parliament created a national church with the king as Supreme Head. Although Henry himself remained hostile to the Lutheran Reformation, the attack on papal authority invited further religious reform. Thus, as part of the confiscation of church revenues, Henry appropriated monastic lands and closed the monasteries, thereby opening doctrinal questions about the penalties of purgatory (which the monks had traditionally been employed to mitigate.) The introduction of an English Bible, moreover, admitted the possibility of lay interpretation of religious doctrine.

The nationalization of the monasteries and the subsequent sale of monastic lands to English investors accelerated profound economic and social change in sixteenth-century England. Encouraged by Tudor economic policy, many English landowners enclosed manorial lands and shifted from traditional agricultural production to raising sheep. This enclosure movement offered lucrative advantages to many property owners and to the merchants who purchased the wool for resale and export. For the propertyless people forced off their rented lands, however, the enclosures brought serious dislocations. Unable to survive with their traditional occupations, many dispossessed people migrated to towns and cities, while others became itinerant laborers who searched the countryside for ways to earn a living.

Even without these major disruptions, life in Tudor England remained extremely precarious.[5] Early deaths, the proximity of plague, and the possibility of famine betrayed the tenuous nature of social relations. In the face of such uncertainty, Tudor Englishmen sought psychological ballast by exalting those social institutions which seemed most permanent—the church, the aristocracy, customs from time immemorial. Yet, in the sixteenth century even some of these venerable institutions appeared to be decaying. The Henrician Reformation had sundered the traditional religious order of the nation and, in the reigns of Henry's children, further discontinuities emerged. Under Edward VI (1547–53), England experimented with Protestantism; Mary Tudor (1553–58), daughter of Henry's first marriage, endeavored to return England to the Church of Rome; Elizabeth (1558–1603) steered a middle course between proponents of radical Protestantism and those who wished to preserve a Catholic liturgy within the Anglican church. Such changes in the national church did not necessarily alter religious worship in the various parishes, but many Englishmen probably wondered at the frequent alterations of the eternal verities.

Mary's attempt to enforce religious conformity led many dissenting Protestants to seek refuge on the Continent. There they imbibed various strains of Reformation doctrine, which toughened their commitment to the Protestant cause. When Elizabeth ascended the throne, these exiles optimistically returned to their native land, expecting the imminent triumph of their Reformation zeal. Instead, they encountered a politically astute Queen who appeared more intent upon protecting her reign by avoiding partisan strife than promoting the Protestant crusade.[6]

Frustrated by Elizabeth's *via media* in religion, the dissenters—who soon became known, pejoratively, as Puritans—commenced a vocal campaign designed to introduce Protestant theology into the Church of England. Few Englishmen viewed the religious settlement of 1559, which defined a middle road between Protestantism and Catholicism, as a permanent arrangement. Puritans therefore could be optimistic about the future and, at the same time, fearful of popish expansion. They objected primarily to the retention of Catholic ceremonies and offices within the Anglican church and proposed instead that England cleanse its religious institutions by basing the ecclesiastical structure solely upon biblical sources. Thus the Puritan dissenters advocated the elimination of historical incursions on the church's purity and urged a return to a primitive, prehistorical church. This denial of time helps to explain why the Puritan appeal, though spearheaded by university graduates and ordained ministers, nevertheless enjoyed a wide following among people of lesser status. Indeed, it was the laity that most resented the visible symbols of the old order—the bowing and kneeling, the wearing of the surplice, and the other vestigial trappings of the Roman Catholic Church.

Besides its demand for ecclesiastical reform, Puritanism offered a distinct theological position. Borrowing from radical Protestants on the Continent, the exponents of Puritanism stressed the omnipotence of God, the sinfulness of mankind, and the need for salvation by faith alone. The cosmic drama began with the idea of human degeneracy following the Fall of Adam. Laden with sin and corruption, a person could enjoy spiritual rebirth only by the blessing of God's grace. The infusion of that grace—the sense of inner conversion—offered the sinner the possibility of immortality among the Elect of God. Assurance of grace therefore became the great goal of life and Puritans, like pietistic people in other ages, resented all obstacles—rituals, ceremonies, or worldly institutions—that obscured that grander vision.

Puritanism brought its adherents a new perspective on all aspects of life. Thus, while Puritans continued to share many values and ideas with less pietistic contemporaries, their religious insight subtly altered their view of traditional institutions, leading them to see social arrangements differently. In a society undergoing major economic and social change, the Puritans reiterated a commitment to a simpler Christian community based on harmony and love. To a people concerned about the avarice of incipient capitalists, the Puritans preached conservative economic ideas and insisted that worldly wealth might sidetrack the search for spiritual treasure. Such notions appealed to people whose lives had been disrupted by enclosure movements or economic inflations. Puritanism, moreover, offered its followers the possibility of spiritual tranquillity amidst the changing worldly order. Once saved by an infusion of God's grace, a Puritan saint could expect peace everlasting, despite the wiles of the devil himself or his minions on earth.[7]

During the Elizabethan era, neither Puritanism nor Anglicanism (as the established church settlement later became known) achieved intellectual uniformity among its proponents. Both religious movements *developed* their ideological positions over time by frequent defenses of specific aspects of thought. Thus there existed important intellectual disagreements among supporters of each persuasion and consequently Elizabethan religious debate lacked the precision associated with later denominational configurations. Furthermore, the clumsiness of the Tudor ecclesiastical structure permitted considerable local autonomy in matters of religion. Within the official church, therefore, variation and deviation remained viable alternatives for dissenting Englishmen. The blurring of lines within the two movements and the absence of monolithic ideologies should not obscure the basic cleavages between supporters of the established church and their dissenting opponents. Anglicans and Puritans, despite their common English Protestant heritage, *perceived* these fundamental differences and evaluated their respective positions accordingly.[8]

The fuzziness vanished quickly from the English religious picture during the reigns of Elizabeth's Stuart successors, James I (1603–25) and his son, Charles I (1625–49). The Stuart monarchs, concerned with protecting the royal prerogative in religious affairs, encouraged the defense of the Church of England against the chorus of Puritan protests.[9] The repeated articulation of religious principles, in turn, hardened the ideological attacks of the rival causes. Public debate accentuated theological differences; Anglicans and Puritans moved farther apart. As the doctrinal arguments entered the political arena, as Parliament increasingly adopted an antiestablishment position, the religious ideologies began to serve more than theological purposes. By aligning with one of the rival groups, Englishmen could locate themselves within the larger social order. People became committed—often in deeply personal ways—to competing ideologies and consequently became less willing or less able to compromise those positions. In this manner, ideological imperatives worked to polarize English society, intensify more traditional disputes, and heighten political tensions.

The sophistication of the intellectual debate also revealed serious divisions within the Puritan movement. By the second decade of the seventeenth century there existed at least three major Puritan subgroups—presbyterians, separatists, and nonseparating congregationalists—and other smaller sects that later formed the groundwork of such denominations as the Baptists and Quakers. Of the larger groups the presbyterians alone advocated a national church, based on synods and presbyters, that could embrace the entire English population. The other groups, technically congregationalist, argued that the visible church on earth should limit its membership to true saints by excluding unregenerate people. Within these groups, however, there was little consensus about how to discover true saints. The notion that each congregation should be autonomous encouraged further variations and divisions. Puritans could unite against a common enemy like the Church of England but would quickly collapse into internecine strife when left alone.

The separatists generally insisted that the Anglican church, by maintaining communion with sinful people, had lost its validity as a Christian church. They therefore chose to withdraw from the Church of England and attempted to create pure enclaves of chosen saints. One such congregation, that of Scrooby, accepted exile in Holland in 1607 in a desperate effort to avoid spiritual corruption; this group, in 1620, provided the "Pilgrim" core of a sparsely populated colony at Plymouth in distant New England. Not all congregationalists accepted the extreme position of the separatists. The nonseparatists—many of whom participated in the colonization of the larger settlements at Massachusetts Bay—suggested that while the Church of England seemed tainted by the retention of Catholic procedures, it nevertheless constituted a true church still capable of being purified.[10] During Elizabeth's reign, this position had proved viable for Puritans who wished to worship as they pleased without departing from the official church structure. Under the Stuart monarchs and the oversight of such scrupulous officials as Archbishop William Laud, this moderate attitude appeared less feasible. Striving for religious uniformity, the Anglican establishment sought to purge the church of all dissent. Such was the price of ideological certainty.

By the 1620s Puritan dissenters had become frustrated by the refusal of the Church of England to accept religious reform. Viewing this failure as a sign of iniquity, preachers and laymen condemned the sinfulness of English society and warned that God would soon punish the nation for its corruptions. Advocates of such institutional reforms as the elimination of the office of bishops and the curtailment of popish ceremonies hoped that parliament would force the king to approve ecclesiastical revision. But in 1629 Charles I dismissed an unfriendly parliament and inaugurated an era of personal rule. Meanwhile, the episcopal officers began to suspend dissenting ministers in an attempt to enforce religious uniformity. As positions hardened, Elizabethan equivocations became untenable.

The dissolution of parliament and the suspension of unorthodox preachers alarmed Puritans throughout England. Catholic victories on the Continent, in France, Germany, and Denmark, added to these fears. Believing that they were engaged in a cosmic struggle against the forces of Antichrist, Puritans worried that human perversity would cause the true church to be destroyed. Yet, at this moment of peril, it appeared to Puritans that God had provided a refuge for His church in America; a timely withdrawal into the wilderness might preserve the true religion until conditions improved at home. Such flight would not only avert direct conflict with the crown, but also might ease the inner anxiety that plagued Puritan consciences.

During the 1620s, several trading companies had attempted, with limited success, to plant settlements along the coast of New England. Then in March 1629, within days of the dissolution of parliament, the royal government approved a charter for the Massachusetts Bay Company, a joint-stock enterprise headed by a group of prominent Puritans. Like other royal patents, this charter granted a vast tract of land in America to the investors of the company. But, for reasons that remain unclear, the charter failed to define a location for the company, thereby enabling the Puritan leaders to transfer their headquarters to New England. With this virtual assurance of autonomy, Puritan reformers prepared to erect a godly commonwealth in America, a citadel of religious purity in a world of spiritual chaos.

Under the leadership of John Winthrop, a member of the gentry of Suffolk, an expedition of eleven ships and nearly a thousand colonists sailed for New England in April 1630. John Cotton, minister of the Boston congregation in Lincolnshire, traveled to Southampton to bid farewell to the migrants. Justifying the uprooting of a people, Cotton explained that "when some grievous sins overspread a country [and] threaten desolation . . . , a wise man," foreseeing the plague, should "hide himself from it." Then, with an eye to the unknown continent, he concluded, "Neglect not walls, and bulwarks, and fortifications for your own defense; but ever let the name of the Lord be your strong tower; and the word of his promise the rock of your refuge."[11]

The Great Migration of the 1630s, which lured nearly 20,000 souls to New England, represented an attempt to preserve the true church free from the corruptions of Stuart England.[12] The Puritan colonists viewed themselves as participants in a cosmic struggle between the forces of God and the agents of the devil. Their adventure in New England enjoined them to uphold the purity of their faith by creating godly institutions to oversee all aspects of life. "We are a company professing our selves fellow members of Christ," declared Governor Winthrop to his fellow travelers aboard the *Arbella*, and "we ought to account our selves knit together by this bond of love, and live in the exercise of it, if we would have comfort of our being in Christ."[13]

Though Winthrop entitled his mid-ocean sermon "A Modell of Christian Charity," the New England enterprise lacked the formal planning associated with later utopian communities. It was the spirit behind the adventure, not the visible arrangements, that seemed unique to the founders of Massachusetts. Indeed, the pluralistic origins of the Puritan ideology—the serious disagreements over fundamentals that later sundered the movement—prevented the formulation or implementation of a specific program. Such shortcomings, nevertheless, do not indicate that less-articulate settlers rejected the Puritan ideology or scoffed at the élan upon which it was based. Regardless of individual variations and idiosyncracies, the colonists of New England generally shared a value system that was *both* English and Puritan and that stressed the importance of creating a godly society in America. That mere mortals fell short of these grandiose ideals did not obviate the vitality of their creed.

The founders of New England not only hoped to build a refuge for the true church; they also wished to create a doctrinally pure society, one that would reflect the inspiration of the holy Scriptures. Given these purposes, they sought to eliminate the historical innovations that had corrupted the church in other places. Above all, they believed that the ecclesiastical structure had to be cleansed of human impurities. Only true saints—people chosen by God for life eternal—would be permitted to participate in the holy sacraments; the invisible church of God must be made tangible on earth. Congregational autonomy, of course, permitted considerable variation (or, as some would say, deviation) in ecclesiastical affairs. Yet generally the churches in New England limited full membership to those who had experienced a spiritual conversion, who could testify that the Lord had imparted His grace into their souls, who could claim to be among the Elect of God. Not everyone in New England could meet thece rigorous standards, but most of those who did not apparently blamed themselves, rather than society, for their inadequacies.[14]

The political order similarly reflected a desire to translate spiritual categories into secular arrangements. The government of Massachusetts derived from the royal charter of 1629, which authorized the formation of a joint-stock company to trade and settle in New England. Theoretically, only stockholders—known as "freemen"—exercised control over company business. However, once in New England, the leaders of the company redefined the notion of "freemanship" to mean "citizenship," thereby permitting the general male populace to participate in "company" matters. In this way a commercial organization became the basis of a political body. This metamorphosis, the Puritan leaders believed, would strengthen communal bonds and encourage social cohesion; consensus, not authority, would bring people together. But the colony's leaders had no intention of departing from the original goals of their enterprise. Thus, as the basis of potential participation expanded, they also instituted a unique standard for determining "citizenship": only church members would be considered freemen. In later decades this policy served to restrict the number of eligible voters. For the first generation, however, it symbolized the spiritual community that underlay the more visible social order. In other places the ownership of land or the accident of residence determined one's political activities. But in New England the spiritual brotherhood preceded institutional arrangements and shaped the political structure of the region.[15]

Prior to the Great Migration, the planners of the Puritan enterprise expected to establish a single Christian community in the wilderness. Within months after landing in Massachusetts, however, the colonists, for unforseeable reasons, dispersed around the Bay and formed separate communities. In subsequent years, as newcomers crowded the coastal areas, the leaders of the colony authorized the creation of interior settlements to accommodate the growing population.[16] Such dispersal destroyed the possibility of building a single community, but it did not weaken the search for a Christian society. By blending various English residential patterns, the Puritan founders adopted a system of town government to implement their social ideals.

The colony government granted land not to individual settlers but to townships, which then subdivided the holdings among the inhabitants. Besides distributing land the town governments provided a variety of public services and structured the economic and social life of their residents. Town meetings, which remained open to nonfreemen, elected local officials, sent representatives to the General Court, and levied taxes; town officials supervised the distribution of alms, hired a schoolmaster, scrutinized economic activities, and kept the meetinghouse in good repair. The importance of town life mirrored the intimacy of social relations. Residents lived together, worked together, and prayed together. Influenced by Christian idealism and family bonds, New Englanders brought a spirit of charity to early town life. Thus, in organizing a town the inhabitants usually convenanted to live according to the Gospel and to uphold the religious ideals upon which the colony had been founded. For later generations such neighborliness became a source of friction and oppression. But for the founders, it signified the joyful harmony of a spiritual brotherhood.[17]

The autonomy of local institutions—the towns and the churches—obviated the possibility of erecting a monolithic society in New England. Moreover, the attempt to institutionalize Puritan ideals created important divisions in the communities. Among the political leaders, Winthrop and Thomas Dudley quarreled about the discretionary powers of the Puritan magistrate in meting out justice. Orthodox ministers like Thomas Hooker and John Cotton disagreed about church policy and the standards of admission to the sacraments. The disputes often revealed the paradoxical basis of Puritan values, the persistent attempt to translate the invisible world of spiritual relations into the palpable language of human affairs. Too often the spirit of Puritanism resisted the practical demands of its exponents. At times charity might contravene justice, or grace contest with benevolence. Such abstractions, in the imperfect world of mortals, caused endless problems.

These tensions not only undermined the spirit of charity, but also led some colonists to seek spiritual peace in new settlements, some as far distant as the Connecticut Valley. Even more serious were the challenges raised by such religious heretics as Roger Williams and Anne Hutchinson, both of whom won considerable followings among New Englanders. Though substantially different, both movements questioned specific attempts to define the pattern of divine relations in secular terms, to make the world of God visible on earth. These dissenting movements, besides illuminating the heterogeneity of the New England way, forced the Puritan establishment to articulate an orthodox defense. As Puritan leaders prosecuted people like Williams and Hutchinson, they defined their own position with greater precision. The effect of these controversies, therefore, was to forge a quasi-official orthodoxy that, while not entirely uniform, nevertheless limited the extent of acceptable deviation.[18]

These ideological developments, together with the institutional patterns of New England, influenced the self-image of the Puritan founders. As natives of England, first-generation New Englanders continued to love the country of their birth and considered themselves Englishmen to their dying days. As exiles in the wilderness, they viewed their careers as part of an international endeavor, one that would see the true church supplant its enemies throughout the world. And for inspiration, they looked to like-minded reformers in England, Scotland, and Germany. By journeying to America, however, the Puritan colonists initiated a process that culminated in the formation of a distinct identity. New Englanders might share ideals, values, and practices with people in England and in Europe, but they alone had ventured across the ocean to build a society based upon these common principles.

During the first decade of settlement, New Englanders prayed fervently that their countrymen at home would see the light and accept the logic of reform. When the English civil wars erupted in the 1640s, New Englanders joyously predicted a victory for the Puritan cause and many returned to England to battle with the Lord. But as internecine quarrels forced English reformers to broaden their doctrine and accept religious toleration, their sympathizers in America frantically withdrew to the sanctity of the New England way. Frustration at the failure of English reform reflected only part of the dilemma facing leaders like Winthrop, Hooker, and Cotton; for the founders of New England unwittingly, and perhaps unconsciously, had become attached to their wilderness society. They had shaped the ideas and institutions of the infant settlements and ironically had become enmeshed with their creations.[19]

Only gradually and reluctantly did the founding fathers realize their growing commitment to New England. Then, overcoming the shock of recognition, they strove to insure the perpetuation of the New England way. In 1646 the Massachusetts General Court summoned a synod of ministers to draft a statement of doctrinal purity. Praying that the glory of God "may still dwell in our land . . . and our posterity may not so easily decline from the good way," the Court expressed hope that the children of the land would "add to such beginnings of reformation and purity as we in our times have endeavored after, and so the churches in New England may be Jehovah's, and he may be to us a God from generation to generation."[20] English exiles in a howling wilderness thereupon became the founding fathers of the colonies in New England. Though Winthrop and his generation would die as Englishmen in exile, they had already adopted, in their own lifetimes, the self-image of patriarchs, symbols that would haunt their children and their children's children for the next century.

The founders of New England, though influenced by their experience in America, continued to evaluate themselves by the standards of European Protestantism. Their descendants, however, men and women who matured thousands of miles from the centers of European society, lacked those cosmopolitan standards. Instead, as children of the wilderness, they measured their achievements against the accomplishments that they ascribed to their parents. The founders had done great things in New England in transforming a virgin land into a settled society. Yet, the grandeur of that metamorphosis concealed basic social problems, weaknesses and fissures that the founders themselves perceived and lamented, but that evaded the myopic vision of their children. Thus when second- and third-generation New Englanders confronted division and conflict in their society, they assumed full responsibility for these problems. In misunderstanding their parents, younger New Englanders fell victim to an inner sense of failure, to guilt, to shame, and to frustration.

Second- and third-generation New Englanders, born and raised in a community dedicated to the principles of Christian love, inherited a pattern of social arrangements badly fragmented by the logic of those ideas. The founders had attempted to institutionalize the spirit of Christian charity by limiting church membership and political participation to visible saints, people who could claim to be among the Elect. The Puritan founders realized, of course, that satanic evil pervaded human society and they expected that some of their neighbors would be hypocrites while others would be simply malevolent. The spirit of Christ would not convert such people, but rather would minimize their impact on the rest of society. For later generations of Puritans, the problem of the unregenerate became more acute. The descendants did not forsake the rigorous standards of their ancestors and continued to believe in the viability of a community of saints. But, for reasons that they could not entirely understand, these children discovered a significant decline in the number of Puritan conversions. Perhaps the relative harmony of New England life eliminated the social basis of religious anxiety; perhaps the younger generations were less pietistic than their parents. Whatever its causes, New Englanders recognized a decline in church membership within two decades of colonization.

In grappling for a solution to this problem, the children of New England discerned another anomaly in their system. The pattern of congregational independence enabled each church to select (or "call") its minister, to establish baptismal practices, and to determine standards of membership. Such autonomy encouraged flexibility and variations, but it also erased the hope of attaining uniformity. Each congregation viewed its own traditions and practices as correct and regarded neighboring churches that pursued different policies as deviant. At times these disagreements led to disputes that involved the entire region; more frequently, it caused serious breaches within single churches.

The problem emerged most clearly in the 1650s and 60s when numerous ministers, concerned about declining church membership, recommended a compromise standard for admission (known to its detractors as the "Half-Way Covenant"). Half-Way members would not be allowed to partake of the Lord's Supper (thus preventing a deterioration of the visible church) but, upon declaring their faith, could have their children baptized. Instead of welcoming the innovation, many congregations denounced their spiritual leaders for introducing heretical reforms; even churches that approved the changes often implemented the new system with regret. Above all, the patchwork compromises that had formed a peaceful façade in the churches collapsed under the pressures of dissent, division, and recrimination. By the later decades of the century, diversity and contention characterized the ecclesiastical affairs of New England.[21]

The disorders in the churches reflected and, in turn, aggravated a variety of secular disputes. Though the children of New England embraced the ideals of social harmony and Christian charity, they nevertheless found numerous occasions for departing from those principles. Sons might remain loyal to their fathers, dwell in the same towns, and pray in the meetinghouse, but they did not necessarily love their neighbors or the newcomers who periodically entered the community. With increasing acrimony townsmen argued about land allotments, tax levies, the selection of ministers, and a host of pettier matters. Many of these quarrels resulted from fundamental social and demographic changes—the maturation of new generations, the growth of population, the reduction of available acreage, and the conservative policy of the General Court in creating new towns.[22]

The demise of the spirit of neighborliness also reflected important changes occurring in the social structure of New England. Though Puritanism condemned worldliness and materialism, it nevertheless instructed people to labor assiduously at their callings. Puritans viewed the profits of such work as a sign of God's favor, intended for spiritual, rather than secular, purposes. Puritan ministers, moreover, enjoined godly parents to increase their estates for the benefit of their posterity. These intellectual imperatives, instead of promoting social harmony, encouraged acquisitiveness and competition. The growth of population, by forcing some children to migrate to new towns or to learn nonagricultural occupations, reinforced these tendencies. Investments in land or in trade became necessary and respectable alternatives to traditional callings. Thus the pursuit of industry undermined the Christian community and replaced it with social mobility, personal jealousy, and family rivalry.[23]

The appearance of these problems, many of them ironic outgrowths of Puritan views, bewildered the children of New England. Committed to parental ideals of social oder, the younger generation lamented their inability to attain those goals and concluded that they were unworthy of their ancestors. At mid-century Puritan ministers developed a conventional sermon style—the jeremiad—which glorified the accomplishments of the first generation, chronicled the failure of their descendants, and warned of impending catastrophes for the spiritual apostasy. For second-generation New Englanders, the jeremiads confirmed the purity and infallibility of the founding fathers and their original ideals. This glorification of the first settlers partially reflected the unconscious longings of the children for a return to their own childhood, to a time of apparent tranquillity when their parents had assumed full responsibility for the welfare of the community. The early years of colonization thus appeared more peaceful and more virtuous; the history of New England became less a narrative of human adventure and more a story of archetypal symbols.[24]

The jeremiads provided more than a denunciation of New England's youth. By linking later generations to the ahistorical exploits of the patriarchs, the apotheosis of the fathers offered later New Englanders a sense of uniqueness in the cosmic scheme. Though most often expressed by the intellectual elite, such idealization embraced all members of the society. Partly geographical and partly tribal, proximity to the heroic deeds of the founders placed the younger generation in the mainstream of Christian history. Thus, while the fathers remained exiles in the wilderness, the sons lived and died as New Englanders—a chosen people, once removed.[25]

The willingness of the second generation—those New Englanders who matured in the middle decades of the century—to deify the founders reflected the absence of alternative symbols with which they could identify. During the 1640s and 50s the course of events in England, particularly the schisms within the Puritan movement, deflected New England idealism. By comparison to the mother country, the colonies seemed tranquil and pure. To be sure, many Puritan sons, including such prominent young men as Increase Mather and Fitz-John Winthrop, sailed to England to enjoy the wider opportunities of a European society. But the Restoration of Charles II in 1660 quickly dispelled whatever dreams these youthful New Englanders may have entertained. Many returned to America bearing tales of frustration, which reinforced colonial distrust of Stuart England.

For New Englanders the Restoration signalled not only the defeat of Puritan reformism but also the possibility of royal intervention in colonial affairs. Though proclaiming loyalty to the crown, the colonists recognized that the English authorities might subvert their political and social institutions. Such policies as basing suffrage on church membership or the persecution of religious minorities like Quakers might lead to the revocation of the colonial charters. These fears explain, in part, the growing importance of the jeremiads as metaphorical defenses against external influences. For in venerating the fathers, later New Englanders were denying that the system itself was at fault. By deploring their own sins, the sons assumed full responsibility for a defective community.

When a royal commission arrived in New England in 1664 to

investigate the colonies, the loyal sons responded with a variety of intellectual defenses and clever evasive tactics. In the short run noncooperation proved successful and the royal officials, stymied by the colonists, returned to England. But the colonial victory, instead of dampening English interest in New England, served to increase it. In subsequent years other royal officials, most notably Edward Randolph, visited New England, scrutinized colonial activities, and recommended that the crown abridge local autonomy. Such advice culminated in the revocation of the Massachusetts charter in 1684 and the establishment of the Dominion of New England, a royally controlled administrative unit that included the colonies of New England and New York.

During this prolonged period of English interference, Puritan stalwarts not only resisted royal control but also competed with a growing number of colonials who advocated accommodation with the crown. Even in 1664 a substantial group of "moderates" had accepted American dependence on the Empire and had urged cooperation with the royal commission; a dozen years later, Randolph found that many colonials endorsed the overthrow of the charter government. This opposition to the New England establishment reflected a series of interrelated discontents–some political, some economic, some personal. Linking them all was the growing realization among certain colonials that the British Empire represented an alternative model to the jeremiad tradition. In explaining New England's problems, various colonials, instead of feeling inadequate for their failure to attain patriarchal perfection, rationalized their shortcomings by indicting the system itself and, by implication, the men who had created it. According to these people, enforced isolation had transformed New England from a citadel of purity into a backwater province. Balking at a return to New England, Fitz-John Winthrop admitted that "I had far rather content myself with a mere competency in a strange country than in a city or place where I am known."[26] Restoration England thus became a prototype of political and cultural sophistication.

In the two decades after the Restoration, relatively few New Englanders accepted the provincial model as an explanation of the region's social problems. For the most part, provincialism–the notion of British cultural superiority–appealed to a minority of the young people who had direct contact with the mother country. In the 1680s, however, a series of political events–the revocation of the Massachusetts charter; the creation of the Dominion under Sir Edmund Andros; the Glorious Revolution of 1689, which overthrew the Andros regime; and the bestowal of a second royal charter in 1691–emphasized that provincialism meant power as well as culture and consequently broadened its appeal. Rising families seeking to legitimate their new status, old families declining in status and power, and a variety of other out-groups–all sought solace under the mantle of royal government. Political instability, by undermining the traditional order, strengthened the appeal of provincial values on all levels, and royal officials inadvertently encouraged the trend by periodically threatening to revoke the charters of Massachusetts and Connecticut.[27]

The political crises of the 1680s and 90s, by challenging the legitimacy of the New England way, introduced a cultural crisis of major proportions.[28] The English officials in the colonies could not be banished, nor their presence ignored. Moreover, as representatives of the metropolis, they scorned the natives of New England, even those who aspired to intellectual and political prominence. Colonials who had viewed themselves as members of a superior culture now confronted an important challenge to that self-image. Most New Englanders, deeply infused with Puritan values, reacted defensively against this external threat; but a few, the younger and more alienated, viewed metropolitan culture favorably. Regardless of one's position, however, the possibility of alternative models could not be denied. And, for as long as English influences would be felt in America–until 1776 when the Declaration of Independence snapped the bonds of empire–New England children would face two equally viable traditions. Never again could Puritan parents predict the cultural loyalty of their progeny.

Defenders of the Puritan tradition defined the royal intervention from the perspective of the jeremiads. Viewing the founding fathers as archetypal heroes, New England men bewailed the decline of spiritual purity and asserted that the sins of the people had brought down the wrath of God in the figure of Sir Edmund Andros and his accomplices. These loyal sons resisted the pull of metropolitan culture and emphasized the spiritual superiority of the colonies. As descendants of the Puritan fathers, they particularly condemned the notion of religious toleration and continued to view the Church of England as anathema. Of all the iniquities perpetrated by the Andros regime, none had rankled so much as the introduction of Anglican services on the hallowed ground of Boston. Thus the jeremiad tradition persisted into the eighteenth century, serving as an important analytic tool for the majority of the population. If New England appeared provincial and inferior by English standards, the fault lay with the children of the age, who had departed from the pure ideals of the patriarchs.

A second group of New Englanders felt the tension of provincialism more deeply than the upholders of the jeremiad tradition. Many young men, instead of being repelled by the intrusion of royal power, found themselves attracted to the more sophisticated metropolitan culture. Men like Fitz-John and Wait Still Winthrop, Joseph Dudley, and Gurdon Saltonstall, alienated from the provinciality of New England society, imitated English manners and paid homage to the cultural leadership of the mother country. "We are some of us English gentlemen and such is your own family," wrote Dudley to Saltonstall, "and we should labor to support such families because truly we want them."[29] Their attempts at attaining respectability, however, were not always appreciated by English officials, who viewed them as pretentious provincials. Such rebuffs had a sobering effect on these men, causing them to reconsider their enthusiasm for metropolitan society. In the end the Winthrops and Saltonstall retreated to the safety of their native New England and accepted the limited rewards it offered. Preaching of the colonial relationship to the mother country, Saltonstall remarked, "We are a little branch of that vine."[30] Others, like Dudley, moved in the opposite direction, choosing to become lesser officials in the wider British Empire. Despite these important differences, however, both types acknowledged the cultural superiority of England and both regarded New England as a mere province of the Empire. Keenly aware of their limitations, Anglo-Americans and provincial New Englanders had much in common. In a society dominated by symbolic fathers, they had contemplated the crime of patricide.[31]

Although internal pressures prevented these provincials from openly attacking the Puritan fathers, at least two New Englanders recognized that the problems of the age reflected not so much the sins of contemporaries as the inadequacies of the first generation. John Hale, pastor of the church at Beverly, Massachusetts, responded to the trauma of the Salem witch trials by accusing the patriarchs of establishing erroneous precedents. "A child will not easily forsake the principles he hath been trained up in from his cradle," admitted Hale, but "most of these principles I here question as unsafe to be used." Hale spoke bravely but nevertheless refused to publish his pamphlet in his lifetime.[32]

Solomon Stoddard, the magisterial preacher of Northampton, was less discreet. Convinced that the disorders in the New England churches revealed the evils of congregational autonomy, Stoddard advocated the creation of a presbyterian polity. His opponents, particularly Increase and Cotton Mather, denounced his proposal as a desertion of the New England way. "The mistakes of one generation many times becomes the calamity of succeeding generations," Stoddard replied. "The present generation are not only unhappy by reason of the darkness of their own minds," he declared, "but the errors of those who have gone before them, have been a foundation of a great deal of misery." Pleading for an "impartial examination" of first principles, Stoddard denounced "an inordinate veneration" of the founding fathers.[33]

Stoddard, impelled by ideological certainty, and Hale, shocked by a legal murder, articulated heretical positions in seventeenth-century New England. Most of their contemporaries, committed to the jeremiad tradition, denied the historical limitations of their ancestors. Week after week, year after year, Puritan ministers invoked the timeless spirit of the founding fathers and urged their congregations to achieve the impossible. Even pious New Englanders could respond only with frustration and self-deprecation. In the latter part of the century, however, the intrusions of English standards presented third- and fourth-generation Puritans with alternative models for self-analysis. The sophistication of English culture suggested that colonial deficiencies did not merely reflect the sins of the people. Although few New Englanders drew such daring conclusions, English patterns remained to tempt provincial children. Thus, when Samuel Johnson announced his conversion to the Church of England in 1722, he merely carried the flirtations of the Winthrops and Saltonstall to their logical end.

NOTES

1. Numerous New Englanders viewed their history as a process of generational succession; see, for example, John Higginson, "An Attestation to this Church-History of New-England" [1697], in Cotton Mather, *Magnalia Christi Americana; Or, The Ecclesiastical History of New-England,* 2 vols. (Hartford, Conn., 1855), 1:13; Increase Mather, *The Order of the Gospel* (Boston, 1700), pp. 10–11; "Instructions of our agent, Jonathan Belcher," December 9 [1728], "Talcott Papers," *Connecticut Historical Society Collections* 4 (1892):146; Thomas Prince, "Dedication," *A Chronological History of New England In the Form of Annals* (Boston, 1736).

2. William Hubbard, Epistle Dedicatory, *The Happiness of a People* (Boston, 1676).

3. For a suggestive treatment of these themes, see Mircea Eliade, *Cosmos and History: The Myth of the Eternal Return*, trans. Willard R. Trask (New York, 1959), especially pp. 46–47. The blurring of the biographical with the archetypal can be seen in C. Mather, *Magnalia,* passim.

4. The religious situation in England is described in Peter Heath, *The English Parish Clergy on the Eve of the Reformation* (London, 1969); for an overview of the English Reformation, see Arthur G. Dickens, *The English Reformation* (London, 1964).

5. For a description of English society in this period, see Peter Laslett, *The World We Have Lost* (New York, 1965).

6. The best study of Elizabethan Puritanism is Patrick Collinson, *The Elizabethan Puritan Movement* (Berkeley, Calif., 1967). For a valuable discussion of Puritanism in the context of the reformed Protestant tradition, see David D. Hall, "Understanding the Puritans," in *The State of American History*, ed. Herbert Bass (Chicago, 1970).

7. For a provocative discussion of the social basis of Puritanism, see Michael Walzer, "Puritanism as a Revolutionary Ideology," *History and Theory* 3 (1963):59–90.

8. John F. H. New persuasively analyzes the metaphysical differences between the two groups in *Anglican and Puritan: The Basis of Their Opposition, 1558–1640* (Stanford, Calif., 1964). For a study that emphasizes the religious consensus of the period, see Charles H. and Katherine George, *The Protestant Mind of the English Reformation, 1570–1640* (Princeton, N.J., 1961).

9. For a discussion of the activity of the Puritan press and pulpit, see William Haller, *The Rise of Puritanism* (New York, 1938).

10. For a fuller discussion of these ideas, see Perry Miller, *Orthodoxy in Massachusetts, 1630–1650* (Cambridge, Mass., 1933) and Edmund S. Morgan, *Visible Saints: The History of a Puritan Idea* (New York, 1963), chaps. 1–3.

11. John Cotton, "Gods Promise To His Plantations," in *Old South*

Leaflets 3 (Boston, n.d.):9, 15. For discussions of the background of the migration of 1630, see Edmund S. Morgan, *The Puritan Dilemma: The Story of John Winthrop* (Boston, 1958); Peter N. Carroll, *Puritanism and the Wilderness: The Intellectual Significance of the New England Frontier, 1629–1700* (New York, 1969), chap. 1; also see n. 12 below.

12. Perry Miller, in "Errand Into the Wilderness," *Errand Into the Wilderness* (Cambridge, Mass., 1956) and in *Colony to Province*, suggested that New Englanders aspired to build a city upon a hill, a beacon of godly perfection that all people would imitate. More recently, Robert Middlekauff has argued persuasively that Miller's view has exaggerated the egocentrism of the founding fathers; see his *The Mathers: Three Generations of Puritan Intellectuals, 1596–1728* (New York, 1971), esp. pp. 32–34.

13. John Winthrop, "A Modell of Christian Charity," in *Puritan Political Ideas: 1558–1794*, ed. Edmund S. Morgan (Indianapolis, Ind., 1965), p. 90.

14. For a fine analysis of these ideas, see Morgan, *Visible Saints*, chaps. 2, 3.

15. For a clear explanation of these changes, see Morgan, *Puritan Dilemma*, chap. 7; see also Stephen Foster, *Their Solitary Way: The Puritan Social Ethic in the First Century of Settlement in New England* (New Haven, Conn., 1971), p. 45.

16. See Carroll, *Puritanism and the Wilderness,* chap. 7.

17. For a discussion of some of these New England towns, see Sumner Chilton Powell, *Puritan Village: The Formation of a New England Town* (Middletown, Conn., 1963); Greven, *Four Generations*; Kenneth A. Lockridge, *A New England Town: The First Hundred Years: Dedham, Massachusetts, 1636–1736* (New York, 1970).

18. For a suggestive treatment of these crises, see Kai T. Erikson, *Wayward Puritans: A Study in the Sociology of Deviance* (New York, 1966).

19. My understanding of this problem has benefited from Miller, *Colony to Province*, chap. 1, and Middlekauff, *The Mathers*, pt. 1.

20. Quoted in *The Creeds and Platforms of Congregationalism*, ed. Williston Walker (New York, 1893), p. 170.

21. For perceptive analyses of the changes of the late seventeenth century, see Miller, *Colony to Province,* passim; Morgan, *Visible Saints,* chaps. 4–5; Robert G. Pope, *The Half-Way Covenant: Church Membership in Puritan New England* (Princeton, N.J., 1969); Paul Robert Lucas, "Valley of Discord: The Struggle for Power in the Puritan Churches of the Connecticut Valley, 1636–1720," Ph.D. diss., University of Minnesota, 1970.

22. For works dealing with this problem, see n. 17 above.

23. The best analysis of this question remains Miller, *Colony to Province.*

24. Writing of a parallel process, Otto Rank has observed that "the entire endeavor to replace the real father by a more distinguished one is merely the expression of the child's longing for the vanished happy time,

when his father still appeared to be the strongest and greatest man, and the mother seemed the dearest and most beautiful woman. The child turns away from the father, as he now knows him, to the father in whom he believed in his earlier years, his imagination being . . . only the expression of regret for this happy time having passed away." See *The Myth of the Birth of the Hero: A Psychoanalytic Interpretation of Mythology*, trans. F. Robbins and Smith Ely Jelliffe (New York, 1914), p. 67.

25. For studies of the jeremiad, see Miller, *Colony to Province*, passim; Middlekauff, *The Mathers*, passim. For a suggestive discussion of this idea, see Sigmund Freud, *The Future of an Illusion*, trans. W. D. Robson-Scott (New York, 1955), pp. 21–23.

26. Fitz-John Winthrop to John Winthrop, Jr., December 19, 1661, *MHS Colls.*, 5th ser., 8 (1882): 269.

27. This discussion has benefited from several secondary studies; see Miller, *Colony to Province;* Jack P. Greene, "Political Mimesis: A Consideration of the Historical and Cultural Roots of Legislative Behavior in the British Colonies in the Eighteenth Century," *American Historical Review* 75 (1969), esp. pp. 343–44; Lucas, "Valley of Discord"; Dunn, *Puritans and Yankees*, pt. 3; Michael Garibaldi Hall, *Edward Randolph and the American Colonies: 1676–1703* (Chapel Hill, N.C., 1960); and especially, Bernard Bailyn, *The New England Merchants in the Seventeenth Century* (Cambridge, Mass., 1955).

28. For an overview of this problem, see Ver Steeg, *Formative Years*, chap. 6; for a revealing analysis of a similar crisis in a different culture, see Kenneth B. Pyle, *The New Generation in Meiji Japan: Problems of Cultural Identity, 1885–1895* (Stanford, Calif., 1969).

29. Quoted in Breen, *Character*, p. 220.

30. Saltonstall, A Sermon, p. 57.

31. The Winthrops have been studied in Dunn, *Puritans and Yankees;* the careers of Joseph Dudley and Gurdon Saltonstall await further study.

32. John Hale, "The Preface to the Christian Reader," *A Modest Enquiry Into the Nature of Witchcraft*, in *Narratives of the Witchcraft Cases: 1648–1706*, ed. George Lincoln Burr (New York, 1914), p. 404. The elderly John Higginson, in a dedicatory preface to the tract, obviously misunderstood Hale's indictment of the founding fathers.

33. Solomon Stoddard, "An Examination of the Power of the Fraternity," printed with *The Presence of Christ with the Ministers of the Gospel* (Boston, 1718), p. 1; see also Lucas, "Valley of Discord," passim.

3

"APPETITES TAME AND PLIABLE"

WHEN NEW England parents spoke of the earliest years of life, they emphasized the burdens of childhood, the risk of early death, the danger of succumbing to sin. Children were ignorant and naive, easily led astray by wicked impulses, overly enamored, in Samuel Johnson's words, "with gilded trifles." In Christian terms, the first stages of life signified the darkness of mankind's temporary abode on earth, the transitory nature of mortal existence and its preparation for a fuller life hereafter. Viewing children as miniature adults, different only in size and age from full-grown people, New Englanders encouraged their children to mature quickly, to pass promptly through this difficult age of juvenile pleasures.[1]

Amidst the "toyish stuff" of childhood, Puritan parents discerned the sin of Adam lurking beneath the innocent faces of their children.[2] The youngsters had to be awakened from sin and "weaned" from the world before they could enjoy the eternal blessings afforded only to the children of God. New Englanders therefore agreed that childhood was a time of discipline and learning. Godly parents endeavored to defeat the corrupt wills of their progeny by instilling a sense of religion into those young minds as early as possible. Such nurturance might not provide assurance of salvation, but it would, at least, influence the visible conduct of the maturing individual. "Train up a child in the way he should go," Samuel Johnson quoted on the title page of his catechism, "and when he is old he will not depart from it."[3] Such godliness not only promised to preserve the individual from sin, but also formed the basis of a virtuous society. "Families are the nurseries for church and commonwealth," preached Increase Mather; "ruin families, and ruin all. Order them well and the public state will fare better."[4] Thus the parents of New England paid homage to the lessons of childhood.

Robert Johnson, a prosperous yeoman of Hull in Yorkshire, listened intently to the Puritan sermon of his pastor, Ezekiel Rogers. For nearly two decades Rogers had served the souls of his people with sincere devotion. Scorning the popishness of the established church, the minister refused to don the required surplice, ignored the traditional ceremonies, and preached the pure Christian Gospel of the Almighty. Like-minded benefactors within the church protected the Puritan preacher from episcopal interference. But the appointment of Archbishop Richard Neile, a staunch Anglican, soon ended the time of peace. Now, in 1637, Rogers softly told his congregation that he could minister to them no more.[5] The Lord, in His infinite wisdom, had permitted the episcopacy to silence the truth—perhaps as a warning to the godly of worse catastrophes to come.

These divine signals persuaded Rogers to seek spiritual peace in the Puritan colonies of New England, and he earnestly invited his loyal parishioners to join his exodus. Robert Johnson did not hesitate. Resolutely, he sold his lands and possessions, gathered his wife and four sons, and journeyed to London to embark for America. Early in 1638, just as the springtime blossoms painted the New England countryside, the Johnson family landed at Massachusetts Bay. The coastal areas had, by that time, become overpopulated and Robert Johnson, together with many of his shipmates, eagerly accepted an invitation to join a group of settlers then forming a community called New Haven on the northern shore of the Long Island Sound.

Sailing from Massachusetts in October, the Johnson family nearly perished when their vessel ran aground in a storm. But, as one of their companions remembered, "God carried us to our port in safety." The family settled in what was called the Yorkshire quarter of New Haven and probably spent their first winter in a partially completed building. Robert Johnson, a devout Puritan, testified to the presence of the Holy Spirit and achieved full membership in the congregational church dominated by its austere minister, John Davenport. Judging from his ranking in the church, Johnson seems to have prospered moderately from his lands, and when he died in 1661 he left a generous estate to his children.[6]

Robert Johnson, the yeoman of Yorkshire, became in New Haven a Puritan patriarch, a first-generation New Englander. His sons apparently respected his position and shared his Puritan values. The eldest, Robert, completed his education at Harvard College and later joined his father's former minister, Ezekiel Rogers, in the pulpit at Rowley in Massachusetts. Two other sons, Thomas and John, migrated to a Puritan settlement at Newark in New Jersey and became founding fathers in their own right. The youngest, William, remained at home until 1651, when he moved to nearby Guilford to marry the seventeen-year-old daughter of Francis Bushnell.[7] None of these sons ever questioned the preeminent position of their father. Yet they themselves could also claim to be first-generation colonists. Each of them had been born in England and each had ventured with his father across the vast Atlantic to settle in the American wilderness. Each could identify with the grand mission of the Puritan leaders and each could find his special place in New England society. This blurring of generations later confused their descendants, who regarded the earliest colonists as founding fathers regardless of their age.

The fertile acreage around the Menunkatuck River, several miles east of New Haven, attracted a group of colonists from Surrey and Kent, who purchased the native Americans' title to the land and established the town of Guilford in 1639. While still aboard ship the settlers covenanted "to be helpful each to the other in every common work, according to every man's ability and as need shall require," and they promised "not to desert or leave each other or the plantation, but with the consent of the rest." Led by their minister, Henry Whitfield, the Puritan exiles attempted to create an autonomous colony based on the principles of congregationalism. The Guilford church restricted membership to visible saints and required parishioners to attest that God had infused His grace in their souls. In forming the church in 1643 the townsmen pledged to "settle and uphold all the ordinances of God in an explicit congregational church way, with most purity, peace and liberty." Then they dissolved the temporary government created in 1639 and instituted a new body politic in which political rights extended only to full church members.[8] This decision signified the closed and cohesive nature of the community. Surrounded by strange natives in a remote wilderness, the residents of Guilford endeavored to build a Christian society based solely on the word of God.

It was into this tightly knit group that William Johnson moved when he married Elizabeth Bushnell in the summer of 1651. A devout Christian like his father, William achieved full membership in the congregational church by attesting to a conversion experience. His industriousness in the fields yielded profitable returns, while his reputation for sincerity and sobriety earned him the respect of his fellow townsmen. In 1665 they chose him to represent the town in the Connecticut General Assembly, a position that he filled over thirty times in the next three decades. William also served the town in numerous local offices–sergeant of the militia, town clerk, surveyor, attorney, school teacher, and town patentee.[9] Each of these positions reinforced his standing in the community. But William most of all cherished his appointment as deacon of the church. For it demonstrated that his neighbors held him above spiritual reproach and trusted him with the weighty responsibility of caring for "the temporal good things of the church."[10]

William Johnson's prominence in town life placed him at the center of colonial affairs. As a member of the Connecticut legislature, he heard disputes between towns, helped to formulate a policy toward the native tribes, recommended the improvement of secondary education, and participated in a variety of other decisions affecting the welfare of the commonwealth. Always he tried to protect the interests of his townsmen. But in 1687 he watched somberly as Sir Edmund Andros, the King's representative, dissolved the government of Connecticut and merged the colony into the Dominion of New England. Two years later he returned to Hartford to learn of the overthrow of the Andros regime and the resumption of the colony's government. No doubt he rejoiced with his colleagues at the news of the Glorious Revolution, which placed the loyal Protestants, William and Mary, on the English throne.[11]

William Johnson was a pious man who attended the church regularly and faithfully. Like his father, he listened closely to the sermons of his minister and searched his soul for confirmation of his sanctity. Though bothered by occasional doubts, William remained confident that he would join the Elect in heaven. When he drafted his last will and testament in 1695, he earnestly committed his soul "into the hands of God my merciful Father in Jesus Christ my merciful redeemer."[12]

Johnson's spiritual vision, however, was not unclouded. For from his seat in the Guilford church he increasingly heard his preacher condemn the decline of religiosity and warn of impending chastisements from God. Such jeremiads echoed from the pulpit of the General Assembly, which Johnson frequently attended. In 1685 he heard Samuel Wakeman's election sermon, *Sound Repentance: The Right Way to Escape Deserved Ruine,* which warned "God's Covenant People" in Connecticut of the dangers of spiritual apostasy. "We are much backsliden from God in our affections and conversations; we have lost our first love and left our first works," Wakeman declared, and "if the footsteps of those that first followed the Lord into this, as then unsowen Land, be inquired after how dim and almost worn-out will they appear?" "Verily, we are gone backward, backward and not forward," he exclaimed, "and verily these backward retrograde God forsaking motions carry such hateful unthankfulness unto God . . . put him to such open shame in the eye of the world" that, he continued, it might justly be feared that God would forsake them and bring ruin to such a people. The troubles with the mother country signified God's displeasure, for "New-England's credit and repute is brought many pegs lower than sometimes." Only sound repentance could bring the Lord to smile upon the land.[13] The following year the election preacher repeated this theme. "Look into families and other societies," he asserted; "is there not too visible and general a declension; are we not turned (and that quickly too) out of the way wherein our fathers walked?"[14]

William Johnson listened and he heard. With his wife he had endeavored to establish a godly household. Elizabeth had borne twelve children in twenty years, but seven had died in childhood, perhaps because Guilford, as a port town, remained exposed to infectious diseases.[15] She herself died at the age of 38, delivering her last child in 1672. Only one son, the eleventh child, born in 1670, survived. William named the boy Samuel and symbolically dedicated him to the church.[16] This Samuel, bereft of his mother at an early age, was a good and loving son, generous, pious, and well-intentioned. But by the time he reached puberty it was evident that he would not enter the ministry. William tried to conceal his disappointment; but when he looked into his family, he perceived "too visible and general a declension."

William Johnson's children afforded their father the same affection and respect that he commanded from the townspeople. All of his children who lived to adulthood—four daughters and a son—remained in Guilford to raise families of their own. Samuel, the son and major heir, lived with his father until 1694, when he married Mary Sage, the daughter of a prosperous landowner of nearby Middletown. He too planted deep roots in the town of his birth and endeavored to imitate the piety and eminence of his parent. The physical rootedness of this generation reflected, no doubt, its acceptance of the values of the patriarch. William Johnson meanwhile presided over the family, indulging his grandchildren and telling stories of the early days in New England. When he died, full of years, in 1702, he was mourned by two generations of loving descendants.[17]

For his first thirty-two years Samuel Johnson lived in the shadow of his father. He worked hard on his lands and attended the church faithfully. With his wife, Mary, he strove to create a Christian household similar to the one in which he had matured. Their first child, born ten months after their marriage, was dutifully named William in honor of his grandfather. But the autumnal air of the seacoast chilled the infant and he died in six weeks. Mary and Samuel, much grieved by their loss, prayed to God to forgive their sins. A year later their prayers were answered; Mary delivered a boy, named Samuel for his father, on October 14, 1696. The elderly William took special pleasure in the lad, watching him grow and learn, and hoped that his earlier dreams for his own Samuel might yet be realized in his grandchild.

For all his industry and sobriety, the elder Samuel failed to attain the stature of his father. When William, deacon of the church, died, the congregation passed over Samuel and appointed James Hooker, a newcomer to Guilford who had married into a prestigious family, to replace him. Samuel's inability to achieve the social distinction of William reflected not so much his lack of piety as a general shift in social relations. Instead of pursuing a career in the ministry, Samuel followed a more worldly calling in "business."[18] Such activity revealed the growing complexity of New England life and signified a larger departure from a simple agrarian society. Many New Englanders criticized these economic trends and viewed them as dangerous symptoms of the secularization of society. In 1685 Samuel Wakeman had condemned "that haughtiness of spirit that predominates among us, [when] every no body would be some body. . . . Men's conditions sit uneasy and their callings suit them not," he remarked sadly. Such antipathy to economic innovation may explain Samuel's problems in Guilford.[19]

The precise nature of Samuel's early activities remains uncertain. But following William's death and the inheritance of the bulk of his father's estate, Samuel became more enterprising. In 1707 the town meeting authorized Johnson to erect a fulling mill on the Menunkatuck River in the northwestern section of the town. This mill, the first of its kind in Guilford, processed wool by stretching and winding the cloth around a smooth wooden log.[20] As Johnson's worldly wealth increased, his neighbors discerned no decline in his religious fervor. Keeping his eye fixed on the spiritual treasure of heaven, Johnson pursued his earthly calling for the greater glory of God. And when Deacon John Meigs died in 1713, Samuel Johnson assumed the ecclesiastical office held earlier by his father.[21]

The second Deacon Johnson managed to maintain the high spiritual standards of the first. When he died, a fairly rich man, in 1727, his son lauded his "sincere and upright devotion towards God." "He was remarkable for a friendly temper and delighted much in hospitality toward strangers and was always ready to deny himself to help such as were in distress," recalled the younger Samuel Johnson. "He spent a great deal of time in visiting the sick . . . and like our Saviour Christ went about doing good. He was exactly circumspect in all his words and actions, open, friendly and plain hearted. . . . In a word I think it may be truly said of him, that he was an Israelite indeed in who there was no guile."[22] By the end of his life, therefore, the elder Samuel Johnson had fulfilled the ideals of William. In his eulogy the younger Samuel acknowledged that fact. But the junior Samuel perceived his father on many levels, not the least of which was his image of how his grandfather William had perceived *his* only son. In reacting to the senior Samuel, the younger felt keenly the presence of the patriarchal William. He understood well how his grandfather had deprecated his father and how his parent had incorporated that low esteem. Three generations of Johnsons had interacted for the first six years of little Samuel's life, and the elder Samuel's later career could never obliterate that primal confrontation.

In October 1696 Fitz-John Winthrop, agent for the colony of Connecticut, negotiated in London with royal officials to prevent the repeal of the colony's charter. Amidst the bustle of the metropolis, he yearned for the tranquillity of provincial life. Simultaneously, the General Assembly of Connecticut, considering "the wonderful goodness of God . . . toward his people," proclaimed a day of "public and solemn thanksgiving." In Guilford, ninth largest town in the colony, the population increased by one (to 126 persons) when Mary Sage Johnson delivered her son Samuel. The town grew slowly in the next decade, numbering but 160 inhabitants in 1706. For the growing boy the surrounding native tribes served mainly as negative symbols of heathenism and barbarism, reminding young Samuel and his playmates of what they were *not.* Occasional fears of warfare further widened the breach separating the two peoples. Years later, in an idyllic description of an imaginary place, Johnson revealed what may well have been a childhood memory of Guilford: ". . . under a gradually rising hill, at the foot of which runs rushing down among the rocks, and sometimes with sudden rapid falls, a most delicious rivulet of pure water . . . taking its rise from a thicket of trees, and . . . losing itself in a gentle winding stream amidst grass and flowers of various hue, in a pleasant meadow below; beyond which, on one side, the sea at a distance . . ., and on the other, a beautiful landscape of pleasant pastures, flocks, and herds, and a delightful country village."[23]

As the first child–three-and-a-half years older than the next sibling–Samuel enjoyed a special place in the Johnson household. Mary Sage Johnson remains a shadowy figure, as do most women of this period; but her oldest son always described her as a "tender mother."[24] Like most infants, Samuel found peace and comfort in her arms–from his narcissistic perspective a sense of cosmic union, a feeling of spiritual universality.

If Mary Johnson accepted the nurturant patterns of her Puritan culture, she weaned her son sometime between his first and second birthdays, perhaps because of a suspected pregnancy.[25] The weaning symbolized not only the disruption of his maternal union but also an abrupt break in his cosmic omnipotence. Perhaps to compensate for the loss of his mother's breast, Samuel developed a tendency to overeat and in later life became "considerably corpulent."[26] As a grandfather he was untypically solicitous about the weaning of a grandchild, suggesting his recognition of the difficulty of the experience.[27] More fundamental, anxiety over separation became a dominant theme in Samuel's unconscious life. In later years he endeavored to recover the maternal union by forming substitute maternal attachments.[28] First in the "mother church" of England, then in the study of Hebrew, "the mother of all languages," Samuel sublimated his desire to incorporate his own mother and the larger cosmos that she symbolized.[29] Even as an adult, Johnson dreaded prolonged separations from his family and openly grieved at the unnaturalness of such departures.[30]

Johnson's fear of separations, of course, reflected more than the trauma of weaning. In Puritan New England, the termination of nursing introduced children to other patterns of child-rearing that reinforced a fear of loss. Weaning children after their first birthday meant that the youngsters had, in most cases, already begun to explore the narrow confines of the New England household, probably upsetting the order of things in countless ways. To prevent domestic confusion, New England parents tried to put the children in their proper place at a young age. In an early sermon Samuel Johnson admonished parents to "keep a strict watch over your children that they run not into sinful courses and to curb sin in its first beginnings." Firm discipline would prevent the children from destroying the peace and order of the family. "If . . . you would have children virtuous," advised Johnson, "you must teach them early to deny themselves, and . . . you must make their inclinations and appetites tame and pliable." Fearing the consequences of overindulgence, he urged parents to establish their authority "by inflexibly insisting on reverence and obedience."[31] At an age, then, when children were adjusting to the weaning experience and learning to stand on their own feet, New England parents attempted to establish precise limits to the autonomy of the young.

Infantile efforts to attain self-control, instead of winning adult approval, provoked parental wrath. Believing that childish willfulness should be destroyed, New England parents forced the children to accept their basic powerlessness. Infants, who had recently enjoyed narcissistic fantasies of omnipotence, were now subjected to harsh dicipline by their parents. This early assertion of adult authority could only undermine the self-confidence of the children. Frustrated by parental rebuffs, Puritan children suffered the psychological consequence of shame—a profound sense of inadequacy for failing to attain their goals. Seeking to master their worlds, the children were defeated *before* they started and were humiliated for their premature efforts. Such a disciplinary tactic enabled New England parents to thwart the willfulness of their children and taught the youngsters to acknowledge the authority of their superiors.[32]

But the fear of contempt that followed from these early defeats affected the children for the rest of their lives. New Englanders remained hesitant about public openness, anxious about visible appearances, and sensitive to the eye of God. Speaking of the problem of vanity, Samuel Johnson chided his congregation to "1. Make no good deed more public than is necessary. 2. Perform as many [good deeds] as we can as private[ly] as possible. 3. And regard chiefly the eye of our heavenly father."[33] Such advice, repeated from numerous pulpits throughout the colonial period, revealed an underlying anxiety about visibility. "There is nothing more uneasy to me," confessed Johnson to an English correspondent, "than to be set in . . . an odius light in the face of the world, and especially [in front] of my great and good patrons and benefactors."[34] These fears reflected a deeper psychological concern about the loss of esteem and the withdrawal of love. Preaching about the sin of rebelliousness, Johnson described "disobedient children" as being "cast out of [the] family." Reconciliation with the father "reinstated [the children] in his family" "as though they had never been disinherited." A profound fear of emotional abandonment–what Johnson would call "disinheritance"–thereby reinforced an earlier anxiety about separation from the maternal universe.[35]

As Samuel Johnson matured he remained extremely sensitive to public opinion and dreaded the isolation associated with personal exposure. When discussing questions of love and marriage with his twenty-year-old son, Johnson preferred sending a letter to the boy to confronting him face to face. Similarly, in broaching a second marriage, the recently widowed Johnson proposed in writing, "because of the great difficulty I should labor under in expressing myself in presence, and because I mortally hate to be talked of." The emphasis on visibility also emerged in Johnson's comprehension of God. "He is an *omnipresent* and *omniscent* God," he preached, "and a constant spectator of all our behavior, of all the thoughts and affections of our hearts, as well as all the actions of our lives." God could see everything and if man would but open his eyes, he would "behold the great Lord of Heaven and Earth gloriously shining in all his works!" When Johnson surreptitiously attended an evangelical revival, he carefully concealed his identity, hoping to remain "incognito."[36] These cases exemplify psychological defenses, unconscious strategies designed to protect him from the omnipresent eye of society.

In the patriarchal society of New England, fathers like Samuel Johnson, senior, served as the major source of discipline. The younger Samuel remembered that his father had been "plain hearted in reproving" errant behavior and he accepted chastisement as a sign of parental wisdom. In numerous sermons, he exhorted children to "submit cheerfully to [the] instruction and government" of their elders, for godly parents best understood the spiritual needs of the young.[37] Johnson's confidence in parental discipline concealed a more fundamental ambivalence about his father's "plain hearted" reprovals. "The child that loves his father" will not "account any of his demands burthensome" and will "freely and readily observe them," Johnson maintained, "for what man will not take good care that he offend not the person he sincerely loves?" Such filial obedience extended from the biological father on earth to the supreme Father in heaven and provided spiritual security for the young. But Johnson realized that such love was not always forthcoming. "So if we love not God," he conceded, "we can't fail of having our minds filled with infinite anxieties, and a most dismal train of fearful expectations."[38] This admission of the existence of such feelings revealed the hidden tensions within New England households. Raised to respect ancestral authority, Puritan children suffered intense emotional stress when they failed to appreciate their disciplining parents.

In stifling infantile autonomy, New England parents released considerable aggression of their own. Such attacks—probably more verbal than physical—created lasting effects on the young. New Englanders remained unusually sensitive to outbursts of temper and extolled the virtues of "temperance and moderation" in human affairs. Preaching a funeral sermon for one of his parishioners, Samuel Johnson praised the deceased for his "more than ordinary firmness and stability of mind"; he was a man "of great moderation and equanimity; never much elated or dejected; and scarce ever ruffled or disordered in his temper." "The duty of meekness," Johnson asserted on a different occasion, implies "an habitual command of our tempers as renders us always calm, mild and patient under such trials and provocations as are apt to occur in the course of our lives." This search for outward tranquillity probably reflected an earlier antipathy to the "disordered" temper of the elder Samuel Johnson.[39]

The confrontations between father and son illuminated the larger tensions of generational interaction. At a time when the elder Samuel probably resented the oversight of the patriarchal William, he found himself threatened from below by the emotional demands of his son. Putting young Samuel in his place enabled the father to assert his own dominance in the Johnson household. Painfully, the boy learned to respect the traditional family order and, by extension, the larger society of which it was a microcosm. In later life Samuel Johnson, like most colonial Americans, stressed the importance of preserving hierarchical arrangements and shuddered at the thought of social disorder. "Family government is grossly neglected in the country," lamented Johnson, and "if it be not reformed in a little time, our youth will be utterly ruined and our commonwealth will sink into a confused jumble of untoward and ungoverned rebels."[40]

If the presence of William Johnson aggravated the problems of his own son, it provided his grandson with important psychological defenses against the resentful father.[41] Seeking to recover an earlier maternal intimacy and frustrated by the paternal will, the younger Samuel supplanted his father *symbolically* by identifying with his grandfather. In this way little Samuel became his father's father and thereby fulfilled his fantasy of controlling the family, if only on a symbolic level. William Johnson's acknowledged superiority to the elder Samuel facilitated this reversal of roles, for in identifying with his grandfather the younger Samuel could assume that same superiority. When the senior Samuel died in 1727, his son abruptly interrupted his eulogy to interject a description of William: "(I well remember my grandfather. He was a most excellent Christian and of a most amiable temper. My Father's character may equally stand for his.)" And over half a century after William's death his grandson recalled that he "was of much note then in their public affairs and esteemed one of the best men."[42]

To little Samuel the aged William represented a founding father, a member of the first generation that already enjoyed a reputation for greatness. William taught his grandson to read and helped him memorize portions of the Bible. When the grandfather visited "the ancient people, his contemporaries," he would take Samuel along and make him recite from memory, "in which he much delighted." These excursions not only revealed Samuel's readiness to identify with his grandfather but also demonstrated William's desire to see the youngster fulfill his earlier dreams for his own son. Little Samuel's precociousness convinced William that the boy "should be bred to learning."[43] On this symbolic level, grandfather and grandson conspired to reinforce the elder Samuel's sense of failure and induced the father to accept a secondary role.

These intergenerational configurations emerged in the younger Samuel's desire to learn Hebrew. "One of the first things he remembered of himself," wrote Samuel in his autobiography, "was an impatient curiosity to know everything that could be known. . . . His grandfather had a book in which there were several Hebrew words, the meaning of which he was very desirous to know, but to his great mortification nobody was able to tell him. . . . This gave him a vast desire to know that language . . . [and] made him always principally delight in the original languages as long as he lived."[44] As a student at Yale College, Johnson excelled in languages and developed an early proficiency in Hebrew.[45] In his later years he became a major advocate for the teaching of Hebrew and published an English and Hebrew grammar.[46]

As his autobiography attests, Johnson traced his interest in Hebrew to his grandfather. He also stressed the inability of anyone in the region to translate this mysterious language. By learning Hebrew, Samuel could reverse the intellectual decline in New England and demonstrate his superiority over his father; he could even aspire to become his father's teacher, a role well suited to a youngster named Samuel.[47] Johnson's penchant for learning, particularly his interest in languages, also reflected a more fundamental reversal of generations. The youngster's "impatient curiosity to know everything that could be known" constituted a symbolic desire to incorporate, not only the knowledge of the universe, but the universe itself. Language, moreover, is an oral function and Johnson observed that Hebrew was "the original language," "the Mother of all language and eloquence." In a revealing statement he remarked that "language is, as it were, the copy of universal nature, and like a picture, supplieth the place of originals."[48] The "impatient curiosity" to learn Hebrew therefore served a dual symbolic function in Samuel Johnson's life. On one level he could surmount his childish impotence and replace his father; on another he could renew the fantasy pleasures of the "incestuous" maternal union.

These psychological constellations framed Johnson's comprehension of the eternal father and influenced the formulation of his mature theology. In nearly all his writings Johnson described God as a tender, loving, amiable, affectionate being. God "delights in providing for the welfare of every one of his spacious family," he preached, "which he does with infinitely greater affection and kindness than the most tender father." In heeding the will of God we obey "not the will of an imperious and spiteful enemy, but of a most kind, tender and indulgent *friend,* and who out of mere friendship and good-will to us does will and appoint what we are required to submit to and obey."[49] To this Puritan grandson God was not the avenging father of Calvin, but rather a compassionate father of mercies, a "tender and indulgent *friend.*"

The prototype of Johnson's God was not his earthly father, Samuel, but his omnipresent grandfather, William.[50] "A Father who begets a Son," declared the younger Samuel, "is, at best, but a mere instrument of bringing him into being, whereas God . . . only is the true and adequate cause, and therefore He only is truly our Father." "God ever beholds us through his dear Son," preached Johnson on another occasion, "as his own offspring, and with the eyes of a most tender and merciful *father,* and must therefore be the best of friends." While Samuel, senior, pursued his "business" and Mary Sage performed her wifely duties, it was the patriarchal William who became "a constant spectator of all our behavior."[51] Fond of his precocious grandson, William indulged his fancies and gently chastised his transgressions. The elder Samuel might discipline the lad and seek to break his sinful will, but the aged William tenderly forgave him and mitigated the paternal wrath. William, the father of Samuel, became the father of all Samuels, the symbolic father of mankind; "He only is truly our Father."[52]

While William lived, the elder Samuel quietly acceded to his father's desire that the boy "be bred to learning." But after William's death, this Samuel, at last freed from the scrutiny of the patriarch, changed his mind and "rather chose to bring [his son] up to business, into which he endeavored to introduce him for four or five years." The younger Samuel later viewed this experience as a sign of his father's intellectual inadequacy. The first settlers of New England "were now gone off the stage," he wrote autobiographically, "and their sons fell greatly short of their acquirements as through the necessity of the times they could give but little attention to the business of education." But the boy, perhaps humiliated by the parent's victory, "could never be reconciled" to his father's business; "he could think of nothing but books." At last the elder Samuel capitulated again and let his son "follow his inclinations." And again the son became parent to the father, reasserting his dominance in the name of William. Confused by his inadequacy and perhaps feeling guilty for betraying his own father, the elder Samuel succumbed to the son's demands and acknowledged his error. Having rejected his father's business, the younger Samuel then dedicated himself to his "impatient curiosity to know everything that could be known."[53]

This final confrontation between father and son occurred in Samuel's tenth year, the age at which most young men in New England adopted a permanent calling.[54] For most children in this rural society there were no decisions to be made; young men and women simply prepared to assume the roles of their parents. The senior Samuel's economic initiative, however, introduced an element of choice. (In this respect, it is significant that the elder Samuel's decision to permit his son to pursue his education coincided with the founding of the fulling mill. By allowing the youth to enact the patriarchal dreams of William, the father found release from parental inhibitions and proceeded to develop a thriving business.) Unlike most New England boys, Samuel Johnson could choose his occupation. Moreover, in deciding to further his education, Samuel delayed the time when he would have to make the final choice. Though most college graduates in colonial New England became ministers, there was nothing inevitable about that outcome. During the next decade the younger Samuel would enjoy a luxury afforded to few sons of New England. He would be allowed to "find" himself in the company of a select group of friends, the intellectual elite of his generation.[55]

NOTES

1. SJ, Sermon before the General Assembly, October 22, 1721, JCU. For provocative discussions of childhood in New England, see Edmund S. Morgan, *The Puritan Family: Essays on Religion and Domestic Relations in Seventeenth-Century New England*, rev. ed. (New York, 1966); John Demos, *A Little Commonwealth: Family Life in Plymouth Colony* (New York, 1970). See also the essay by Joseph E. Illick in Lloyd deMause, ed. *The History of Childhood* (New York, 1974). For comparison see Joseph F. Kett, "Adolescence and Youth in Nineteenth-Century America," *Journal of Interdisciplinary History* 2 (1971):283–98. The metaphor of childish ignorance appears frequently in Puritan

sermons; see, for example, Joseph Moss, *An Election Sermon* (New London, Conn., 1715), p. 19.

2. Anne Bradstreet, "Childhood," quoted in Elizabeth Wade White, *Anne Bradstreet: "The Tenth Muse"* (New York, 1971), p. 45.

3. Samuel Johnson, *A Short Catechism for Young People. . . .* (New York, 1765), printed in *SJ Papers*, 3:590. The text is Proverbs 22:6.

4. Increase Mather, *A Discourse Concerning the Danger of Apostasy*, printed with *A Call From Heaven to the Present and Succeeding Generations* (Boston, 1679), p. 91.

5. This discussion is based on Isabel MacBeath Calder, *The New Haven Colony* (New Haven, Conn., 1934), pp. 67–72.

6. James Shepard, "The New Haven and Wallingford (Conn.) Johnsons," *NEHGR* 56 (1902):132–33; *New Haven Town Records*, ed. Franklin Bowditch Dexter, 2 vols. (New Haven, Conn., 1917–19), 1:106, 272, 496–97; John Winthrop, *Winthrop's Journal, "History of New England" 1630–1649*, ed. James Kendall Hosmer, 2 vols. (New York, 1908), 1:291; Michael Wigglesworth, "Autobiography," *NEHGR* 17 (1863): 137.

7. "Genealogical Notes," in "Records of the Town of Newark [N.J.]," *Collections of the New Jersey Historical Society* 6, supplement (1866): 121–22; Guilford Town Records, Liber A, Guilford Town Hall, Guilford, Conn.; George Eleazer Bushnell, *Bushnell Family Genealogy* (Nashville, Tenn., 1945), p. 32.

8. Trumbull, *Complete History of Connecticut*, 1:107–9; [Thomas Ruggles, Jr.], "A Sketch of a History of Guilford, in Connecticut," *MHS Colls.*, 1st ser., 4 (1795):186; [Thomas Ruggles, Jr.], "Extract of a Letter . . . ," *MHS Colls.*, 1st ser., 10 (1809):91; Lucas, "Valley of Discord," pp. 32–35. The Guilford covenant, dated June 1639, is printed in Alvan Talcott, *Chittenden Family: William Chittenden of Guilford, Conn. and His Descendants* (New Haven, Conn., 1882), p. 6.

9. For William Johnson's tenure as representative to the General Court, see *Pub. Recs. Conn.*, 2–4, passim. His other offices are described in R. D. Smith, *The History of Guilford, Connecticut, from Its First Settlement in 1639* (Albany, N.Y., 1877), pp. 76–77, 182, and in Bernard Christian Steiner, *A History of the Plantation of Menunkatuck and of the Original Town of Guilford, Connecticut* (Baltimore, Md., 1897), pp. 112, 172–73, 211–12, 397.

10. Smith, *History of Guilford*, p. 105. "The Cambridge Platform" [1648] described the qualifications for deacons: the candidates should be "*Grave, not double tongued, not given to much wine, not given to filthy lucre,* they must first be *proved* . . . being found *Blameless*." "The office and work of the *Deacons* is to receive the offrings of the church, gifts given to the church, & to keep the treasury of the church: & therewith to serve the *Tables* which the church is to provide for: as the *Lords Table*, the table of the *ministers*, & of

such as are in *neccessitie,* to whom they are to distribute in simplicity." See Walker, *Creeds and Platforms*, pp. 213–14.

11. *Pub. Recs. Conn.*, 3:227, 248, 251, 253, and passim.

12. Probate Records, New Haven, Connecticut, microfilm, 2:294, Connecticut State Library, Hartford.

13. Samuel Wakeman, *Sound Repentance. The Right Way to Escape Deserved Ruine* (Boston, 1685), pp. 18, 23, 24, 27, 31, 33.

14. John Whiting, *The Way of Israels Welfare* (Boston, 1686), pp. 35–36.

15. William's children are listed in Bernard C. Steiner, "Supplementary Notes on the Johnson Family," *NEHGR* 56 (1902):298 and, with slight variations, in SJ, "Liber Dierum," *SJ Papers*, 1:60. Sparse genealogical information on his wife can be found in Bushnell, *Bushnell Family*, p. 32. The high infant mortality among William Johnson's children contrasts markedly with the findings for the healthier interior town of Andover; see Greven, *Four Generations*, p. 28.

16. In naming their children, Puritans frequently considered the biblical significance of the nomenclature. According to 1 Samuel, 1:28, Samuel was "lent to the Lord" to serve him as long "as he liveth." Moreover, 1 Samuel 19:20 describes Samuel as appointed over the school of prophets. These symbolic references were well known in New England and appeared in several published works; see *The Necessity of Reformation* [1679], printed in Walker, *Creeds and Platforms*, p. 437, and Solomon Stoddard, *The Way for A People to Live Long in the Land that God hath Given Them* (Boston, 1703), pp. 12–13. The symbolic nomenclature probably influenced Samuel's self-image; most certainly, it influenced his own son Samuel (b. 1696) in fundamental ways. For a brief discussion of some Puritan names see Franklin Bowditch Dexter, *Biographical Sketches of the Graduates of Yale College*, 6 vols. (New York, 1885–1911), 1:268.

17. For William's children, see Bernard Steiner, "Supplementary Notes," 1:298. The will of Samuel Johnson's father-in-law, David Sage, is printed in Charles William Manwaring, ed., *A Digest of the Early Connecticut Probate Records,* 3 vols. (Hartford, Conn., 1904), 2:109. Much about William's later years can be inferred from SJ, "Autobiography," pp. 3–4. The rootedness of the second-generation Johnsons parallels the patterns found in Andover; see Greven, *Four Generations*, pp. 39–40, 97–99.

18. Smith, *History of Guilford,* p. 127; SJ, "Autobiography," p. 4.

19. Wakeman, *Sound Repentance,* p. 27. Johnson's relatively low social status in 1710 is indicated by the ranking of his son at Yale; he was placed eighth in a class of nine (the ranking being based on social position); see Dexter, *Biographical Sketches,* 1: 117.

20. Smith, *History of Guilford,* p. 33; Steiner, *History of Guilford,* p. 250. For a description of the mill, see Jared Eliot, *Essays Upon Field Husbandry in New England,* ed. Harry J. Carman and Rexford G. Tugwell (New York, 1934), p. 8. Eliot, a native of Guilford, was the town's schoolmaster while Johnson was establishing the mill.

21. Smith, *History of Guilford,* p. 105; Steiner, "Supplementary Notes," p. 298; Guilford Town Records, Liber D, p. 11.

22. SJ, "Liber Dierum," p. 68.

23. Dunn, *Puritans and Yankees*, chap. 13; *Pub. Recs. Conn.*, 4: 175, 181, 468; 5: 6; [Knight], *Journal*, p. 39; SJ, "Raphael," *SJ Papers*, 2: 521.

24. For a genealogy of Johnson's family, see Steiner, "Supplementary Notes," p. 298, and, with some variation, SJ, "Biographical Notes," *SJ Papers*, 1: 60. References to Mary Sage Johnson appear in SJ, "My Present Thoughts of Episcopacy" [1719], *SJ Papers*, 3: 8 and "Liber Dierum," p. 67.

25. The interval between Samuel (b. October 1696) and his next sibling, Mary (b. March 1700 N.S.), is longer than all the birth intervals of the first nine children. This suggests that Mary may have had a miscarriage or stillbirth while Samuel was still an infant. Puritan weaning is discussed in John Demos, "Underlying Themes in the Witchcraft of Seventeenth-Century New England," *American Historical Review* 75 (1970): 1311–26. For the practice among English Puritans, see Alan Macfarlane, *The Family Life of Ralph Josselin: A Seventeenth-Century Clergyman. An Essay in Historical Anthropology* (Cambridge, 1970), pp. 87–88. In addition there are references in the diaries of Samuel Sewall and Cotton Mather that suggest the importance ascribed to weaning.

26. Thomas B. Chandler, *The Life of Samuel Johnson, the First President of King's College in New York* (New York, 1805), p. 126.

27. SJ to W.S.J., June 16, 1760, JCU: "Pray how did M[istress?] Polly bear her weaning? Kiss her for me and give my Love to . . . all the Children. . . ."

28. For a psychoanalytic discussion of this problem, see John Bowlby, "Separation Anxiety," *International Journal of Psychoanalysis* 41 (1960): 89–113. Robert Jay Lifton has suggested that "separation anxiety" reflects not merely the birth trauma and other childhood separations and survivals but also a more fundamental fear of death; see *Death in Life: Survivors of Hiroshima* (New York, 1967), pp. 485–86.

29. The metaphor of the "mother church" appears frequently in Johnson's writings, but only in relation to the Church of England, the established church of the mother country. For his reference to Hebrew as the mother language, see Samuel Johnson, *An English and Hebrew Grammar* ([London], 1765), p. 6 of the MS copy in JCU. See chap. 4 below.

30. Upon leaving Stratford to assume the presidency of King's College in New York, Johnson begged his son to forgive his departure: ". . . it looks more unnatural for parents to leave their children than vice versa. But I beg you will think as favorably of me as you can, and believe that it has been the greatest shock to my mind to leave you, that I ever met with." Johnson ascribed the necessity of his absence to the providence of God. See SJ to WSJ, May 14, 1755, *SJ Papers*, 4: 35. Johnson wrote a similar revealing letter to WSJ, April 20, 1755, JCU.

31. SJ, Notes for Sermon XLVI: On Religion Recommended to Children, August 24, 1718, JCU; "Raphael," pp. 555–57.

32. This discussion of the effects of severe discipline at an early stage of child development is based on the theories of Erik H. Erikson. In

explaining this process, I have tried to "work backwards" without engaging in circular reasoning. According to Erikson, a sense of the loss of self-control at the stage when a child is trying to "stand on his feet" evokes a sensitivity to shame; these ideas are presented briefly in *Childhood and Society,* rev. ed. (New York, 1963), pp. 251–54. My analysis of Johnson's writings suggests not only that he encouraged early and firm discipline (see n. 31), but also that he himself experienced a variety of emotions associated with shame. For very provocative studies, see Gerhart Piers and Milton B. Singer, *Shame and Guilt: A Psychoanalytic and a Cultural Study* (Springfield, Ill., 1953), pp. 11–17, and Helen L. Lynd, *On Shame and the Search for Identity* (New York, 1958), pp. 31–37. For the Puritan context, see Demos, *A Little Commonwealth,* chap. 9.

33. SJ, Minutes of Sermons on Christ's Sermon on the Mount, August 1741, JCU. The third item was entered by Johnson at a later time.

34. SJ to SPG, November 30, 1751, *SJ Papers,* 1: 152.

35. SJ, Six Sermons on Psalm 36, July-August 1766, JCU, sermon 6, p. 37. Piers and Singer, in *Shame and Guilt,* pp. 16–17, have written: "Behind the feeling of shame stands not the fear of hatred, but the fear of *contempt* which, on an even deeper level of the unconscious, spells fear of *abandonment,* the death by emotional starvation."

36. SJ to WSJ, July 7, 1747, S.J. to Mrs. Anne Watts, January 15, 1759, *SJ Papers,* 1: 127, 280; S.J., Ten Sermons on the Lord's Prayer, March 1736, JCU, sermon 5; S.J., A Sermon: Of the All-Sufficiency of God . . ., September 2, 1744, JCU, postscript. Explicit references to shame appear throughout Johnson's writings. He shared these emotional patterns with other members of his culture. Thus one election preacher declared, "If Honour be the reward of Vertue; then shame and disgrace shall be the punishment of Vice and of a Neglect of God." See Nathaniel Chauncey, *Honouring God the True Way to Honour* (New London, Conn., 1719), pp. 41–42. For further discussion, see also Demos, *A Little Commonwealth,* pp. 137–39.

37. SJ, "Liber Dierum," p. 68; Notes for Sermon 46, August 24, 1718, JCU.

38. SJ, Sermon: Concerning the Love of God, March 19, 1721, JCU.

39. SJ, Sermon at the Funeral of Coll. John Burr, January 15, 1750, appended to A Sermon: Concerning the Ascension and Intercession of Christ, June 1751, JCU; SJ, Minutes of Sermons, August 1741, JCU. These ideas appear widely in New England sermons; see, for example, Timothy Cutler, *The Firm Union of a People Represented* (New London, Conn., 1717), p. 10.

40. SJ, "Raphael," p. 556.

41. The following discussion has been informed by two essays by Ernest Jones: "The Phantasy of the Reversal of Generations" and "The Significance of the Grandfather for the Fate of the Individual," both of which are printed in *Papers on Psychoanalysis,* rev. ed. (New York, 1919); see also Karl Abraham, "Some Remarks on the Role of Grandparents in the Psychology of Neurosis" [1913], in *Clinical Papers and Essays on*

Psychoanalysis, ed. and trans. Hilda C. Abraham (London, 1955), pp. 44–47. Very illuminating is R. D. Laing's *The Politics of the Family and Other Essays* (New York, 1971), esp. p. 77.

42. SJ, "Liber Dierum," pp. 68–69; SJ to WSJ, January 6, 1757, Smyth MSS, New Haven Colony Historical Society. Johnson's reminiscence of his father revealed a similar glorification of paternal benevolence, but the elder Samuel lacked, in his son's eyes, the greatness of William.

43. SJ, "Autobiography," pp. 3–4.

44. Ibid.

45. Benjamin Lord to Ezra Stiles, May 28, 1779, in Dexter, *Biographical Sketches,* 1: 115–16; Judah Monis to SJ, March 2, 1716, JCU. The latter letter was written in Hebrew because "you [i.e., Johnson] take particular pleasure in the Hebrew tongue."

46. SJ, *An English and Hebrew Grammar* (London, 1765).

47. See above, n. 16. This reversal of roles was made explicit in the eulogy for the elder Johnson; see below, chap. 7.

48. SJ, "Autobiography," p. 3; *English and Hebrew Grammar,* p. 6; [S.J.], *The First Easy Rudiments of Grammar, Applied to the English Tongue* (New York, 1765), p. 6.

49. SJ, Sermon: Concerning the Love of God, March 19, 1721, JCU; Ten Sermons on the Lord's Prayer, March 1736, JCU, sermon 5.

50. A classic statement of the personification of nature is in Freud, *Future of an Illusion,* p. 38.

51. SJ, The Great Crime and Ingratitude of Forgetting God, January 1754; Ten Sermons on the Lord's Prayer, March 1736, both in JCU.

52. New England parents were keenly aware of the tendency of grandparents to spoil their grandchildren. John Robinson, whose writings were influential in the seventeenth century, observed that "grandfathers are more affectionate towards their children's children, than to their immediates, as seeing themselves further propagated in them, and by their means proceeding to a further degree of eternity, which all desire naturally, if not in themselves, yet in their posterity. And hence it is, that children brought up with their grandfathers, or grandmothers, seldom do well, but are usually corrupted by their too great indulgence." Quoted in Philip J. Greven, Jr., ed., *Child-Rearing Concepts, 1628–1861: Historical Sources* (Itasca, Ill., 1973), p. 13.

53. SJ, "Autobiography," pp. 3–5. The narcissistic dynamics of such confrontations are suggested in Gerald H. J. Pearson, *Adolescence and the Conflict of Generations: An Introduction to Some of the Psychoanalytic Contributions to the Understanding of Adolescence* (New York, 1958), p. 44.

54. For a suggestive treatment of this problem, see Demos, *A Little Commonwealth,* pp. 145–50.

55. The broader implications of the discontinuities between generations are discussed in Margaret Mead, "The Implication of Culture Change for Personality Development," *American Journal of Orthopsychiatry* 17 (1947): 633–46, and Kingsley Davis, "The Sociology of Parent-Youth Conflict," *American Sociological Review* 5 (1940): 525–35.

4

"HIS RULING PASSION"

WHILE THE elder Samuel Johnson launched his fulling mill in Guilford, his son commenced "the business of education" under the tutelage of the town schoolmaster, Jared Eliot. The ten-year-old Samuel, "having such a thirst after learning, . . . made a pretty rapid progress" in such subjects as Latin and Greek and quickly became "his master's favorite." But Eliot's departure from Guilford interrupted the boy's education. Samuel soon found other teachers among the neighboring ministers and managed to obtain sufficient proficiency in the classical languages to be admitted to Yale College before the age of fourteen. By that time he had not only acquired a basic scholastic education but had also imbibed a pattern of cultural values that structured his image of the world. When Samuel Johnson traveled to the college at Saybrook in 1710 to pursue his "thirst after learning," he already possessed a strong sense of his place in the world and a firm notion of what he wanted to become.[1]

Like his father and grandfather, Samuel Johnson had been raised in the jeremiad tradition of New England. From the weekly sermons of Guilford's minister, Thomas Ruggles, had learned that the Puritan fathers had been extraordinary men, noted for their piety and godliness, and that God had blessed this people with His grace. For boys like Samuel, this glorification of the first settlers created idealized ancestral symbols, models worthy of respect and imitation.[2] The jeremiad sermons also denounced the children of New England for failing to uphold the original purity of the founders. "That generation has not been long removed," remarked one Connecticut preacher, "and yet we are greatly degenerated." This loss of religious zeal threatened the peace of the colony, for an angry God would surely punish His back-sliding people.[3] To forestall the "impending judgments," the Connecticut legislature endeavored to suppress "all profaneness and immorality" and urged the clergy "to excite and stir up their good people to . . . a reformation of [the] provoking evils."[4] Thus, while bewailing the spiritual decline, the jeremiads cried for the restoration of a pure religious community, one that could continue to claim the special favor of the Almighty.

The future of the godly society demanded the transmission of Puritan ideals to later generations of New Englanders. From the earliest years of colonization, Harvard College had served as a seminary of learning, providing both an orthodox and a liberal arts education. But by the early eighteenth century many conservative New Englanders detected alarming innovations at Harvard—a movement toward latitudinarianism that hinted at heresy. These fears, together with a desire for a local college, led a group of ministers to propose the creation of a collegiate school in Connecticut, a bulwark of orthodoxy against what seemed to be a floodtide of secularism and immorality. The founders of the school (later known as Yale College) recalled that the Puritan fathers had migrated to the American wilderness to preserve the purity of the Protestant religion, but "their unworthy posterity" had unfortunately neglected "this grand errand." Now, in 1701, "sensible of our equal obligations . . . to prosecute the same end," the Connecticut divines proclaimed the importance of a "liberal and religious education of suitable youth." Ten years later, as Samuel Johnson completed his first year of collegiate studies, the Connecticut election preacher praised the Lord for providing the colony with "nurseries of learning," and urged the people to continue their support of the "school of prophets among us."[5]

The attempt to reinvigorate the Puritan tradition in eighteenth-century Connecticut reflected not only a concern about internal disintegration but also a fear of interference from England. The failure of the colonies to coordinate military affairs during Queen Anne's War (1701–13), the American counterpart of a larger war between England and France, had revealed a fundamental weakness in the British Empire, and royal officials seriously contemplated the repeal of the colonial charters. These imperial problems alarmed loyal New Englanders, who recognized that the preservation of the New England way depended upon the maintenance of the traditional "liberties and privileges."[6]

Besides this political threat, the emergence of the Church of England further challenged the visible harmony of Puritan New England. By the early eighteenth century migrations from England and Ireland had brought a few dozen Anglican families to Connecticut, most of whom settled in the southwestern region of the colony around Stratford. Vastly outnumbered by the descendants of Puritans, these Anglicans confronted a deliberate policy of religious discrimination. But in 1701 the English crown chartered the Society for the Propagation of the Gospel in Foreign Parts, a missionary organization designed to strengthen the episcopal church in the colonies.

From nearby New York, Caleb Heathcote, a prominent member of the provincial elite, encouraged the SPG to support missionary activity among the "dissenters" of New England. Accompanying an Anglican preacher to Connecticut, Heathcote encountered massive resistance from third- and fourth-generation Puritans. The dissenters viewed the Church of England as the "most dangerous enemy they have to grapple withall," Heathcote reported to London, and "half of the people in that government think our church to be little better than the papist." Despite a warm reception from the colony's Anglicans, Heathcote harbored no illusions about the task before him. "We are here in an enemy's country," he admitted, and "all the ground we can propose to gain amongst them must be by soft and gentle means, for should the friends of the Church do otherwise, the whole country would soon be in a flame." But even if the Anglican missionaries posed no immediate threat to the Connecticut establishment, their presence could not be denied by the Puritan clergy. Orthodox ministers might take "abundance of pain . . . to persuade and terrify the people" from listening to Anglican sermons, but they could never silence the ecclesiastical arm of the British government.[7] For the children of New England, therefore, the much-maligned Church of England served as a visible reminder of the superiority of British power and of the existence of an alternative metropolitan culture.

Fear of Anglican expansion, together with a more general concern about spiritual decline, convinced the Connecticut orthodoxy that ecclesiastical reform should be instituted in order to forestall "heresy and apostasy." In 1708 the General Assembly summoned the colony's ministers to a series of conferences to consider ecclesiastical revision. The resulting system—known as the Saybrook Platform—organized the churches into county "consociations," which were supervised by a ruling council of ministers. This arrangement enabled the clergy to oversee the affairs of individual congregations in such important matters as the appointment of pastors.[8] By curtailing local autonomy, the Saybrook Platform attempted to eliminate the pervasive discord within the churches and promised a return to the tranquillity of the first generation. "Remember ye our brethren," declared the reforming ministers, remember "that the practical piety and serious religion of our progenitors is exemplary and for our imitation, and will reflect confounding shame on us, if we prove degenerate."[9] With such solemn exhortations, the children of New England swore to maintain their symbolic attachments to the founding fathers.[10]

In the autumn of 1710 Samuel Johnson enrolled at Connecticut's collegiate school to satisfy his "impatient curiosity to know everything that could be known." This "thirst after knowledge and truth," he later remarked, "was always his ruling passion separate from every other consideration."[11] Johnson's desire to master all knowledge represented, on a symbolic level, an attempt to incorporate and control the known universe. By establishing such intellectual hegemony, he could create, at least symbolically, a sense of cosmic universality. The vision of becoming the most learned man in Puritan America also meant that he would attain unsurpassed eminence in the Christian world. Such accomplishments would reverse the spiritual decline among God's people and would enable the young intellectual to reaffirm his personal superiority over his father's generation. Johnson's fantasies of intellectual omnipotence—what he called his "ruling passion"—though perhaps only partially conscious, became an idealized object that he struggled to attain during his student years at Yale.

Despite a heavy emphasis upon theology and matters of religion, the Yale curriculum offered more than a ministerial education; it endeavored to produce men well versed in the liberal arts. Yale freshmen concentrated on the classical languages, recited from Tully and Virgil, translated the Greek Testament, and read the Psalms in Hebrew. Sophomores grappled with the problems of logic, while upperclassmen moved from natural philosophy to mathematics and metaphysics. The study of rhetoric, ethics, and theology—subjects examined by all classes—completed the Yale education. Besides listening to the lectures of their mentors, the undergraduates participated in syllogistic disputations designed to sharpen their minds and improve their oratorical skills. Four years of such study qualified a student for graduation in a ceremony characterized by formal academic recitations.[12]

Because Yale College ranked its students according to the social status of their families, Samuel Johnson stood next to last in a class of nine.[13] His intellectual accomplishments, however, brought him greater distinction. Having acquired a superior preparatory education in the classical languages, Johnson surpassed most of his classmates. Benjamin Lord—a schoolmate whom Johnson once saved from drowning—remembered him as the "greatest proficient" in the languages and acknowledged his "genius" in composition and what passed for oratory. Johnson's academic reputation earned him an early appointment as schoolmaster of his native town, a position he held until he received a more prestigious assignment as a tutor at Yalc in 1716.[14]

Johnson later confessed that his undergraduate success had "served to blow him up with a great conceit that he was now an adept." These illusions satisfied important emotional needs for Samuel Johnson—his desire for intellectual supremacy and his search for fame and distinction. A contemporary description of the Yale commencement in 1714, at which Johnson obtained his bachelor's degree, captured the pomposity and presumptuousness of the students. "I hear that the Athenian Oracle is held at Seabrook College," quipped a friendly observer, and "that all knotty questions (although twisted as hard as the Gordian one) may be resolved and untied; and that they'll do it, although with Alexander's sword." If they succeed, he averred, "for their reward they shall have . . . an empire, but not of the whole known, but of the unknown world."[15] Thirsting after universal knowledge and the personal recognition it would bring them, Samuel Johnson and his classmates prematurely accepted the veneer of scholarship as proof of their intellectual achievements.

Besides the formal academic exercises, Yale students attended divine services regularly at the college and transcribed the sermons into their notebooks. While Samuel Johnson studied at the collegiate school, preachers like Tutor Phineas Fiske and Thomas Ruggles appeared frequently before the undergraduates and expounded various themes within the jeremiad tradition.[16] From these exercises the scholars not only absorbed the lessons of orthodox Puritanism but also learned the art of preaching. Samuel Johnson readily accepted the theological ideas of his mentors, and his earliest religious writings reveal the influence of the jeremiad cosmology. In one significant passage, for example, he affirmed the validity of New England's ecclesiastical structure, and specifically rejected the polity of the Church of England ("there is no place for a hierarchy, or a rather a *hier*-slavery," he stated bluntly).[17] Johnson's acceptance of the dominant Puritan values, together with his intellectual curiosity, persuaded him to embark on a career in the ministry. In provincial Connecticut, clergymen were expected to be pious and "capable of divining the word of truth aright"; they also had to be "competently well skilled in arts and languages" and "well studied and well principled in divinity."[18] The young scholar, academically successful and eminently orthodox, seemed well suited for the task.

Johnson's commitment to intellectual achievement led him to draft a comprehensive system of all knowledge—an "encyclopedia" that passed through five "editions" between 1713 and 1715. In a late version, consisting of 1,271 theses written in Latin, he divided knowledge into archetypes and types and then further subdivided the units into the general arts of grammar, rhetoric, arithmetic, physics, and theology. This early endeavor reflected the scholastic basis of a Yale education in the early eighteenth century. Following Petrus Ramus's theories of logic, Puritan intellectuals had drafted universal systems of knowledge since the sixteenth century.[19] But for Samuel Johnson these philosophical abridgments also served to reinforce his self-image as an intellectually superior person capable of knowing everything that could be known. In marginal annotations he described himself as "Samuel, the wise, the virtuous, Johnson." Such heady conclusions seemed thoroughly reasonable to a successful student like himself. If New England represented the highest level of cultural achievement (as the jeremiad tradition repeatedly maintained), and if he had already demonstrated his intellectual brilliance by successfully reducing all learning to 1,271 propositions, was he not then entitled to indulge his fantasy of Samuel, the wise and the virtuous?[20]

Although Samuel Johnson viewed his encyclopedia as simply the epitome of his intellectual development, his preoccupation with philosophical synthesis also satisfied important emotional needs. The decision to pursue a ministerial career eliminated many of the dilemmas associated with growing up. But like all young people, Johnson still had to transcend the painful stage of puberty, a time of rapid physical growth, a period of reawakened sexuality. In biological terms, he found his body making sexual demands that could not be satisfied within the accepted pattern of moral values. Nor could the young man maintain his emotional attachments to his earliest love objects, his parents. Indeed, his enforced absence from his family while at college (a sociological characteristic of the New England apprentice system as well) may have functioned to obviate those primal emotional drives. Thus, to satisfy his growing emotional needs—what he once called "our hot youth's folly"—Johnson shifted his "ruling passion" away from his family connections and turned instead to an intense pursuit of higher learning.[21]

The transition from his original love objects to more socially acceptable forms of expression involved fundamental psychological changes. Johnson's fantasies of intellectual omnipotence constituted an early alternative object of love. Enamored of a dream of self-fulfillment, Johnson gradually shifted his attention away from his family and onto himself. This narcissistic pattern, common to many young adolescents, also influenced the next stage of his emotional development. During his years at Yale, the young scholar forged an intimate friendship with his classmate Daniel Browne. Johnson idealized this friend and later described him as "one of the most hopeful youths his country ever bred." In Browne, Johnson found traits and characteristics that he himself desired and that he could possess vicariously through their close acquaintance. "Dearest friend," Johnson elaborately addressed Browne, "most excellent among the learned, endowed with splendid learning." Such eloquence revealed that Johnson had successfully transformed his love for self into a love for an external object, a love for an ideal, a passion for learning. In Johnson's eyes, Browne had attained their common goal.[22]

This crucial shift of emotional energy from himself to the ideal of learning underlay Johnson's repeated attempts to perfect his synthesis of all knowledge.[23] In one letter he advised Browne "not to live wholly without diverting . . . your mind [with] feminine society a little whereof I conceive to be pleasant and yet not hurtful."[24] Instead of shunning his emerging sexuality, of repressing his feelings by denying their existence, the young man intellectualized his desires, made them socially acceptable by abstracting them, and then indulged his fantasies.[25] In a revealing letter to Browne, Johnson depicted his encyclopedia as his wife, "that most excellent Lady Techne," and portrayed its philosophical attributes in anthropomorphic terms of feminine beauty.[26] In writing and revising the encyclopedia, the young man could seduce and be seduced by his secret mistress. Johnson could embrace the Lady Techne without challenging the dominant social values, and by transforming his "ruling passion," he could even aspire to be Samuel "the wise, the virtuous."[27]

If Samuel Johnson believed that he had attained his dream of becoming the most learned man in the Christian world, his accidental discovery of Francis Bacon's *Advancement of Learning* in 1714 swiftly shattered the young man's "towering imaginations." To his surprise, "he soon saw his own littleness in comparison with Lord Bacon's greatness." Johnson's ignorance of this book reflected the shortcomings of a Yale education, but the writings of Bacon had been available to other colonial students.[28] A second discovery, however, clearly betrayed the provinciality of New England culture. In 1714 Connecticut's agent in London, Jeremiah Dummer, procured a sizable library of new books for the Connecticut college. These volumes, which included, in Johnson's words, "the works of our best English poets, philosophers, and divines," appeared "like a flood of day to his low state of mind."[29]

Johnson's discovery of the "new learning"—the writings of

such men as Locke and Newton—represented, on a personal level, a microcosm of the larger cultural crisis in New England. Once the vanguard of Western civilization, the Puritan colonies now appeared hopelessly remote from the metropolitan centers of learning, mere provinces of the greater British Empire. For young Johnson, the introduction of the Dummer library brought intense psychological distress. Believing himself capable of becoming the most learned man in the world, he abruptly discerned that even the most brilliant man in New England, even Samuel "the wise, the virtuous," could not measure up to metropolitan standards. Johnson's initial reaction—a feeling of "his own littleness"—revealed a profound sense of shame for seriously miscalculating the state of his achievement. These feelings of "littleness" and the frustration of misplaced trust in the New England way, by undermining his image of the world and his place in it, produced a crisis of identity.[30] No longer confident of his self-image, young Johnson now attempted to integrate his past accomplishments with the new vistas opened by the Dummer library.

Intent on salvaging his identity as the most learned man in the world, Samuel Johnson plunged into the "new learning" and ransacked the tomes of such men as Locke, Newton, Boyle, and Descartes. Perhaps if he could master the new ideas, perhaps if he could incorporate these newly found worlds, he could still retain his sense of intellectual superiority. With the advice of his friend Daniel Browne, Johnson reexamined his cosmology and began to draft a new version of his encyclopedia. Completed in 1716, this revised synthesis revealed the persistence of Johnson's dream of embracing all knowledge. Philosophy, asserted the young intellectual, "is an universal and complete . . . system . . . of all learning, mental or intellectual acquirements or ideas, whether human or divine, natural or revealed.[31]

Although the emotional substrate of the revised encyclopedia remained unchanged, the new synthesis revealed Johnson's valiant effort to master the new learning.[32] Seeking to embrace eighteenth-century rationalism, Johnson modernized the language, eliminated the scholastic theses of the undergraduate exercises, and adopted the style of his English mentors. In the end, he seemed satisfied with his revision and later insisted that the new work proved that he "was wholly changed to the New Learning."[33]

Such exaggerated statements, however, could not conceal the fact that the revisions were often more apparent than real and that fundamental assumptions linked the later work with its scholastic predecessors. Yet the new synthesis demonstrated a mental strategy that Samuel Johnson repeated throughout his life. Accepting the superiority of English culture, he borrowed selectively from metropolitan writers and sought to harmonize their ideas with his own. Most important, he refused to relinquish his self-image as Samuel, the wise and the virtuous, and clung tenaciously to his dream of becoming the most learned man in the world.

The introduction of the new learning not only affected the content and structure of Samuel Johnson's philosophical writings, but also influenced the young man's attitudes toward religion and theology. Johnson later remembered that he had been "designed for the pulpit" from his earliest years and he had begun to preach occasional sermons while teaching school at Guilford. To Daniel Browne, Johnson acknowledged that preaching was "formidible and difficult at first," but became somewhat easier as he went along and in the end appeared "most sweet." Johnson planned to be ordained during the summer of 1715 but for unknown reasons postponed his examination until the following March. According to the practices established by the Saybrook Platform, ministerial candidates had to pass the scrutiny of the county association before being licensed to preach. Easily demonstrating his orthodoxy and his command of the liberal arts, Johnson passed this examination and the New Haven association deemed him "qualified for the work of the gospel ministry."[34]

Samuel Johnson's earliest sermons, written during 1715, reflect an orthodox Puritan mind. Tightly structured and carefully planned, these pieces articulated the traditional Protestant ideas of man's Fall from grace, the intervention of Jesus Christ as a mediator, the need to seek salvation by renouncing sin and by accepting the sovereignty of the Lord. The sermons stressed the power of "an angry and offended God" and emphasized that man could expect nothing without God's grace. "Had not God mercifully of his rich and free grace been pleased to reveal a way of salvation," asserted the young minister, "we should have been miserably in the dark about it." Only the grace of God could provide sinners with assurance of salvation, a sense of spiritual security.[35] In these sermons, then, the novice preacher simply imitated the style and content of his Puritan mentors.

During the following year, however, a time when Johnson grappled with the problem of revising his encyclopedia, the sermons reveal a subtle, and probably unconscious, transformation. Johnson now spoke less of the arbitrary nature of God's sovereignty and emphasized instead the essential rationality of the universe. "God's will," he declared, "is nothing but what is highly reasonable." "The soul of man," said Johnson, is "his rational spirit," and consequently man had to glorify God "in a rational manner." Insisting that "the life of a saint is a rational life" and that "the saint's happiness is all intellectual," he predicted that God would reward the faithful with "an ocean brim full of intellectual pleasure forever to be swallowed up in"[36] In theological terms, then, no less than in purely philosophical ones, Samuel Johnson achieved a sense of cosmic harmony by intellectualizing the world.

In these later sermons Johnson described religion not as a mysterious search after spiritual joy, but rather as "a science or doctrine acknowledging the glorious and adorable being and perfections of a deity with a just sense of our duty flowing therefrom." For the young scholar, religion seemed more an affair of the head than of the heart and he earnestly asked his friend "whether illumination of the mind (I mean spiritual) is not sufficient for conversion?" To his diary, Johnson confessed with pride that "more rational thought of religion increaseth in my mind and fanatical principles wear out."[37] This fundamental denial of religious enthusiasm, of the passion and intensity associated with religious conversion, reflected Samuel Johnson's search for inner peace. Haunted by emotional forces that threatened his equilibrium, he sought psychological ballast by rationalizing his religion, by repudiating his emotions, by repressing his passions.

During the late summer of 1716, while Samuel Johnson struggled with his religious convictions and worked on the revised encyclopedia, he received two offers of employment. The first was a call from First Church of Newark, New Jersey, to minister to their souls;[38] the second was an invitation to become a tutor at Yale. Without hesitation Johnson accepted the latter position. As a Yale tutor the young scholar would have a unique opportunity to reverse the intellectual deterioration in New England. By introducing curriculum reforms, by imparting the new learning to provincial students, Johnson could lead the Puritan colonies to a higher level of cultural achievement. Such a role seemed ideally suited to a young man named Samuel, for the biblical namesake too had been appointed to head the school of the prophets.[39]

Johnson's desire to raise the intellectual standards of the provincial college became more feasible in 1717, when the Yale trustees appointed Daniel Browne to assist him in his tutorial work. The two scholars "joined their utmost endeavors to improve the education of their pupils by the help of the new lights they had gained." Locke and Newton promptly entered the Yale curriculum and the Ptolemaic astronomy gave way to the Copernican. Johnson himself overcame his early dislike for mathematics and learned enough geometry and algebra to read Newton with "great pleasure."[40] For the young intellectuals, the success of the pedagogical reforms promised an early fulfillment of their dreams.

These aspirations, however, were soon dashed by a prolonged political dispute over the location of the college. Two factions—one centering around Hartford, the other at New Haven—vied for legitimacy and Johnson, as a representative of the New Haven group, became an innocent victim of provincial politics. Despite an act of the legislature, the Hartford faction refused to accept New Haven as the college seat, and it operated an independent school until a second legislative act ordered all students to attend the established college. The Hartford scholars, while obeying the order, endeavored to embarrass the New Haven college by attacking its leaders. Drafting a "collection of faults," which included accusing the tutor of mismanagement of the upper classes, the dissident students questioned the adequacy of Samuel Johnson's learning. "Their objections," replied Johnson, "were all of them either designed misunderstandings or misrepresentations or else absolute falsehoods." The Board of Trustees, after hearing the charges, denounced the students for raising unfounded allegations and defended Johnson "as a man of good learning, and in that respect very well accomplished for the charge he is in."[41]

The peace of the college nevertheless required that some concessions be made. Jonathan Edwards, who as one of the dissident students had left New Haven in protest, reported that the Trustees "have removed that which was the cause of our coming away, viz., Mr. Johnson, from the place of a tutor." Johnson himself never explained his departure from Yale in 1719. But while the Trustees rewarded him "for his extraordinary service," it is likely that he resigned his academic position to avoid further problems.[42]

For Samuel Johnson, the student rebellion, like the earlier discovery of the new learning, brought profound psychological turmoil. Determined to become the most learned man in the world, the young intellectual found himself thwarted by his provincial neighbors, felt again the sting of public exposure, and suffered anew the shame of misplaced confidence. Once again the New England way had failed to satisfy Johnson's emotional needs.[43] Seeking greater certainty, the young man accepted an invitation to become the minister at West Haven, only four miles from the college, and he began his pastoral duties there in March 1720.

While Tutor Johnson was studying the new learning and mediating with the Hartford dissenters, he continued to preach sermons from various pulpits around New Haven. These religious pieces reflected Johnson's persistent commitment to the jeremiad tradition of his culture. He spoke often of the special blessings of the people of New England and of the need to maintain spiritual godliness. "We had better be [pagan] worshippers of the sun," he asserted, "than live and die in disobedience to the gospel in New England." In another sermon he exhorted the congregation to pray for the continuance of divine favors so that "God may delight in us for good." The jeremiad structure also enabled the preacher to denounce the sins of the land and Johnson often chided his listeners for the decay of "true holiness" and the persistence of "contentions and divisions among God's people."[44] In this way he maintained connections with his spiritual roots.

For all his apparent orthodoxy, however, Johnson had commenced a serious inquiry into the origins of Christianity, which culminated in his repudiation of the New England way. Reading in the Dummer library, Johnson discovered numerous works by Anglican divines that seemed to demonstrate the superiority of the Church of England. Further study of the Anglican Prayer Book and conversations with churchmen in Connecticut convinced the young man of the "reasonableness and great advantage" of episcopal government. By the time that Johnson accepted the pulpit at West Haven, he had acknowledged that "episcopacy was truly the primitive and apostolical form of church government, and that the apostolic office was designed to be a settled standing office . . . to the end of the world."[45]

Samuel Johnson's espousal of the Anglican church reflected his pervasive dissatisfaction with the religious institutions of New England. First, he disliked the emotionalism of the evangelical churches and preferred the more rational liturgy of the Church of England. Thus he disapproved the extemporaneous preaching of the Puritan ministers and felt that "preconceived well-composed forms were infinitely best." Johnson's distrust of the irrational also made him "much embarrassed with the rigid Calvinistic notions in which he had been bred." Believing in the reasonableness of God's universe, the young man found spiritual comfort in the "golden mean" of the Anglican church.[46]

This psychological basis of Johnson's antipathy to religious enthusiasm emerged in his criticism of the ecclesiastical structure. In condemning the congregational form of church government, "in which every brother has a hand," Johnson pointed to the "endless feuds, censoriousness and uncharitableness" that "issued in great animosities and often in virulent separations." He became convinced that a popular form of church government could "not long subsist . . ., but must from the nature of it crumble to pieces, as every individual seemed to think himself infallible."[47] For Johnson, the congregational autonomy of the New England way had destroyed the spiritual peace that had characterized the primitive church. Theological variation had served only to encourage bitter discord and further schism. Searching for cosmic universality and fearful of separations, Johnson naturally found spiritual rest in the more authoritarian structure of the Church of England.

Johnson's disgust with the "contentions and divisions among God's people" contrasted with the unity and harmony he perceived in the episcopal church. "I am persuaded," he wrote at the time of his ordination at West Haven, "that there ought to be and originally was . . . an external and visible unity" of Christ's church. "And for this reason I am no less persuaded that an external uniformity ought to be . . . established by the authority of the church, and that the measures of such an external and visible uniformity . . . ought to be held as sacred and inviolable." The episcopal church, Johnson concluded, appeared best suited "to promote, preserve and maintain the peace and unity . . . of the true religion."[48] By 1720, then, Samuel Johnson had articulated a sophisticated rationale for his conversion to the Church of England. And yet in that year he accepted ordination as the minister of a Puritan church.

In justifying this paradoxical decision, Johnson later insisted that while he understood the advantages of episcopal ordination, "he did not yet see it necessary in point of conscience to conform; so he made himself easy and went on." Fearing that a public announcement "would be of vastly more disservice to the church," would provoke "fatal jealousies" at the college, and would expose the young man "to great dangers and difficulties," Johnson preferred to live with his doubts. "I may in the meantime be doing some service to promote the main interest of religion," he wrote in rationalizing his decision, "though it be not in a method so desirable."

Johnson's failure to act also revealed a fundamental unwillingness to break with his cultural roots. Thus, while he condemned needless separations from a particular church, he nevertheless accepted schisms made for the sake of conscience. In this way, Johnson could maintain his affinity for "our honest progenitors, who first came over to this land." Similarly, in listing his reasons for acquiescing in presbyterian ordination, Johnson paid primary homage to "the passionate entreaties of a tender mother," who begged her son to reconsider.[50] In placing preeminence upon this maternal influence, Johnson unconsciously expressed the primal symbolism of his interest in the "mother" Church of England. Frustrated by the disharmony of the New England way and by such petty quarrels as Hartford's reluctance to relinquish the college seat, Samuel Johnson craved the cosmic equilibrium of his earliest life and ironically discerned in his own mother the major obstacle to his spiritual tranquillity. She nevertheless remained a powerful force, and he preferred, for the time, to appease her demands rather than cause her unhappiness.

In accepting the offer from West Haven, Samuel Johnson fulfilled his grandfather's desire that the lad be "designed for the pulpit." Yet, in Johnson's eyes the position involved much more than a permanent calling. "He had much better offers, but he had no worldly aim," wrote Johnson of himself; "his grand point in view was to improve his mind in knowledge, and therefore for the sake of being so near the college and library and the conversation of his dear friends, Mr. Cutler and Mr. Browne, though his place was but poor, he chose to settle there."[51] For Johnson the West Haven position provided a safe retreat from the intellectual skirmishes of the college. Beset by serious doubts about his religion and the validity of the New England way, confused about his personal ideals and his place in the world, bewildered by his inexplicable emotional pulls, the young man found temporary solace—a psychological "moratorium"—by performing the well-defined functions of a Puritan minister. While at West Haven, Johnson enjoyed the luxury of contemplation and delay—and if he desired companionship he could travel the short distance to Yale, where he could expect a friendly greeting.[52]

In his ordination sermon, the new pastor explained his attitude toward the ministry and articulated positions that defined his entire career as a clergyman. A minister should 'be thoroughly studied and well informed in the principles of religion," maintained Johnson, "for the faithful discharge of that work" requires a "thorough insight into the doctrines and duties of Christianity." He nevertheless warned that "speculative knowledge of divine things" was insufficient for the "holy calling" and that a godly minister also "should have a feeling and realizing and affecting sense" of spiritual grace. Finally, Johnson advised that ministers "take good heed that their doctrines be true and orthodox." But Johnson's definition of orthodoxy ("All . . . doctrines . . . must be formed from or brought to the gospel as the test and touchstone") remained sufficiently broad to allow him to use the liturgy of the Church of England as the basis of his sermons. Moreover, in establishing procedures for the administration of the sacraments, the minister adopted a liberal practice that required a potential communicant to profess a belief in the doctrines of Christianity, declare repentance for one's sins, and swear obedience to God's church.[53] For Johnson, then, the autonomy of the New England churches protected the security of his moratorium.

Though Samuel Johnson spent most of his time at West Haven

reading divinity, ethics, and Christian history, he also made time for the study of physics, mathematics, and metaphysics. Wherever possible he attempted to systematize his learning, to reduce his knowledge to concise, but universal, formulas. From one English author he derived a "scheme of religion" in which "all the doctrines and duties . . . might appear in a short compass and be beheld in a more direct view." By "methodizing" his thought "upon every particular subject," he hoped to improve his memory.[54] In a tract on Logic, Johnson attempted to systematize the rules of reasoning. "My method . . . shall consist in giving a plain and historical account of our several intellectual powers," he wrote optimistically, "and prescribing rules for their direction everywhere according as they shall be found needful and wherever erroneous bias and tendency of our minds requireth any."[55] Shortly thereafter Johnson drafted a comprehensive program for collegiate studies.[56] Entirely derivative, these writings revealed the persistence of Samuel Johnson's dream of incorporating everything that could be known.

Nor could Johnson long escape his dilemma regarding the necessity of episcopal ordination. In his synopsis of the "chief heads of divinity," he reiterated the importance of an episcopacy for the proper maintenance of church government. And in comparing the English churches with continental Protestantism, he declared that the Puritan dissenters were "guilty of schisms in refusing obedience" to the established church.[57]

It was in the "Logic," however, that Johnson launched a fundamental attack on New England's religious anomalies. People are led into error, he remarked, because of ignorance, or laziness, or an "aversion to books and study." These visible excuses, however, concealed more basic motives—"a fear that a more careful examination of a matter would oblige them to part with some opinion . . . in which their present interest is concerned," forcing them to "embrace one contrary to it." The problem, Johnson continued, was that people too easily deferred to the authority of others. "A great veneration" for such opinions "will dispose us to resign our minds and take what they say for true without examining it. Now," he concluded, "though it becomes us to have a reverence for the judgments of the great and ancient and men of experience . . ., yet we ought to endeavor to weigh well their reasons."[58]

For Samuel Johnson, the founding fathers, people like his

grandfather William Johnson, remained great men. But as mere mortals, they too were fallible. In departing from the Church of England a century before, they had inadvertently opened the way for religious error, for the disruption of the harmony of the true church of Christ. The contention within the New England churches reflected not so much the failures of the children as a fundamental weakness in the system of religion itself.

After 1720 Samuel Johnson's sermons reveal a deliberate search for a resolution to his theological quandry. "We ought to be no less concerned to actually believe all Christ's doctrines, than to obey all his commands," he preached in a sermon delivered before the provincial legislature; "yet it is to be feared that there are many Christians, that content themselves with an actual belief of some of the articles of our faith . . . and yet don't live under a lively sense of the rest."[59] In retrospect, Johnson's message to the legislature can be seen as an oblique attack on the New England way. But no one noticed and Johnson was content to keep his secret.

In a subsequent sermon on the "Excellency of Charity," the young minister stressed the importance of organic union among Christians. We all have "the same father, who is God," he asserted, "and one and the same Mother, who is the Church and we being many are one body in Christ." The organic nature of social relations therefore required people to accept their place in the world. Nothing is so hateful to God, he declared, as a factious, rebellious spirit, which threatened the cosmic order. Thus individuals had to obey laws and government, "submitting to every ordinance of man for the Lord's sake." Only then could mankind enjoy peace and harmony in the world.[60]

One month later, at the invitation of Gurdon Saltonstall, Samuel Johnson addressed the legislature with the text "The Fashion of the World passeth away."[61] Seven months after that he traveled to Stratford to consult with the Anglican missionary George Pigot. And three months thereafter, in the library of Yale College, he announced his conversion to the Church of England. "I thought it my bounden duty to come over to the Episcopal side," he averred, "that I might live and die in the unity of the church."[62] The quest for cosmic unity had ended.

In converting to the Church of England, Johnson rejected the jeremiad tradition of his father and grandfather. His ability to indict the founding fathers was made considerably easier (if not necessary) by the failure of the New England way to satisfy his personal needs. The startling discovery of provincialism in 1714, followed by the student rebellion in 1718, had threatened Johnson's identity in fundamental ways. In repudiating the founding fathers, in identifying with the established church of the metropolitan culture, Johnson could maintain his self-image as a learned man and indulge his fantasy of cosmic incorporation. In short, Johnson rejected his native culture because it had already rejected him.

NOTES

1. SJ, "Autobiography," pp. 4–6. During this period the average age of entering students at Yale was nearly sixteen. Johnson therefore was slightly younger than his classmates; see Richard Warch, "Yale College: 1701–1740," Ph.D. diss., Yale University, 1968, p. 291.

2. SJ's sermon notes indicate that Guilford's Thomas Ruggles preached in the jeremiad tradition; see Notes from Sermons, 1714–15, JCU.

3. Samuel Whitman, *Practical Godliness the Way to Prosperity* (New London, 1714), p. 36.

4. *Pub. Recs. Conn.,* 4: 468; 5: 436.

5. Proceedings of the Board of Trustees, November 11, 1701; SJ, "Some Historical Remarks Concerning the Collegiate School," November 20, 1717, both printed in Dexter, *Documentary History,* pp. 27, 149; Stephen Buckingham, *The Unreasonableness and Danger of a Peoples renouncing their Subjection to God* (New London, Conn., 1711), p. 21.

6. Address of Fitz-John Winthrop [May 1705?], printed in *MHS Colls.,* 6th ser., 3: 290; see also Dunn, *Puritans and Yankees,* passim.

7. SJ, An impartial and candid state of the case . . . [1763], JHP; Caleb Heathcote to SPG, November 9, 1705, SPG MSS, ser. A, vol. 2, no 117; Caleb Heathcote to SPG, January 1, 1707–8, October 1706, both in *HP*, 1: 35, 18–19.

8. The Saybrook Platform is printed in Walker, *Creeds and Platforms.* See also *Pub. Recs. Conn.,* 5: 51.

9. "A Preface" to the Saybrook Platform, in Walker, *Creeds and Platforms,* p. 520.

10. Samuel Johnson's minister, Thomas Ruggles, endorsed these changes; see [Ezra Stiles], *Extracts from the Itineraries and other Miscellanies*, ed. Franklin Bowditch Dexter (New Haven, Conn., 1916), pp. 335–37.

11. SJ, "Autobiography," pp. 3–7.

12. The best analysis of the Yale curriculum at this time is Warch,

"Yale College," chaps. 7–8. Also helpful are Norman S. Fiering, "President Samuel Johnson and the Circle of Knowledge," *William & Mary Quarterly* 28 (1971): 199–236; Norman S. Fiering, "Moral Philosophy in America, 1700–1750, and Its British Context," Ph.D. diss. Columbia University, 1969. Johnson's description is in "Autobiography," pp. 6–7.

13. Dexter, *Biographical Sketches,* 1: 117. Johnson's low ranking may have contributed to his alienation from the social system that placed him so low; for a provocative statement, see Cedric B. Cowing, *The Great Awakening and the American Revolution: Colonial Thought in the 18th Century* (Chicago, 1971), pp. 28–29.

14. Benjamin Lord to Ezra Stiles, May 28, 1779, in Dexter, *Biographical Sketches,* 1: 115–16; Steiner, *History of Guilford,* p. 398; SJ, "Autobiography," p. 5.

15. SJ, "Autobiography," pp. 6–7; Ebenezer Williams to Thomas Foxcroft, December 24, 1714, quoted in Warch, "Yale College," p. 284.

16. Johnson's extensive notes of sermons are in various notebooks in JCU.

17. SJ, "An Encyclopedia of Philosophy" [1714], *SJ Papers,* 2: 175. This quotation is significant not only for its rejection of the Church of England, but also because it reveals that Johnson (as well as other members of his culture) was aware of the existence of an alternative ecclesiastical structure. Johnson's earliest religious writing, a personal diary of spiritual confessions, was mutilated (probably in the nineteenth century). The biblical citations in the margin, however, suggest an acceptance of the jeremiad tradition; Liber Dierum, JCU.

18. *Pub. Recs. Conn.,* 4: 405.

19. Two versions of the encyclopedia, dating approximately from 1714, are printed in *SJ Papers,* 2: 23–186. For the existence of five editions, see the original manuscript, JCU. The influence of Ramus is analyzed in Perry Miller, *The New England Mind: The Seventeenth Century* (New York, 1939).

20. The doodles that appear in the original manuscript read as follows: "Shemuelihah Sophronius Aretianus Johnsonius" and "Samuelijah Aretius Johnson." In the preface to the Encyclopedia, Johnson linked the New England cosmology with the greatest philosophical movements; see *SJ Papers,* 2: 61.

21. SJ, "Autobiography," p. 7; Sermon before the General Assembly, October 22, 1721, JCU. This discussion of adolescence has benefited from the insights of Peter Blos, *On Adolescence: A Psychoanalytic Interpretation* (New York, 1962), and Anna Freud, "The Ego and the Mechanisms of Defense," *The Writings of Anna Freud,* rev. ed. (New York, 1966), 2.

22. See Blos, *On Adolescence,* pp. 72, 77–78. The quotations are in SJ, "Autobiography," pp. 17–18; SJ to Daniel Browne, February 1714, *SJ Papers,* 2: 189–90. I am grateful to my former colleague James Tracy for translating the original Latin.

23. See A. Freud, "The Ego," pp. 159–62.

24. SJ to Daniel Browne, June 20, 1715, *SJ Papers,* 2: 193.

25. Anna Freud writes: "The abstract intellectual discussions and speculations in which young people delight are not genuine attempts at solving the tasks set by reality. This mental activity is rather an indication of a tense alertness for the instinctual processes and the translation into abstract thought of that which they perceive." "The Ego," pp. 161–62.

26. SJ to Daniel Browne, February 1714, *SJ Papers,* 2: 189–90.

27. The question of Johnson's overt sexuality is impossible to document. It is likely that he enjoyed friendly relationships with women, as his letters to Daniel Browne imply. Moreover, in giving advice to his own son, Johnson confessed to "frequent [social] intercourse" with members of that "tender and unwary sex." But he could have been referring to relationships that occurred somewhat later in his life; see SJ to WSJ, July 7, 1747, *SJ Papers,* 1: 128–29. Shortly after returning from London in 1723 (while still unmarried) Johnson read a popular volume that warned of the debilitating effects of masturbation; the book is described in Robert H. MacDonald, "The Frightful Consequences of Onanism: Notes on the History of a Delusion," *Journal of the History of Ideas* 28 (1967): 423–31.

28. SJ, "Autobiography," p. 7; Fiering, "President Samuel Johnson," pp. 209–10.

29. SJ, "Autobiography," p. 7; "Some Historical Remarks," p. 151.

30. Erik Erikson writes: "The nature of the identity conflict often depends on the latent panic pervading a historical period. Some periods in history become identity vacua caused by three basic forms of human apprehensions: *fears* aroused by new facts, such as discoveries and inventions . . . which radically expand and change the whole world-image; *anxieties* aroused by symbolic dangers vaguely perceived as a consequence of the decay of existing ideologies; and the *dread* of an existential abyss devoid of spiritual meaning"; see "Autobiographic Notes on the Identity Crisis," *Daedalus* 99 (1970): 733. For other incisive comments, see Lynd, *On Shame,* pp. 37, 43–44.

31. SJ to Daniel Browne, August 3, 1716 and August 27, 1716; S.J., "The Revised Encyclopedia" [1716], all in *SJ Papers,* 2: 194, 197, 198, 208–9.

32. The best analyses of Johnson's philosophy are Fiering, "Moral Philosophy" and "President Samuel Johnson." The work is printed in *SJ Papers,* 2: 202–15.

33. SJ, "Encyclopedia of Philosophy" [1714], *SJ Papers,* 2: 186, marginal note written later.

34. SJ, "Autobiography," p. 10; S.J. to Daniel Browne, June 20, 1715, *SJ Papers,* 1: 192–93; Samuel Whittlesey to SJ, March 28, 1716, JCU, 1. The guidelines for ministerial examination that were used in Fairfield County (and that presumably did not vary much from those in New Haven County) are printed in Trumbull, *A Complete History,* 1: 489–90. At Johnson's ordination Joseph Moss preached a sermon that the candi-

date dutifully copied into his notebook; see Miscellaneous Notes, March 28, 1716, JCU, 1.

35. Johnson's first sermon is printed in *SJ Papers,* 3: 293–312. The others are in JCU. Quotations are from sermon 1, *SJ Papers,* 3: 296 and sermon 5 ("My Examination Sermon").

36. The emphasis upon rational religion appears in sermons 6–8 (published in *SJ Papers,* 3) and in sermons 9 and 11 (in JCU). Quotations are from *SJ Papers,* 3: 317, 324, 326, 327, 338.

37. SJ, Sermon 7, *SJ Papers,* 3: 329; SJ to Daniel Browne, August 27, 1716, *SJ Papers,* 2: 198; Liber Dierum, entry November 1716, JCU.

38. Dexter, *Biographical Sketches,* 1: 123; "Records of the Town of Newark, [N.J.]," printed in *Collections of the New Jersey Historical Society* 6 (1866): 127, does not mention Johnson's name, but one of the members of the search committee was a first cousin of Johnson's father.

39. See above, chap. 3, n. 16.

40. SJ, "Autobiography," pp. 8–9; "Mundas Novas" [1717], *SJ Papers,* 2: 247; Notes on Plane Mathematics, 1717–18, JCU.

41. SJ, "Autobiography," pp. 8–9; "Some Historical Remarks," pp. 160–61; *Pub. Recs. Conn.,* 6: 98–100.

42. Jonathan Edwards to Mary Edwards, March 26, 1719; Proceedings of the Trustees, September 9, 1719, both printed in Dexter, *Documentary History,* pp. 192, 198; SJ, "Autobiography," p. 10.

43. Timothy Cutler, who as Rector of Yale knew Johnson intimately, later remarked that his friend deserved "a better character than some in a higher station." See Cutler to Zachary Grey, April 7, 1725, "Copies of Letters of Timothy Cutler . . .," MSS, New-York Historical Society.

44. SJ, Sermon 17 (April 28, 1717); Notes for a Thanksgiving Sermon (November 5, 1718); Notes for a sermon at a Private Fast (February 28, 1716–17), all in JCU.

45. SJ, "Autobiography," pp. 10–12; "My Present Thoughts of Episcopacy" [1719], *SJ Papers,* 3: 3–8. An Anglican schoolmaster of Westchester, N.Y., claimed to have "first induced" Johnson "to be a favourer" of the Church of England while the young man was a tutor at Yale. See William Forster to SPG, November 19, 1723, SPG MSS, ser. A, 17: 246.

46. SJ, "Autobiography," pp. 10–12.

47. Ibid., p. 12.

48. SJ, "My Present Thoughts of Episcopacy," pp. 3, 5, 6.

49. SJ, "Autobiography," p. 12; "My Present Thoughts of Episcopacy," p. 8.

50. SJ "My Present Thoughts of Episcopacy," pp. 4, 8.

51. SJ, "Autobiography," p. 10.

52. The best analysis of the idea of an adolescent moratorium is Erikson, *Young Man Luther.*

53. SJ, An Ordination Sermon, March 9, 1720, JCU; "Autobiography," p. 12; The Method I shall observe in the administration of the holy sacraments, May 20, 1720, JCU.

54. SJ, "A Common Place for the Chief Heads of Divinity," January 1719–20, *SJ Papers,* 3: 601.

55. SJ, "Logic" [1720], *SJ Papers*, 2: 220.

56. SJ, "The Best Method (to me) of Scholars' Studies While at the College" [1720], *SJ Papers,* 2: 250.

57. SJ, "A Common Place for the Chief Heads of Divinity," p. 623; "Selections from a Book of Collections . . ." [n.d., but pre-1722], *SJ Papers,* 2: 253–54.

58. "SJ, "Logic," pp. 236–38.

59. SJ, Sermon, October 16, 1720, JCU.

60. SJ, Sermon: Concerning the Nature and Excellence of Charity, October 14, 1721, JCU.

61. See chap. 1 above.

62. SJ "My Present Thoughts of Episcopacy," p. 8, postscript.

5

"IN UNITY WITH THE BODY OF CHRIST"

IN ANNOUNCING his conversion to the Church of England in 1722, Samuel Johnson endeavored to resolve the crisis of identity that had plagued his soul for half a decade. After considerable hesitation and self-examination, he now realized that only by rejecting certain institutions of the New England way could he fulfill his personal aspirations and find inner tranquillity. Could we have stifled our desire for episcopal ordination, observed Johnson in retrospect, "we might have had the greatest applause of all our friends and acquaintances." But so great was our love of episcopacy, so strong our religious convictions, "as to make us leave fathers, mothers, brothers, sisters, houses and lands."[1]

Johnson's statement greatly exaggerated his renunciation of his heritage. While repudiating the jeremiad tradition of his ancestors, he nevertheless retained fundamental aspects of his more youthful identity. His insatiable "thirst after knowledge" remained a "ruling passion" and dominated his subsequent intellectual development, culminating in revised encyclopedias and improved schemes of learning. Similarly, Johnson still craved public recognition and visible fame, an emotional tendency that structured his relations with friend and foe alike. These personal traits, residues of Johnson's earliest experiences, constituted basic features of his adult personality.

The conversion to the Anglican church nevertheless represented a positive assertion of Johnson's mature identity. Unlike most of his neighbors and friends, he perceived himself affirmatively as a disciple of the established church of the mother country. This self-image possessed a negative side as well: Samuel Johnson was not a loyal son of New England. The simple dichotomy, however, required confirmation from other people, for Johnson, like other human beings, measured himself in the context of his culture. In provincial Connecticut, Samuel Johnson's emerging identity found ready reinforcement from other members of the society. Anglicans like George Pigot welcomed his conversion, while staunch Puritans within the West Haven congregation rebuffed his conciliatory gestures.[2]

The implications of such external attitudes, however, did not emerge completely until Samuel Johnson visited England in 1722 to obtain episcopal ordination. As a convert to the metropolitan church, he anticipated full membership in the English episcopal community. But shortly after arriving in England, he experienced a curious mishap: "we were by mistake directed to a [dissenters'] meeting," he noted in his diary.[3] For all Johnson's self-image as a sincere Anglican, other Englishmen did not perceive him as an ordinary countryman. The initial error, of course, was easily, if not humorously, rectified. But throughout his sojourn in the mother country, Johnson experienced similar feelings of estrangement. Despite his religious orthodoxy, he remained a mere visitor from distant shores, a cultural outsider. Thus the voyage to England further awakened Johnson to what he was not. Only after encountering the metropolitan society did the child of the provinces recognize the full limitations of his personal situation; only then did he forge his adult identity as a provincial churchman.

In October 1722 Samuel Johnson bade farewell to his congregation at West Haven and, with Daniel Browne and Timothy Cutler, began the overland journey to Boston to embark for England. The three would remain travel companions during the overseas adventure and later would be joined by James Wetmore, another of the Yale converts. Supporters of the Anglican church welcomed the young men to the provincial capital, still a Puritan stronghold where preachers like Increase and Cotton Mather struggled to preserve the glory of the first colonists. In November, one day before sailing, the converts took communion in the Church of England. "How devout, grand, and venerable was every part of the administration," Johnson remarked. In the traditional rituals of the established church, he had found spiritual peace.

But still ahead lay the terrors of the Atlantic passage. A century earlier the voyage to New England had served to reinforce a sense of community among the founding fathers. All members of that first generation survived the ordeal, and the crossing became for them an initiatory ritual, a series of common experiences that seemed to separate them from the remainder of mankind, that demonstrated their chosenness.[4] For Samuel Johnson and his friends the ocean voyage functioned in a similar way. In order to explore new worlds beyond the seas they too endured a "boisterous and uncomfortable voyage" lasting five weeks and four days. In later years, Johnson viewed that journey as a sign of distinction, an event that separated him from most provincials, a symbolic experience that he shared with all Anglican ministers who had sailed to England for episcopal ordination.

The young travelers, already predisposed to extol the wonders of metropolitan culture, found that the attractions of England exceeded their provincial imaginations.[5] On the first day ashore they attended services at the Cathedral of Canterbury and paused to view "the ancient magnificence" of the city. In London, where Johnson spent nearly six months, the Americans toured the famous buildings and monuments and praised the glory of the mother country. Of St. Paul's Cathedral Johnson wrote, "it is perhaps one of the finest buildings in the world—an amazing mass of stones!" They attended the Houses of Parliament, saw numerous dramatic performances in Drury Lane, chanced upon "a wondrous clock that performed all sorts of music," and kissed the hands of the Princesses. "Glorious things!" asserted Johnson after inspecting the trophies of Sir Francis Drake.

Besides such "curiosities" as the water works, the palaces, the gardens, Johnson seemed especially struck by the antiquity of European culture. In New England time had begun less than a century earlier, in the lifetime of William Johnson. Even the great moments of New England's past had been transformed into a chronicle of symbolic time. Memory, instead of placing people in history, carried them to the timelessness of the founding fathers.[6] But in England human history permeated the nation's institutions. The aristocracy, the church, the monuments—all bespoke the passage of human time, a sense of the past that Samuel Johnson tried to understand. In London the American tourist visited numerous historic sites, and in brief journeys to the universities at Oxford and Cambridge he scrutinized the old manuscripts, the medals, and the memorabilia and "antiquities" of past centuries.

The Puritan migration to New England had severed Johnson's ties with his national roots and he now attempted to restore those bonds, searched to locate a place in history. As a recent convert to the Church of England, Johnson directed his interests toward the early defenders of the episcopal church, particularly to those Anglicans who had opposed the Puritan cause a century before. At Westminster Abbey he observed the handwriting of Archbishop William Laud, a firm opponent of Puritanism, and viewed the signatures of the Puritan regicides; on another occasion, he paused to visit the place of King Charles's execution. These excursions into the past provided Johnson with lasting historical symbols, ancestral figures with whom he could identify. Such commitments reinforced his identity as a loyal churchman. Years later, during another outburst of religious enthusiasm, he condemned the "horrid murder of one of the best Kings that sat upon the English throne" and described the Puritan rebellion as a "dismal tragedy, the shame of our nation."[7] This identification with the English past, by linking Johnson to distant time, satisfied an emotional need for a feeling of immortality. As part of an ancient tradition, the American convert could reach beyond the limits of his lifetime and obtain a sense of historical transcendence.

Johnson's travels to the English universities also reinforced his self-image as a learned man. Both Oxford and Cambridge, influenced by sympathetic members of the SPG, awarded him honorary Master of Arts degrees, distinctions that Johnson cherished throughout his life. Such honors, rare indeed among provincial scholars, visibly confirmed his intellectual superiority to other graduates of American colleges. The sojourns at the universities also enabled the young intellectual to extend the range of his knowledge. One friendly professor demonstrated various anatomical curiosities with his microscope, while Johnson himself described with pleasure the sight of numerous antique relics, including Roman urns and Egyptian mummies.

While these intellectual adventures provided great satisfaction for the American tourist, the discovery of England's historical treasures heightened Johnson's sense of provinciality. After his return to the colonies Johnson drafted an essay that revealed the impact of European culture upon his consciousness. Imagine a "poor peasant who had never seen anything greater or finer than a little mean thatched house or hut underground" suddenly carried to one of the palaces of Europe, wrote Johnson. There he would view "the exquisite architecture, the fine statuary, the beautiful painting, the surprising clockwork, the curious water-works, and delightful gardening." An "ecstacy of ravishment" would overcome him, suggested Johnson, and he would be "surprised, amazed and astonished!"[8] Johnson's response of wonder, characteristic of all provincials, not only convinced him of the poverty of American culture, but also shaped his mature identity as a colonial intellectual. However much he would praise the accomplishments of English learning or aspire to metropolitan standards, Johnson well understood his personal limitations as a child of the provinces.

In justifying his conversion to the Church of England, Samuel Johnson emphasized the necessity of episcopal ordination. By rejecting the office of bishops and by permitting laymen to participate in ordination ceremonies, he argued, the Puritan fathers had broken the apostolic succession. Only by traveling to the bishops of the mother country could colonial Anglicans restore the spiritual bonds. To be sure, the first ministers in New England, despite their hostility to episcopacy, had originally been ordained within the established church. It was their children and grandchildren who had first administered the sacraments without proper authority. "I am sure the *present* can't be called the *original* churches of the country," wrote Johnson in attacking the New England way, for "there is a vast difference between the original and present state of religion here."[9] Ironically, the jeremiad tradition that had condemned the sinfulness of New England's children now served the Anglican cause. For Johnson, only a properly administered episcopacy could reestablish peace within the churches of Christ.

Upon arriving in London, the young converts began a flurry of visits to various ministers, who promised to assist them in obtaining episcopal ordination. To the SPG, Samuel Johnson appealed for an appointment as missionary to the Anglicans at Stratford, Connecticut. Though he had lost "the good will" of most of his West Haven congregation, Johnson insisted that "a very considerable number of the most serious of them" desired him to return to the neighborhood so that they would not have to "submit to the administration of any dissenting teacher." Emphasizing the advantages of the Stratford pulpit, Johnson admitted "the greatest reluctance" to leave his native country, but agreed nevertheless to settle wherever the Society assigned him.[10] After brief discussion, the SPG granted his request and also appointed Daniel Browne to Bristol, Rhode Island, and Timothy Cutler to the new Anglican church in Boston.

Young men seeking ordination in the Church of England had to demonstrate their knowledge of the Bible, the Book of Common Prayer, Latin, Greek, and church history, as well as subscribe to the Thirty-Nine Articles. Dr. William Green, the Bishop of Norwich, tested the young converts and approved their ordination. "After that," noted Johnson, "we were about town to provide robes" for the ordination ceremony. Having received confirmation, the New Englanders then obtained ordination, first as deacons, later as priests. For Johnson, these rituals provided a valid basis for his acceptance of the ministry; no longer would he worry about being separated from the body of the church.

Once ordained, Johnson petitioned the SPG for an American pulpit, a request that required him to preach a probation sermon before the episcopal authorities. The examination proved a mere formality, and in June Johnson received his license from the Bishop of London. Two weeks later, he visited the Archbishop of Canterbury at Lambeth Palace and received "his solemn apostolical benediction by imposition of hands." The ceremony confirmed Johnson as a missionary for the SPG, an apostle of the true church of Christ. Johnson's diploma from Oxford had expressed hope that "by his ministry, another and the same Church of England" would be born in America.[11] This statement became, for Johnson, a guiding principle of his life.

The acquisition of episcopal ordination fulfilled Samuel Johnson's search for cosmic unity and provided a feeling of spiritual coherence. "It is far from being a matter of indifference what communion we are of," asserted Johnson in defense of his conversion, "whether we are in unity with the body of Christ, or in a state of separation from it." Christ had intended the church to be unified and universal and yet Johnson observed the "christian name broken into innumerable sects and parties, divisions and subdivisions." By participating in the Church of England, Johnson hoped to restore the universality of his spiritual relations, to reestablish his sense of self.[12]

Besides achieving this symbolic union, Johnson's ordination also bolstered his assault on the Puritan fathers of New England. "You think your fathers were very good men, and came here for the sake of religion and you can scarcely be persuaded to think they could be mistaken," he wrote to a congregational critic. "I think as charitably of your fathers as any of you do," Johnson continued, significantly adopting the second-person pronoun: "I am ready to believe that they meant well, and endeavored to please God according to the best of their light: but I don't therefore think they were perfect. On the contrary," he asserted, "I am persuaded, they greatly . . . erred in some things; and indeed I suppose you think so too, for you have greatly departed from them in several instances, and are ashamed of many of their notions and practices."[13] In accepting episcopal ordination, Johnson broke irrevocably with the jeremiads' veneration of the Puritan settlers. The problems of the American churches, he believed, derived from the anomalies established and institutionalized by the first generation. As an apostle of the true religion, his duty now required him to enlighten the minds of his friends and neighbors, to explain the virtues of the Anglican church, to restore harmony and order to the spiritual life of New England.

Johnson's relationship to the established Church, for all its apparent orthodoxy, nevertheless revealed the subtle impact of the young man's provincial background. While awaiting examination by the Bishop of Norwich, the New England converts had arranged to be rebaptized in the Anglican church. "Having grave doubts" about the validity of presbyterian baptism, wrote Johnson in explaining this step, we "received private hypothetical baptism. If this be right," he added, "may God approve it; and if otherwise . . ., may He pardon it."[14] The New Englanders' attitude toward presbyterian baptism, though apparently consistent with their belief that only episcopally ordained ministers could administer the sacraments, contradicted the established doctrines of the Church of England. By the early eighteenth century, the bishops of the Anglican church (with few significant exceptions) had attempted to preserve the Protestant succession of the Hanoverian monarchs by compromising with the presbyterian dissenters.

In exchange for the political loyalty of the dissenters, the bishops accepted the validity of presbyterian baptism (though not of ordination); only then could the bishops hope to maintain a united front against the more orthodox, but politically less reliable, Tories. Thus the New Englanders' position placed them on the side of the conservative "High Church" group that opposed a rapprochement with the dissenters. The denial of presbyterian baptism, however, by ignoring the political basis of the established church in England, revealed the provinciality of American Anglicanism.

The unwillingness of New England churchmen to support compromises with English dissenters reflected the special problem facing the episcopal church in the colonies. Surrounded by hostile congregationalists and presbyterians and subjected to verbal abuse and political discrimination, New England Anglicans resented the political power of the dissenters in the mother country that prevented ecclesiastical reform in America. Provincials like Samuel Johnson gained support from Edmund Gibson, Bishop of London, who not only opposed concessions to English dissenters, but also advocated the appointment of a bishop for the colonies to facilitate the expansion of the Anglican church. During Johnson's sojourn in London he conversed frequently with the Bishop and shared his vision of a stronger episcopal church. Throughout the colonial era, however, men like Gibson represented but a tiny minority within the episcopacy. Politically impotent, Gibson's plans to improve the Church in America repeatedly foundered against the shoals of Whig expediency. In supporting Gibson, therefore, colonials like Samuel Johnson further manifested their provinciality, their inability to understand or to accept the political machinations within the established church. Their High Church orthodoxy and their optimism about ultimate success betrayed their lack of touch with English religious trends.[15]

Johnson's voyage to the mother country not only introduced the young man to the wonders of English culture and the grandeur of the established church, but also exposed him to the greatest terror of metropolitan life in the eighteenth century: the smallpox. Shortly after arriving in England, Timothy Cutler contracted the disease, "but by God's will recovered" quickly. Describing the mishap, Daniel Browne asserted "we are not greatly concerned about it, leaving the matter to the divine disposal."[16] But Cutler's illness delayed their ordinations until the spring, allowing time for the pox to strike again.

Now the victim was Daniel Browne. "God grant him safe deliverance," exclaimed the worried Samuel Johnson, who prudently moved his lodgings to another house. In a week Browne was dead. "O Father, not my will, but thine be done! O my grief! I have lost in him the best friend in the world,—a fine scholar, and a brave Christian," lamented Johnson in his diary. "It is thy will, O God; let me be silent . . . . But my flesh trembles for fear of Thee, and I am afraid of thy righteous judgments. O give me grace to be resigned, and to get good by it," implored the shaken man. "O save and spare me, if it may be thy will, for Christ's sake."[17] Frightened and grieved, Johnson sought solace in the church and comfort from his friends, who tried to divert his somber thoughts. Yet he never recovered from this brush with death and Browne's memory haunted his soul to his dying day.

Johnson's initial reaction to Browne's death—an extreme anxiety about his own death—reflected his sense of increased vulnerability. Death had claimed not an evil man but "a brave Christian." How fragile indeed were Johnson's circumstances. But if death, particularly such sudden death, revealed the will of God, had not the young men tempted the Lord by deliberately exposing themselves to the scourge? Had they not deserted the sanctity of rural New England to attend to business in the unhealthy air of the city? Perhaps their separation from their native land had provoked the Lord? For Johnson, death anxiety and separation anxiety became intertwined. His dread of separation from his family usually betrayed a fear of death, particularly a fear of the smallpox. Thus, in rejecting several offers of prestigious employment in such provincial centers as New York, Newport, and Philadelphia, Johnson emphasized the danger of contracting the disease. Such prudence was commendable in the eighteenth century. But Johnson's anxiety seemed pervasive and compulsive, as though he viewed the pox as a divine punishment for overexposure.[18]

The fact that Johnson had been saved while his best friend, "far worthier" than he, had died, produced intense feelings of guilt. Yet, for Johnson, survival also indicated divine favor. In cataloguing the remarkable providences of his life, he stressed his escape from the smallpox "when friends of his about him much less exposed took it and died." These "deliverances," he asserted, became "mighty obligations to render his life as useful as ever he could." Thus survival in London confirmed Johnson's feeling of chosenness, his sense of being providentially selected to fulfill his personal mission.[19] The Lord, he concluded, had saved him for some special purpose.

In July 1723, three months after Daniel Browne's death, Samuel Johnson departed from England and arrived in Boston in mid-September. He stayed there to hear his friends, Timothy Cutler and James Wetmore, preach at the King's Chapel and then "hastened home to his father's house" in Guilford, having been absent for a year and a day.[20] During that brief time Johnson had a new and stronger sense of himself and had established a keener notion of his place in the world. The wonders of England had introduced him to unsurpassed "raptures" and he readily appreciated the advantages of metropolitan life. These experiences had reinforced a sense of provinciality, led to a realization of his inability to compete with the celebrities of London, Oxford, or Cambridge.

England remained an ideal culture for Samuel Johnson; he referred to Oxford as a "paradise" and regretted his departure from that "happy island."[21] Later in life he doodled on envelopes in such a way as to make them appear addressed "to Dr. Johnson at London."[22] Yet, for all his wishful thinking, he understood that as a child of New England he belonged in the provinces. Though he continued to view America as a "raw uncultivated country," he learned to accept his role as an apostle of the true religion and an advocate of the new learning. "It would . . . be a very nice refreshment to me if I could now and then take a ride to Oxford, whither I am very often carried in my imagination," Johnson confessed to an English acquaintance. "However, that article of faith . . ., the communion of saints," offers the pleasing thought "that we are one and together in heart and arm, though situated at a great distance from one another in body. In this respect," he declared with resignation, "faith supplies the want of vision even of an earthly felicity."[23] Samuel, the wise and the virtuous, had come home.

In November 1723 Johnson arrived in Stratford to assume the pulpit from George Pigot. "God . . . spared me another year," he wrote in his diary, "and returned me safe to my father's house and to my charge." The Lord had taken his best friend but had spared him. "What can I do less," he asked, "than devote my life thus preserved by Thee to Thy service to do all the good I can for thy glory and the good of the souls of men!" Now that I am "perfectly well satisfied as to the lawfulness and regularity of my mission," he declared, "so I propose by thy Grace, both to adorn my profession, by an holy life as a Christian and faithfully to fulfill my ministry as a clergyman, by doing all the service I can to the souls committed to my care. Let thy good Spirit ever be with me to preserve me from error, and lead me into all truth. So direct me in my ministry and succeed my labors," he concluded, "that I may have many souls for my crown and rejoicing in the day of the Lord Jesus. Amen."[24] With such solemn oaths Samuel Johnson dedicated himself to the task that occupied the remainder of his life. As a preacher, a pedagogue, and a missionary, he would seek to enlighten and convert his provincial countrymen.

NOTES

1. SJ. to SPG, March 30, 1750, *HP*, 1: 259–60. See also his, A Sermon of the City of God, November 14, 1737, JYU.

2. See chap. 1 above. Identity formation involves both positive and negative images and commitments. Erikson writes: "Identity formation normatively has its negative side which throughout life can remain an unruly part of the total identity. The *negative identity* is the sum of all those identifications and identity fragments which the individual had to submerge in himself as undesirable or irreconcilable. . . ." Erikson, "Autobiographic Notes," p. 733.

3. Johnson kept a journal of his trip to England, SJ's Book Being a Journal of his Voyage to, Abode at, & Return from England in Anno 1722 . . .; the original is in JCU and a nineteenth-century copy is held at the New Haven Colony Historical Society, New Haven, Connecticut.

Large portions appear in Beardsley, *Samuel Johnson*, chaps. 2–3. Quotations in this chapter, unless otherwise cited, are from the Journal.

4. The ocean voyages, of course, affected all European colonizers of America. But the Puritan settlers viewed their experiences as unique and saw the successful crossing as a sign of providential distinction; see Carroll, *Puritanism and the Wilderness*, chap. 2.

5. Besides Johnson's Journal, one document written by Daniel Browne has survived. It suggests that the men reacted to England in similar ways; see Daniel Browne to Joseph Browne, February 15, 1722/23, Smith MSS, Hawks Papers, Church Historical Society. For a larger study of Americans abroad in this period, see William L. Sachse, *The Colonial American in Britain*, (Madison, Wis., 1956).

6. See chap. 2 above.

7. Sermon: Of the Trial of the Spirits, prefatory note dated "King Charles's Martyrdom 1746/7," JCU.

8. [SJ], Letter to the *New York Gazette*, March 1729, *SJ Papers*, 2: 255–56.

9. SJ to Thomas Foxcroft, August 24, 1726, HU.

10. SJ's Representation to SPG, January 18, 1722 [/23], *HP*, 1: 61.

11. SJ, "Autobiography," p. 30.

12. SJ to Thomas Foxcroft, July 5, 1726, HU. Johnson applied similar metaphors to explain the conversion of other New Englanders to the mother church: "they were persuaded in their consciences that it is safer to retire into the unity of the Church than to live and die in a state of schism from her." See SJ to Edmund Gibson, November 4, 1725, Fulham MSS, Lambeth Palace.

13. [SJ], *A Letter From A Minister of the Church of England to His Dissenting Parishioners. . . .* (New York, 1733), printed in *SJ Papers*, 3: 27.

14. Beardsley, *Samuel Johnson*, p. 34n.

15. The complex history of the Church of England at this time is discussed in several works; see George Every, *The High Church Party: 1688–1718* (London, 1956); Norman Sykes, *Edmund Gibson, Bishop of London, 1669–1748: A Study in the Politics & Religion in the Eighteenth Century* (Oxford, 1926); Norman Sykes, *From Sheldon to Secker: Aspects of English Church History, 1660–1768* (Cambridge, 1959). For the question of lay baptism in New England, see Bruce Edward Steiner, "Samuel Seabury and the Forging of the High Church Tradition: A Study in the Evolution of New England Churchmanship, 1722–1796," Ph.D. diss., University of Virginia, 1962.

16. SJ, "Autobiography," p. 17; Daniel Browne to Joseph Browne, February 25, 1722–23, Smith Mss.

17. SJ, Journal; "Autobiography," pp. 17–18.

18. This discussion has benefited from Lifton, *Death*, especially pp. 481–93. On the question of separation anxiety, Lifton writes: "Psychologically speaking, the survivor's actual death immersion is itself a symbolic reactivation of earlier 'survivals'—of childhood experiences associated with separation and loss, including the birth process—which serve as 'models' for

later death anxiety. . . . [E]ven in adult life images of death, loss, and separation remain, to a considerable extent, psychologically interchangeable. A survivor's death encounter, therefore, may be symbolically reactivated by exposure to any of the three, as well as by experiences specifically reminiscent of that encounter" (*Death*, pp. 485–86).

19. SJ, "Autobiography," p. 5. Johnson revealed a similar attitude when a granddaughter survived a serious accident: "I hope it is an argument that her life is designed for some good struggle, that it was so signally preserved when all human means failed." SJ to WSJ, December 1, 1760, JCU, 2.

20. *Boston Gazette*, September 23–30, 1723; SJ, "Autobiography," p. 19.

21. SJ to ?, January 25, 1724, *SJ Papers*, 3: 218; SJ to Francis Astry [1724], JHP.

22. The doodles, apparent statements of unconscious wishes, appear on the back of many letters written after 1755 (significantly, the latter stages of Johnson's life); see, e.g., William Smith to SJ, July 23, 1755, JCU, 1; Charles Inglis to SJ, March 22, 1768, February 5, 1771, June 17, 1771, all in JHP.

23. SJ to George Berkeley, Jr., October 27, 1755, JCU, 1; SJ to Mr. Hayward, August 10, 1729, JHP. Timothy Cutler shared Johnson's low estimation of provincial learning: "The state of New England is too near that of the barbarous ages," he wrote to an English correspondent. See Cutler to Zachary Grey, September 4, 1732, "Copies of Letters," New-York Historical Society.

24. SJ, "Liber Dierum," pp. 64–65.

6

"A FRIEND TO HIS COUNTRY"

IT WAS at Stratford, Connecticut, a small rural village in the southwestern corner of the colony, that Samuel Johnson embraced his life's work as a minister of the Church of England. There was "work enough for Sunday laborers in the Lord's harvest," assured George Pigot upon surrendering his pulpit to the new minister. The Stratford congregation, the largest in the colony, numbered about fifty families, and scattered Anglicans in the region increased Johnson's flock to about 120 families. As the only Anglican minister in Connecticut, he faced the formidable task of satisfying their diverse spiritual needs.[1] But in a large measure Johnson was ideally suited for that role.

Ordination in the episcopal church had alleviated Johnson's major anxieties. Having established a coherent sense of himself, his attention now shifted away from questions of identity and focused instead upon his effectiveness and competence as a mature individual. The sense of inner harmony that he now possessed enabled him to pursue his ministerial career with the same intensity that earlier he had devoted to the resolution of his crisis of identity. That energy, powerful and single-minded as it was, promptly brought him into conflict with the native culture that had nourished him.

By the 1720s Puritan New England had lost much of the religious spirit that had dominated the seventeenth century. Congregations quarreled openly with their ministers, argued about church procedures, scrambled for prestigious seats in the meeting house.

Worse still, a secular shadow hovered above the land, a growing worldliness that was manifested by increased absenteeism on the Sabbath. New England had not yet forsaken its sense of chosenness, as Samuel Johnson soon would learn, but the confidence, the spiritual clarity, the evangelical certainty had drained from the land.

There was one element, however, one lingering catalyst that could still evoke the old passions and arouse the children of New England. That was the specter of episcopacy, the ugly dragon that had driven the founding fathers into the wilderness. By the eighteenth century, this abiding dread of the Church of England betrayed not so much a spiritual righteousness as a tenuous, fractured balance within the orthodox churches. For the Anglican church, united under the aegis of the royal authority, contrasted vividly with the religious chaos that was New England. To the loyal Puritan children therefore, the episcopal threat never appeared greater than now.

Against this trembling backdrop, Samuel Johnson emerged as the devil incarnate. His conversion to the Church of England symbolized not only the danger of metropolitan invasion but also the internal decay eating at the core of New England society. More fundamental, he exhibited, even flaunted, the self-confidence and optimism of a true convert. He had not returned to Connecticut like the prodigal, beaten and ashamed, but had ridden home proudly, head erect, dedicated now with a convert's zeal to uplifting his benighted neighbors. By all sober accounts, he had returned as the enemy within.

In these initial encounters Samuel Johnson nevertheless demonstrated a remarkable optimism, a strange innocence that verged on the naive. By converting to the Church of England, he had discovered peace, harmony, and unity, and he sincerely believed that other people would find his joyful message irresistible. "You may depend upon it," he declared forthrightly, "that in proportion as true knowledge increases in the country, a veneration of the Church of England will [also] increase."[2] Such confidence left Johnson ill-prepared for the onslaughts from the New England establishment, the Puritan descendants whom Johnson usually described, with more than a trace of superiority, as "Independents" or "Dissenters."

These orthodox believers, challenged as never before, fought back desperately, defending what they recognized as the very essence of their culture. Johnson's conversion, by questioning the sanctity of the first generation, imperiled the meaning of their own lives. Such apostasy, total as it was, could only be interpreted as an expression of evil. Any doctrinal arguments merely concealed a bedrock of sin. Thus Saltonstall's successor, Governor Joseph Talcott, advised Bishop Gibson that the Anglicans of Connecticut "can not be much recommended for their zeal for religion or morality." Their only motives, he explained with apparent seriousness, were "to appear singular, or to be freed from a small tax."[3]

Such conclusions, of course, ignored the sincerity of religious conversion. But it was not that the Puritan establishment was dishonest—though Johnson himself bitterly denounced Talcott's description. The problem, rather, was that the New England orthodoxy lacked the intellectual apparatus to explain the conversions in any other way. To an age that still believed in the uniformity of religious truth, any deviations, however disguised with Christian rhetoric, constituted a fundamental threat to the cosmic order, a perverse assault on an otherwise harmonious system. This perspective, moreover, revealed the persistence of a viable religious cosmology, despite the visible decline of religiosity. It was only because the Puritan descendants remained committed to religious principles that they refused to accept Samuel Johnson with the secular indifference associated with the modern temper.

Governor Talcott's confusion nevertheless possessed a modicum of truth. In provincial Connecticut the Anglican missionaries appealed most effectively to poorer people, to men and women of lesser status, presumably to members of social groups who already felt estranged from the dominant culture.[4] These demographic patterns served to rationalize Talcott's analysis, his vision of Anglicans as outsiders. Such prejudices also encouraged the further denigration of provincial Anglicans. "The dissenters are daily spitting their venom," complained Johnson. Converts to the Church of England, he explained, "can have no expectation from the government and generality of people but to be laughed at and looked awry upon." In a culture in which people developed sensitivity to sanctions associated with shame, with visible appearances, and with public exposure, such open ridicule was particularly degrading. Anglican proselytes in eighteenth-century New England appeared "singular" not simply because they represented alienated groups, but also because the congregational majority deliberately thrust them out of the community. The penalty for questioning the symbolic fathers remained ostracism and humiliation.[5]

Nor were these attacks confined to private relations. Fearing the consequences of a viable episcopal church, the Connecticut authorities mobilized the provincial government to extirpate their enemies. Relying upon legislation that required all inhabitants to support "orthodox" ministers, colonial officials compelled the episcopalians to pay the ecclesiastical rate for non-Anglican preachers. Protests by the churchmen eventually persuaded the royal government in England to order an end to the discriminatory policy. Only then did the New England "establishment" concede "dissenting" status to the Anglican minority. Yet Connecticut officials, believing in the importance of regular divine worship, insisted that such "dissenters" as Anglicans and Quakers first justify their claim for tax exemptions by regularly attending services in their churches. This requirement was not easily met, for throughout the colonial period Connecticut churchmen often lacked an established pulpit to attend. The shortage of Anglican ministers—even after Samuel Johnson had won other converts among the ministers—thus provided the New England governments with a convenient rationale for subverting the royal instructions. And when provincial Anglicans protested the discriminatory policy and refused to pay the regular rates, New England officials responded by seizing their property or incarcerating them. Missionaries like Johnson cried in vain for more equitable treatment.[6]

Despite this persecution, or perhaps because of it, Samuel Johnson failed to realize the similarity between his religious certitude and that of his opponents. Like more orthodox New Englanders, Johnson believed in a monolithic universe ruled by a single God and a unitary system of religious truths. As a missionary, moreover, he felt compelled to elucidate his doctrine, to impart his religious insight to people of other persuasions. A clear explanation of the Anglican theology, he was convinced, would promptly convert his opponents and end the "inveterate enmity" against the Church of England.

Johnson's first task, therefore, was to emphasize the similarity between Puritanism and Anglicanism. Thus, when orthodox New Englanders criticized the Church of England for teaching that people might attain salvation merely by performing good works, Johnson replied that "there is no inward change of heart, no being a new creature, without obedience to all the outward ordinances of Christianity . . ., without the outward observance of religion." Accused of advocating an open communion, the apostle warned of the contrary danger of "voluntary excommunication of ourselves." It was much worse, he advised, to receive communion from "one whose authority to administer may be justly disputed" —an obvious attack on the New England ministers who lacked the apostolic benediction.[7]

Throughout Johnson's exegeses there ran a tone of self-evident truth, a persistent sense that—to borrow a Puritan phrase—rightly informed consciences would inevitably agree. Johnson thus ascribed his failure to persuade his opponents to their prejudices, their ignorance, their spiritual obstinacy. Frustrated by these seemingly unreasonable obstacles, he became more determined in his efforts and, in consequence, more shrill and petulant in his language. When Thomas Foxcroft, a presbyterian minister of Boston, asked the Stratford missionary to explain the "extraordinary turn you took" in exchanging "your [Puritan] cloak for [an Anglican] gown," Johnson snapped that "the turn and change I lately made, is not so very extraordinary." The Anglican Church could hardly be accused of heresy, he seethed, "whatever some crackbrained inconsiderate people may have done."

Johnson proceeded to argue that the differences between Anglicans and Presbyterians could be reduced to two questions: "whether the Church should be governed by bishops as superior to presbyters? and whether it be expedient to worship God by a public state liturgy?" Johnson even conceded the latter point, since he did not regard it as essential. But the question of episcopacy, he averred, remained fundamental, "or else I would never have left your communion." "And then," Johnson asked in anger and frustration, "why all this noise and nonsense against the Church of England in the country? Why so much ill blood and fury, so much distance and aversion, that a man must be branded with all the marks of dishonor, and treated with all the odium, baseness and ill usage imaginable, merely because he thinks it his duty to conform to the established church?"

As the debate persisted, Foxcroft became more defensive, Johnson more assertive. Denying that the New England Way was "schismatical and dangerous," the Boston clergyman castigated Johnson for "the open reproach you have cast on the presbyterian communion." The Anglican replied that "episcopacy was truly appointed a remedy against schism," for it was "the most likely form of government... to prevent divisions and disorders." Such structural virtues, Johnson affirmed, reinforced the spiritual blessings of the Church of England. "Our persuasion as much tends . . . to inward, vital, pure, practical... experimental religion as yours can do," he maintained, "and I think a good deal more."

Johnson terminated the debate by recommending that Foxcroft read the works of some English scholars who had analyzed the problem of episcopal ordination. Arguing from authority, he observed that "it is not likely that such little men as we in this country are" would have more to say. Foxcroft, a mere New Englander, could appeal no higher. In this manner the provincial consciousness laid siege to the jeremiad orthodoxy. To Johnson, the superiority of English culture had thoroughly demonstrated the inadequacy of the New England way.[8]

Despite his growing bitterness, Johnson remained optimistic about his ultimate success. But because the provincial government successfully thwarted Anglican demands and perpetuated its discriminatory policies, he turned increasingly to the English establishment for support. To the Bishop of London he suggested that the Puritans' "insolence" derived from the charter government, which protected their autonomy, and he proposed a revocation of that charter.[9] A royal government, he urged, would end the overt persecution of churchmen and place the Anglican church on an equal footing in the competition for souls.

Besides these political changes, Johnson also advocated the appointment of an American episcopate to oversee the Church of England in the colonies. "The fountain of all our misery is the want of a bishop," he exclaimed. The creation of a colonial diocese would facilitate the ordination of new ministers who presently were "loath to expose themselves to the danger of the seas and of distempers" by sailing to England.[10] An American bishop, moreover, would function as a bulwark of religious orthodoxy, protecting godly people from "wretched maxims" and "a great many other perverse principles." The institutional strength of the episcopacy might then defeat the stubborn resistance of the New England way.[11]

Convinced that his suggestions were eminently reasonable, Johnson chafed at the lethargy of the English authorities, their apparent unwillingness to seize the initiative. In Johnson's mind such inertia revealed not the cumbersome workings of the English bureaucracy or the pragmatic problems of political expediency, but a perplexing spiritual indifference. "We in New England . . . lament the languishing state of religion in Old," remarked Timothy Cutler. In Connecticut, Samuel Johnson heartily concurred, pointing to "a spirit of infidelity" spreading across the mother country.[12] What these provincials were condemning was the growing secularization of the age, the deliberate demystification of the universe.

In speaking their apprehensions about English society, people like Cutler and Johnson betrayed an ambivalence typical of provincials in all ages. Certainly they appreciated the wonders of the metropolis and, as Thomas Foxcroft could surely attest, they deferred to the sophistication of English thought. But as outsiders they still viewed the mother country with suspicion. For all its glamor England had nurtured the extremes of infidelity and atheism; sophistication had bred luxury, immorality, and vice. This paradoxical image of Europe dominated colonial culture down to the American Revolution and beyond. For Americans of all persuasions, England remained simultaneously a seat of enlightenment and a den of iniquity.

These cultural attitudes, pervasive though they were, seldom were articulated directly. In Johnson's case, however, they became manifest when he attempted to transplant the English religious system to the colonies. Frustrated by the New England establishment and, more important, ignored by his potential proselytes, he began to question the viability of the Anglican church in a colonial situation. In an elaborate plan submitted to the episcopal authorities in 1732, Johnson requested permission "to abate, in some circumstantial matters," certain tenets of the Anglican worship. These changes, he maintained, would enable him to devote his full energies to the "vitals of religion." The scheme, moreover, would outflank the prejudices of the New England orthodoxy by eliminating the most offensive, but "circumstantial" practices.

Though it was a serious attempt at ecclesiastical revision, Johnson's proposal betrayed more of his personal limitations than his grasp of the problems facing the Church of England in America. Despite a decade of bitter rivalry, he still believed that New Englanders could be persuaded through rational appeal to join the episcopal church. This impression followed from his expectation of the collapse of the New England way—a situation in which, as he explained, the churches were "hastening . . . toward an utter dissolution" because the people "were sick and weary of their present" condition. Finally, Johnson badly overestimated the indulgence of the English bishops. Metropolitan haughtiness argued against liturgical change, while diocesan jealousy blocked the appointment of a bishop. Isolated in America and remote from English currents, Johnson's voice indeed cried in the wilderness.[13]

In the face of this adversity, Johnson's tenacity revealed the power of his emotional commitments. This theological certainty was intimately related to Johnson's personal fantasy of becoming the most learned man in the world. Even when overwhelmed by startling discoveries—first by the Dummer library, later by his expeditions to Oxford and Cambridge—he refused to surrender his self-image as an intellectually superior person capable of knowing everything that could be known. Though Johnson frequently acknowledged his dependence upon English learning, he always strove to keep abreast of the latest ideas, attempted to master the newest trends. Thus, when he arrived at Stratford and dedicated himself to the expansion of the true church, he also resolved "to pursue his former beloved studies, and to improve himself in all parts of learning."[14] By exploring the rational order of the world, Johnson hoped to reestablish intellectual sovereignty over the universe. Those aspirations, however, could lead in dangerous directions.

The Anglican missionary's quest for greater knowledge brought him into contact with William Burnet, the royal governor of New

York, the son of Bishop Gilbert Burnet, and the possessor of one of the finest libraries in America. Like other Englishmen in the provinces, Governor Burnet welcomed the opportunity to display the sophisticated thought of the metropolis to interested Americans. When the young Benjamin Franklin, then a struggling printer, passed through New York, Burnet received him warmly and encouraged his curiosity. Samuel Johnson, better educated than Franklin, enjoyed similar favor. Impressed by Johnson's interest in learning, the governor invited him to frequent conversations and permitted him to borrow his books. Johnson, eager to demonstrate his own abilities, avidly read the volumes suggested by Burnet and modestly offered his opinions about the authors.

Attracted by Burnet's status and sophistication, Johnson initially ignored the content of his thought. As a disciple of eighteenth-century rationalism, however, the royal governor had moved toward a deistic position, which stressed the reasonableness of the universe and consequently depreciated the value of traditional Christianity with its emphasis upon divine revelation. For a man like Benjamin Franklin, already suspicious of orthodox Christianity, Burnet's rationalism posed no threat. But for Johnson, a scrupulous Episcopalian, the latitudinarian principles challenged the most basic assumptions of his personal cosmology. Burnet, hopeful of converting the Anglican to the new intellectual currents, offered his library as "a great temptation."[15]

Johnson's commitment to rational inquiry, together with his willingness to believe the best of metropolitan learning, nearly destroyed his religious certainty. Taken with the "artifice and subtleties" of the English rationalists, the provincial intellectual found himself "in the utmost danger . . . of being finally borne down before their mighty reasonings." At the last moment, however, Johnson recoiled. Instead of rational security, he abruptly realized that his addiction to "reasoning on the great objects of faith" had led him inexorably along the path of error.

"The greatest and worst sorts of trouble and uneasiness," he later asserted, "are endless doubts, scruples, uncertainties, and perplexities of mind," thoughts that "violate the plain dictates of our minds," that cause "a perplexing contradiction and inconsistency with ourselves." The intellectualization of religion, so promising in Johnson's adolescent years, now threatened the meaning of his beliefs. In psychological terms, he suffered a sense of spiritual imbalance, a loss of religious assurance. Horrified by these tendencies, he halted his explorations and firmly resolved "not to indulge in speculations upon articles of faith as though they were subjects of philosophical reasoning and inquiry, but to consider them as revealed facts."[16] Thereafter, Johnson devoted his energies to proclaiming the essential harmony between orthodox Christianity and human reason.

As a near victim of eigheenth-century rationalism, Johnson feared that other contemporaries also might succumb to the logic of the new thinking. From his study in Stratford he perceived that "Arianism and Latitudinarianism so much in vogue often issue in Socianism and that in Deism and that in atheism and the most dissolute living." He observed too that "the more gentlemen pretended to reason and deep speculation the more they dwindled in faith . . ., the more irreligious and immoral they grew." Such tendencies explained the moral decline of the mother country, the political machinations that prevented the appointment of an American episcopate, the failure to effect ecclesiastical reform at home and in the colonies.

"It seems the enemies of Christianity are resolved to leave no stone unturned in order to demolish it," Johnson remarked upon hearing the latest news from England. Such trends challenged not only the Church of England but religion itself, and he begged his Congregational opponents to cease the dissemination of atheistic books. "Can you be insensible that these men are as really enemies to you as to us," he queried, "and that they equally design the ruin of us all?" In "faithfulness to the Gospel," he implored his persecutors, "join with us against the common enemy."[17] For Johnson, the personal crisis of belief explained the problems facing orthodox Christianity everywhere.

The belated discovery of the dangers of "freethinking" convinced Johnson that he should advise other provincials of the inherent pitfalls of rational inquiry. When William Bradford's *New-York Gazette* appealed to "ingenious gentlemen" to submit articles for the "instruction of mankind," Johnson responded with an essay on the compatibility between reason and revelation. The perfection of the physical universe, he declared, the precision of Newtonian mechanics proved the existence of God and demonstrated "that almighty cause to be infinitely wise and good."[18]

Johnson frequently reiterated these ideas in his pulpit oratory. In a sermon called "The Necessity of Revealed Religion," the Anglican preacher reaffirmed the impossibility of attaining religious insight without God's assistance. What "a treacherous thing [is] our reason," he remarked; how easily are we led into error "by false appearances." Such inquiry, moreover, threatened to disrupt the tranquillity of our minds. By permitting "our imaginations to rove" in the divine areas of revelation, "we entangle ourselves in doubts and perplexities"; instead of finding peace and satisfaction, we acquire "endless toil and uneasiness." Only true religion promised solace from this unnatural condition. The plain principles of virtue, Johnson reported, freed our souls "from all perplexing doubts, intricacies, and uncertainties, and from all worrying, enslaving, restless, and impetuous lusts and passions, and consequently from the stings of guilt and fearful expectations." How profound had been Johnson's spiritual crisis, and how simple its resolution! By accepting "the clearest and most evident truths," by avoiding "high soaring speculations," he embraced anew the "pleasure and contentment" of his Christian faith.[19]

Johnson's search for a philosophy that harmonized the new learning with orthodox Christianity ended with his conversion to the writings of George Berkeley, Dean of Derry, later Bishop of Cloyne. In 1729, as part of a plan to erect an episcopal college in the New World, Berkeley arrived in Rhode Island and remained in the colony for nearly three years. The Stratford missonary, anxious to meet "so extraordinary a genius and so great a scholar," arranged for an introduction and, to his pleasure, discovered an immediate affinity with the great man. As in his earlier relationship with Daniel Browne, Johnson idealized his English friend, magnified his stature, and deferred to his accomplishments. "He was a gentleman of vast learning and equal benevolence," Johnson recalled, "and [he] came hither with the most extensively benevolent intention of promoting both religion and learning throughout America among the heathen as well as Christians."[20] This statement readily described Johnson's vision of himself. But as a child of the provinces, the Connecticut minister acknowledged the Dean's preeminence. By establishing proximity to Berkeley, however, by becoming his friend and disciple, by expounding the importance of the Dean's work, Johnson could claim some of that greatness. The personal alliance also enabled the American scholar to reassert his superiority over other provincials—particularly the "dissenters" of New England—who lacked familiarity, much less intimacy, with one of the leading philosophers of the age.

Dean Berkeley's philosophical "immaterialism," his denial of matter and his consequent insistence upon the omnipresence of God, satisfied Samuel Johnson's need for a theocentric cosmology based upon the new learning. According to Berkeley's epistemology, ideas could not exist outside some perceiving mind, either human or divine. Abstract ideas, which could not have originated in the minds of mortals, must have existed previously in the mind of God. Thus the perceptual philosophy confirmed the existence of a divine being. Moreover, Berkeley's system assumed the ubiquity of God, his continued interaction with the minds and souls of human beings. As Johnson viewed it, Berkeley's analysis presented "the most striking apprehensions of [God's] constant presence with us and inspection over us, and of our entire dependence on him and infinite obligations to his most wise and almighty benevolence." No wonder Johnson depicted Berkeley's speculations as "the most surprisingly ingenious I have ever met with" and declared that "the Dean's way of thinking . . . utterly precluded scepticism and left no room for endless doubts and uncertainties."[21]

In emphasizing the omnipresence of a divine mind, Berkeley endeavored to vanquish the arguments of deists and atheists, who had diminished the role of an active God. A decade earlier, the English prelate had denounced the spread of "a cold indifference" to religion and called for a revitalization of the faith.[22] In provincial New England, Samuel Johnson avidly endorsed those assertions. Preaching before Dean Berkeley in 1730, he proclaimed the compatibility of orthodoxy and learning. "The religion taught us in the word of God," Johnson declared, "is truly a divine philosophy, a most excellent and compendious method of living happily." "The teachers of this religion," he asserted in a revealing statement of his self-image, are "the teachers of the best philosophy that ever appeared in the world" and therefore "have the justest title to be esteemed and called the best philosophers." For Johnson wisdom and virtue remained inextricably connected. He urged his audience of ministers to pursue their scholarly studies, to master the "sacred original languages," to read the best Christian authors "that we may furnish our minds with a large store of divine knowledge." Intellectual diligence, by revealing God's truth, promised to uplift the spiritual state of the nation.[23]

Johnson's optimism about the role of education also found reinforcement in Berkeley's definition of knowledge.[24] As a product of mental perception, learning involved the acquisition of ideas taken from a favorable environment. Books, conversations, virtuous living—all were indispensable for intellectual development. By supplying these necessities, by providing an environment conducive to mental perceptions, Johnson hoped to transcend his provincial condition.

These attitudes led the Anglican minister to draft a new synthesis of all knowledge, what he called "A General View of Philosophy, or a Prolegomena to the Arts and Sciences." "It has been a custom here," Johnson explained to Berkeley, that "besides instructing the youth in each particular science," scholars also obtained "a general view of all the sciences, the subjects they treat on and the relation they bear one to another and the general end pursued through them all." Johnson approved this synthetic approach, but criticized the existing compendiums. He therefore proposed to write "a short general view of all the parts of learning in the compass of a sheet or two of paper which the scholars might easily transcribe and have by them."[25] The plan, in other words, represented a modernization and adaptation of Johnson's earlier attempts to systematize his extensive reading.

This "Outline of Philosophy," published in London in 1731, revealed significant departures from Johnson's earlier encyclopedias, particularly in the organization of knowledge.[26] The work also demonstrated his persistent attempt to resolve the dilemmas of provincialism. Lamenting the backward state of learning in America, Johnson exhorted his young countrymen "to apply themselves with the utmost zeal" to a mastery of classical scholarship. Unless they obtained these rudiments, he advised, "they will always be of small account in the eye of the learned and polite world." The general advancement of learning would not only "enrich our minds," but also attract "the notice of the learned world abroad." Provincial Americans might then attain the intellectual distinction of such European scholars as George Berkeley. "For nature doubtless makes as good geniuses here as in other parts of the world," Johnson announced optimistically, "and nothing is wanting but a regular education to polish and cultivate them, that they may exert and display themselves and appear to the best advantage."[27]

Johnson's relationship with Dean Berkeley accentuated the American's feelings of provincial inferiority. "I should be very thankful for your assistance," wrote Johnson to his mentor, "if it were not a pity you should waste your time . . . in writing to a person so obscure and so unworthy of such a favor as I am." In a subsequent missive the Connecticut minister apologized for his ignorance, explaining that he had "been bred up under the greatest disadvantages."[28] Such phrases reflected more than a stylized deference to one's superiors. Thus, on his thirty-third birthday, scarcely one month after apologizing to the Dean, Johnson privately thanked the Lord for "that tranquility of life I enjoy" and expressed satisfaction with his "circumstances of life." Yet, in a parenthetical statement designed for no one's eyes but his own, he admitted that he craved "a greater frequency of the conversation of learned men and a larger scope for being serviceable and doing good in the world."[29] Two weeks later these feelings of inadequacy led Johnson to apply for a more prestigious position in Boston. Denying any interest in what he called "temporal advantage," he insisted that his only motive was "the prospect of being more serviceable in promoting the interest of religion."[30] Such disclaimers could not conceal Johnson's ambitiousness, his desire for visible advancement, his thirst for recognition. The presence of men like Dean Berkeley served as a painful reminder of his provincial accommodation, his feeling of "littleness."

Shortly before his departure from America, Berkeley sent Johnson a collection of books and encouraged the missionary's efforts "to promote religion and learning in this uncultivated part of the world." Berkeley's support of Johnson culminated in 1733, when the philosopher bestowed a large gift, including the deed to his Rhode Island farm, to Yale College. The New England orthodoxy distrusted this largess and worried that it might breed such heresies as Arminianism or, worse, episcopacy. Such ingratitude insulted

Johnson and he promptly denounced the petulance of the dissenters, for the child of the provinces took special pride in his role as a friendly intermediary in the affair. He identified with Berkeley and, through the Dean's generosity, found personal fulfillment as the dispenser of knowledge, the apostle of learning.[31]

As a young man Samuel Johnson had imagined himself as Samuel, the wise and the virtuous. He never relinquished that dream. By associating with sympathetic Englishmen–first with William Burnet, later and more permanently with George Berkeley–the provincial intellectual endeavored to attract the recognition he felt he deserved. Johnson's scholarly distinction, however, depended not merely upon his personal achievement, but also on the level of culture in his native land. For Johnson to attain his goal, he first had to convert his provincial neighbors to the wisdom of the metropolis. As an Anglican minister he worked to extend the Church of England; as a provincial pedagogue he strove to impart English learning. In both cases he attempted to Anglicize the colonies. Only then would Samuel Johnson win visible approval and thereby find inner satisfaction.

NOTES

1. SJ's Answer to Bishop Gibson's Queries, July 1, 1724, Fulham MSS; George Pigot to SPG, January 13, 1723/24, *HP* 1: 87; SJ, "Autobiography," p. 19, gives slightly higher figures.

2. [SJ], *A Second Letter from a Minister of the Church of England to his Dissenting Parishioners* (Boston, 1734), printed in *SJ Papers,* 3: 39; SJ, "Raphael," 2: 570.

3. Joseph Talcott to Edmund Gibson, December 1, 1725. "Talcott Papers," p. 65. For a similar attack on Johnson personally, see William Douglass, *A Summary, Historical and Political of the First Planting, Progressive Improvements, and Present State of the British Settlements in North America,* 2 vols. (Boston, 1755), 2: 149–50, 336; for Johnson's response, see SJ to William Douglass, December 20, 1751, JCU, 1.

4. For a persuasive discussion of the social basis of the Anglicans, see Bruce E. Steiner, "New England Anglicanism: A Genteel Faith?" *William & Mary Quarterly* 27 (1970): 122–35. Cowing has pointed to the low ranking among Yale converts; see his *Great Awakening,* pp. 28–29 and Dexter, *Biographical Sketches,* 1 passim.

5. SJ to Zachary Grey, [ca. January] 1724/25; SJ to SPG, March 20,

1724/25, both in JHP; SJ to Edmund Gibson, January 18, 1724, SJ to John Berriman, January 1, 1725, *SJ Papers,* 3: 217, 219. Various levels of the debate are analyzed in Miller, *Colony to Province.* See also Carl Bridenbaugh, *Mitre and Sceptre: Transatlantic Faiths, Ideas, Personalities, and Politics, 1689–1775* (New York, 1962).

6. The history of Anglicanism in eighteenth-century Connecticut is discussed in the following works: E. Edwards Beardsley, *The History of the Episcopal Church in Connecticut,* 2 vols. (New York, 1865–68), 1; Arthur Lyon Cross, *The Anglican Episcopate and the American Colonies* (New York, 1902); Maria L. Greene, *The Development of Religious Liberty in Connecticut* (Boston, 1905); numerous primary sources are printed in *HP.* Shortly after returning from England, Johnson traveled to New London to appeal to the Governor for a redress of grievances; see SJ to Gurdon Saltonstall, June 20, 1724, JHP.

7. SJ, Notes for a [Fast] Sermon, April 15, 1724; Sermon: Of the Nature of sanctification, February 1726; Notes for a Sermon, March 1, 1723/24, all in JCU.

8. The debate between Johnson and Foxcroft can be followed in several letters exchanged in the summer of 1726. The MSS are in HU; one of Foxcroft's letters is printed in *SJ Papers.* 3: 9–16 and two slightly revised letters by Johnson appeared in an appendix to [James Wetmore and SJ], *Eleutherus Enervatus; Or an Answer to a Pamphlet, Intituled, The Divine Right of Presbyterian Ordination* (New York, 1733).

9. SJ to Edmund Gibson, September 26, 1726, JHP.

10. George Pigot to SPG, October 3, 1722, *HP,* 1: 59; SJ to Edmund Gibson, January 18, 1724, *SJ Papers,* 3: 217–18. When a debate between two Anglican ministers flared in Boston, Johnson seized the opportunity to plead for a bishop; see SJ to Edmund Gibson, October 9, 1724, JHP.

11. SJ to Edmund Gibson, January 18, 1723/24, *HP,* 1: 93; SJ to John Talbot, December 16, 1724; SJ to Edmund Gibson, February 1, 1725, *SJ Papers,* 3: 218–19, 221. See also Bruce Steiner, "Samuel Seabury," pp. 36–37.

12. Timothy Cutler to Zachary Grey, October 8, 1736, "copies of Letters," New-York Historical Society; SJ to Dr. Delaune, August 10, 1725, *SJ Papers,* 3: 222; idem to Mr. Hayward, August 10, 1725, JHP; idem to John Scullard, December 2, 1727, *SJ Papers,* 1: 80.

13. SJ to Edmund Gibson, April 5, 1732, and "Proposals relating to . . . the more successful reformation and propagation of religion in America" [April 1732], both printed in *HP,* 1: 151–54. In his proposal Johnson expressed an ambivalent position regarding the colonial charters. Probably to appease potential converts, he asked if the existing governments could be preserved. Yet he suggested that a revocation of the charters would benefit not only the Church, but also "the people themselves" (p. 154).

14. SJ, "Autobiography," p. 20.

15. Ibid., pp. 20–22; S.J. to William Burnet, December 16, 1724, JHP;

William Burnet to SJ, January 31, 1727, August 14, 1727, *SJ Papers,* 1: 76–78; *The Autobiography of Benjamin Franklin,* ed. Jesse Lemisch (New York, 1961), p. 46.

16. SJ, "Autobiography," pp. 21–22; True Philosophy, or the Wisdom of Religion and Virtue, May 15, 1731, *SJ Papers,* 3: 396.

17. SJ, "Autobiography," pp. 22–23; S.J. to John Berriman, August 18, 1734, *SJ Papers,* 1: 83–84; [SJ], *A Second Letter,* pp. 99–100.

18. *New-York Gazette,* January 28–February 4, 1728 [/29], March 4–10, 1728 [/29]. Johnson's piece appeared on March 17, 1728/29, and is printed in *SJ Papers,* 2: 254–59.

19. SJ, The Necessity of Revealed Religion, September 27, 1727; True Philosophy . . ., *SJ Papers,* 3: 373, 374, 397–98, 403.

20. SJ, "Autobiography," pp. 24–25.

21. Ibid., p. 25; SJ to George Berkeley, September 10, 1729, *SJ Papers,* 2: 263. Johnson's relationship to Berkeley can be traced in their correspondence, most of which is printed in *SJ Papers,* 2. For studies of Berkeley, see A. A. Luce, *The Life of George Berkeley, Bishop of Cloyne* (London, 1949); John Wild, *George Berkeley: A Study of His Life and Philosophy* (Cambridge, Mass., 1936).

22. George Berkeley, "An Essay towards preventing the Ruin of Great Britain" [1721], in *The Works of George Berkeley, Bishop of Cloyne,* ed. A. A. Luce and T. E. Jessop, 9 vols. (London, 1948–57), 6: 69–70.

23. SJ, Concio ad Clerum: A Sermon, May 18, 1730, JCU.

24. For a fuller analysis of this relationship, see Joseph J. Ellis III, "The Puritan Mind in Transition: The Philosophy of Samuel Johnson," *William & Mary Quarterly* 28 (1971): 26–45.

25. SJ to George Berkeley, July 24, 1730, JYU.

26. For a sensitive analysis of these works, see Fiering, "President Samuel Johnson," p. 220 and "Moral Philosophy," pp. 285–86 and passim.

27. SJ, "Advertisement," in "An Outline of Philosophy,"*SJ Papers,* 2: 314–15.

28. SJ to George Berkeley, September 10, 1729, February 5, 1729/30, *SJ Papers,* 2: 268, 275.

29. SJ, "Liber Dierum," p. 70.

30. SJ to Edmund Gibson, October 27, 1729, Fulham MSS. Seven years later Johnson used similar language in soliciting a position at Newport, Rhode Island, the town where Berkeley had tarried for three years. Besides seeking visible advancement the Connecticut minister probably sought to legitimate his unconscious identification with Berkeley. For a description of the affair see SJ to James Honyman, May 1738; SJ to SPG, June 7, 1738, both in *SJ Papers,* 1: 89–91; James Macsparran to SPG, "The State of Trinity Church in Newport, Rhode Island," [October], 1750, SPG MSS., ser. B, 18: 66.

31. SJ to George Berkeley, July 24, 1730, JYU; George Berkeley to SJ, September 7, 1731, *SJ Papers,* 1: 81; SJ, "Autobiography," pp. 26–27; Elisha Williams to Benjamin Colman, January 11, 1732/33, printed in

Dexter, *Biographical Sketches,* 1: 470–71; [Ezra Stiles], *The Literary Diary of Ezra Stiles,* ed. Franklin Bowditch Dexter, 3 vols. (New York, 1901), 1: 205–6 (see also n. 30 above). Berkeley's gift provided for the creation of a scholarship for the most promising students of the classics. Applicants were to be examined by the rector of the college and by a minister of the Church of England. It was this latter provision that alarmed the local orthodoxy.

7
"OUR FATHER'S HOUSE"

AS A young man Samuel Johnson committed himself to the pursuit of knowledge and resolved to master "all parts of learning." He remained faithful to that goal, reading voluminously throughout his life, digesting the latest English publication, following the elaborate and at times bitter debates among eighteenth-century philosophers and theologians. Yet, when Ezra Stiles, perhaps the most learned man of a later generation of provincial Americans, assessed Johnson's career, he described the Anglican minister as "a man of general, but not profound and solid or deep erudition," and he quoted with obvious relish the remark of Thomas Ruggles, Jr., one of Johnson's boyhood acquaintances and the son of Johnson's first pastor, that "Dr. Johnson was always of the opinion of the last book he read." "Some geniuses," Stiles concluded, "with half the observation and reading of Dr. Johnson, would make ten times greater men."[1] Such harsh judgments, coming from two staunch opponents of the Anglican church in New England, reflected the acrimony of Johnson's "bitter enemies"; the statements remained no less accurate for that.

In the isolation of his study in Stratford, Connecticut, Samuel Johnson struggled to harmonize the contradictions and disagreements expounded by the disparate thinkers he admired and respected. Though characteristic of many eighteenth-century writers, this search for intellectual unity nevertheless betrayed the limitations of Johnson's mind and demonstrated not his synthetic skills, but rather his eclecticism. The problem of philosophical integration also illuminated the derivative nature of Johnson's thought, his dependence upon the intellectual output of metropolitan writers, his inability to question beliefs inherited from his Anglo-Puritan past, his uncritical acceptance of widely held ideas about society.[2] Thus, despite the sophisticated language of his writings, Johnson's image of the world remained typical of many other people within his culture. His pulpit oratory and philosophical explications, representative as they were, manifested many of the underlying, even unconscious, assumptions shared by provincials of all status groups and of all denominations in eighteenth-century New England.

In articulating his ideas Samuel Johnson embraced a cosmology that not only expressed the dominant strains of his culture, but also satisfied his emotional needs. Just as his ministerial and pedagogical activity represented a logical fulfillment of personal commitments, so too the *content* of his thought mirrored his innermost feelings. Thus he emphasized the beneficence of God, the order and justice of the universe, the interrelationship of all human affairs. Many other New Englanders, for reasons that remain unknown, shared his vision of the cosmos. Yet, in Johnson's case, these culturally approved ideas also derived from specific aspects of his personality. In fundamental ways, his world view constituted a projection of his emotional life, his relations within the family of his childhood, and the patterns of family life he created as an adult.

Johnson himself appreciated the subjective basis of human commitments. His difficulties as an Anglican missionary, particularly his inability to overcome the hostility of the New England orthodoxy, had demonstrated the shortcomings of rational persuasion. Similarly, his flirtation with eighteenth-century rationalism had revealed the theological limitations of logical inquiry. Such experiences slowly persuaded Johnson that reason alone did not motivate human activity. "Great allowances must be made for human frailty," he observed regretfully, "and the unaccountable prejudices arising from temper, custom, vogue, education, or some untoward association of ideas which may strangely warp our minds and bias the train of our thoughts."[3] Johnson's mature writings manifested these same frailties–revealing the convergence of "temper, custom, vogue, education," and some less-easily defined emotional pulls.

The emotional structure of Samuel Johnson's youth—his fear of separations, his search for unification, his primary identification with his grandfather—had emerged from the three-generational interaction within the Johnson family. Such configurations had led logically, though not inevitably, to the young man's conversion to the Church of England in 1722. Those patterns persisted beyond that crucial event and shaped Johnson's subsequent relations with his aging parents, particularly with his father, and with his younger siblings. The models of Johnson's earliest attachments also influenced the formation of his own family—his marriage to Charity Floyd in 1725, his attitudes toward child-rearing and, in the largest sense, his notion of parenthood.

If communion within the Church of England provided Samuel Johnson with a sense of cosmic universality and a feeling of maternal union, it also offered symbolic alternatives to the paternal figures of the jeremiad tradition. The episcopal hierarchy—the deans, bishops, and archbishops—traditionally served as symbolic fathers to the souls of God's church. Johnson's friendly reception in England reinforced his attachment to these cultural images. Thus Johnson recalled that Dean Stanhope, the first Anglican prelate to receive the American converts at Canterbury, "like a father gave them . . . his most kind advice and direction," while the Archbishop of York "treated them as a most kind father." Similarly, the Connecticut missionary always ended his correspondence to Bishop Gibson with the traditional compliment, "your most dutiful son."[4] Such identifications facilitated Johnson's separation from the church of his father and grandfather. Perhaps these factors also explain his enthusiasm for the appointment of an American episcopate.

Johnson's commitment to the Church of England accentuated the paternal problems of his own father, the elder Samuel Johnson. While operating the fulling mill in Guilford, Deacon Johnson had continued to serve the town's Congregational church, annually accepting election to the "Society's Committee." But in December 1722, just three months after the Yale conversions, the congregation passed over the deacon's name; never again did it appear in the church records.[5] Thus the townspeople punished the parent of the apostate. The elder Johnson nevertheless attempted to maintain peaceful relations with his life-long neighbors, strove to mitigate the shock of his son's decision, and tried, in the final analysis, to save face.

These tendencies brought a new dimension to the symbolic interaction occurring within the Johnson family. The elder Samuel never repudiated his son's conversion and, in his surviving letters, referred to his child as "my dear and kind son." It was, moreover, to his father's house in Guilford that the Anglican missionary "hastened" upon returning from England. In their subsequent conversations the son introduced the father to the writings of the Anglican divines, explained the theological importance of episcopacy, and ultimately convinced the older man of the advantages of the Church of England. He was "entirely reconciled to the Church in point of charity," wrote the Anglican minister upon learning of his father's death in 1727, "and would have communicated with us if he had lived, . . . nay would have done it before now, had it not been for the bitter and uncharitable tempers of the country, which prevailed upon him for peace's sake to abstain."[6] By serving as his father's mentor, the younger Samuel Johnson carried the reversal of generations to its logical conclusion. The child became parent to the father, providing instruction and guidance for the older man. William Johnson, twenty-five years in his grave, had had the final word.

Samuel Johnson's mother, Mary Sage Johnson, had died in the winter of 1726 following "a long and tedious sickness." Her eldest son was deeply grieved over the loss of "so near and dear a relation, one so every way desirable, endowed with so many graces" and fervently prayed for a "happy meeting" hereafter in the kingdom of God.[7] Yet it was the death of Deacon Johnson the next year that the Anglican minister regarded as "the heaviest affliction I ever felt." Mourning the loss of his "dear, tender and indulgent father," Samuel Johnson extolled the deacon's virtues, stressing his godliness, his piety, his friendliness. With traditional Christian metaphors, the minister prayed that the calamity would reclaim him from his sins and "that our father's death may be the means and occasion of the new life in all our souls."[8]

Prior to his death, the elder Johnson had bestowed a modest inheritance on his oldest son, part of which the minister used to purchase a house at Stratford. The deacon divided the remainder of his estate among his surviving children. This legacy, including shares in the fulling mill, permitted all the remaining children who had reached their majority to enter the bonds of matrimony within eleven months of their father's death. By 1730, however, only one male heir, Nathaniel Johnson, remained in Guilford to purchase his brother's shares of the inheritance, while both surviving females, Mary and Abigail, married into old Guilford families and spent their entire lives in their native town.[9] These demographic patterns, typical of New England society, reflected the problem of overcrowding in the eighty-year-old town. As younger generations matured, population pressure apparently forced the children of Guilford to delay matrimony until adequate estates became available, or compelled them to seek suitable homesites in other locations. This process persisted throughout eighteenth-century Connecticut, causing a general rise in land values, leading some children to adopt nonagricultural pursuits and encouraging frequent migrations to interior settlements, where land was cheaper. The dispersal of Deacon Johnson's family thus represented part of a larger, though still rudimentary, transformation of provincial society.[10]

After settling at Stratford, Samuel Johnson maintained contact with his younger siblings in Guilford, visiting them frequently, often to discuss the doctrinal validity of the Church of England. These missionary labors within the family eventually bore fruit. Barely a decade after the death of the elder Samuel, Nathaniel Johnson announced his conversion to the episcopal church and, ten years later, George Bartlett, husband of Abigail Johnson, followed him into the Anglican fold. After the formation of an episcopal congregation in Guilford, in which Johnson's relatives played a prominent role, the Stratford minister preached periodically in his native town, administered the sacraments, and worked to overcome the resistance of the nonepiscopal townspeople.[11] In this manner Samuel Johnson became the symbolic head of the Johnson family.

As a young man Samuel Johnson's search for spiritual peace had dominated his emotional life. Uncertain about himself and of the meaning of his life and his work, he avoided relationships that might have complicated his predicament. Years later, he expressed regret about his inability to share emotional bonds during that earlier time of crisis. Urging his son to be "careful while you are in a state of celibacy to guard against anything that may have the least tendency to make any [woman] miserable," Johnson depicted the hazards of "a frequent intercourse with [women] when no thoughts of anything further than mere conversation are intended. This is an affair of great tenderness," he confessed, "and has occasioned in time past a great deal of grief to me, and were I to go over life again I would never frequently or much converse with a person I had not even remote thoughts of making a partner in life, or when I was in no condition for it."[12] Johnson had released his emotional energy in the pursuit of learning and had relied heavily upon the like devotion of Daniel Browne. Not until 1725, when the Anglican minister had effectively resolved the major dilemmas of his life, did he enter a matrimonial union.[13]

In colonial America, marriage constituted the final stage in the achievement of adulthood. This status was symbolized by the formation of an independent household, separate from the domiciles of other relatives. Once married, people assumed complete responsibility for their own welfare—for their living expenses and the cost of bearing children. In the Old World, such obligations served to delay marriage until the young people possessed sufficient estates to live independently. Prior to the colonization of America, therefore, English children usually waited until their mid- or even late twenties to be married. But in New England, where land was more abundant, people could afford to marry sooner; the average age of marriage consequently dropped significantly in the seventeenth century. By Samuel Johnson's lifetime, however, these trends had begun to reverse, largely because population growth reduced the available acreage. Even so, Johnson's marriage at the age of twenty-nine was somewhat later than the age of marriage of most of his contemporaries. For reasons peculiar to himself, it had taken him longer to find what he called "the partner of his life."[14]

Johnson's spouse, Charity Floyd Nicoll, descended from one of the most prominent families of Long Island, in the neighboring province of New York. Her high social status enabled the girl to obtain more than a rudimentary education and her personal library contained the writings of Chaucer, volumes on history and geography, as well as the traditional Christian tomes. Some time around her twentieth birthday Charity Floyd had married Benjamin Nicoll, a young man with a bright future in provincial politics. She bore him three children, William, Benjamin, and Glorianna, before his premature death.[15] It was in her early widowhood that Charity Nicoll first met Samuel Johnson. They married on Long Island in the early autumn of 1725 and returned together with her children to Stratford. In October Charity Johnson communicated in her husband's church for the first time and then returned Sunday after Sunday for over forty years to hear him preach the words of the Lord.[16]

In explaining his marriage, Samuel Johnson emphasized the woman's role of "keeping house" and the importance of finding "a person of experienced and noted good economy." He found in Charity Johnson not only an available companion but also the mother of three children. Four years his senior and more experienced in marital relations, she provided Johnson with security and stability. He, on the other hand, offered paternal guidance for the fatherless youngsters. As a stepfather Johnson promoted the education of the boys and prepared them for admission to Yale College. Many years later William Nicoll, the last surviving child of the family, traveled to Johnson's home in Stratford "personally to acknowledge your great goodness and care of my younger years, which I gratefully do on every remembrance of you."[17] Such praises, coming from a stepson, bespoke the gentleness and genuine benevolence of Johnson's paternalism.

Samuel Johnson became a natural father two years after his marriage, when Charity gave birth to "a very likely son." Thus, wrote the happy father, "no sooner am I deprived of a father but I am provided . . . with a son to supply the demands of our mortal condition of the world." If such terms suggested the biological reversal of generations, the boy's name further completed the circle. Johnson called the boy Samuel, referred to him frequently as Sammy, but officially christened the lad William Samuel Johnson. Such symbolic nomenclature not only venerated the dead and perpetuated their memories but also subtly justified Johnson's sense of generational superiority. In 1731, thirty months later, Charity delivered a second son, who was also named William. The father dedicated both sons to God. "Let them live to do a great deal of good in the world," he prayed, and "let me live to see them well educated and engaged in thy service! Give them sound and healthy constitutions," he begged, "capacious understandings, teachable and obedient tempers and above all sanctified hearts and virtuous lives."[18] Through his children Samuel Johnson hoped to extend his own values and sought to perpetuate himself, to achieve a symbolic immortality.

Johnson's attitude toward family life and his relationship with his wife and five children reflected his acceptance of the values of his culture. In the Stratford household Johnson attempted to implement those ideals by raising children who embraced his image of the world, who shared his commitment to education and virtue, who would bring credit to the family name. Yet he also had to reconcile those communal values with his personal feelings about family bonds, about matrimony, parenthood, and child rearing. Johnson's remarks about the family, particularly his emphasis upon harmony, balance, and order, revealed a congruence between the conventional wisdom of provincial New England and the particular needs of his own personality.

The secularization of Western culture had altered communal attitudes toward marriage, allowing children greater freedom in selecting their mates. Though arranged marriages still existed, especially among the upper classes, it was becoming more common for young people to marry for love than for familial convenience. It is significant therefore that Samuel Johnson introduced his bride to his family *after* his marriage. Nor did this procedure offend his parents. I pray that "my good god will bless you both," declared the elder Samuel Johnson, pleased that his son had found "a companion [that] you take such satisfaction in."[19]

For Johnson, therefore, the marital bond was based upon the "tenderest love and fidelity." Though married people might disagree about specific matters, he urged them to "communicate their minds and not have any reserves." Such openness, what Johnson called "an entire intimacy," assured a happy relationship. In emphasizing these intangible bonds, however, Johnson could not resist his rationalistic tendency to define the world as a system of reciprocal obligations. The main end of marriage, he preached, was "to promote [the] mutual good" of the couple. They had mutual responsibilities, in other words, "to accommodate each other's tempers," to "guard against what is troublesome." Those phrases, stiff and stylized as they appear, obscured Johnson's personal sensitivity. But in a culture that denied the public expression of feeling, Johnson lacked an alternative mode of discourse.[20]

For similar reasons, Johnson seldom spoke directly about sexual matters, usually relying upon the traditional Christian ideas of chastity, fidelity, and moderation. He viewed bodily passions with suspicion and warned of the dangers of polluting or defiling the soul by pursuing the physical appetites. God had prohibited "all filthy thoughts, entertaining our imagination with them," he preached, and therefore we must suppress our "impure desires so far forth as they gain the least consent of the soul, or the least delight." We must not feed ourselves "too highly what provokes lust," he asserted in a metaphor of orality, and "should rather fast." "All excess even in lawful gratifications," he suggested, was to be avoided, "for these tend to sensualize the soul."[21] Johnson's fear of sensuality reflected both traditional Christian asceticism and his personal distrust of the passions. In the intimacy of his family, no less than in his articulated theology, Samuel Johnson idealized a life of reason, of order, of self-control.

Such virtues, he believed, had to be inculcated in children from their earliest years. Johnson's approach to child rearing borrowed heavily from John Locke's *Some Thoughts Concerning Education,* a work he read shortly after the second birthday of his oldest son. As a parent Johnson demanded "all submission and dutiful obedience" from his offspring and he expected them to "avoid everything that is untoward and undutiful." As a pedagogue and preacher, moreover, he denounced the "foolish fondness" of parents, which made them prey to "the little perverse humors of their tender offspring." Advising parents to establish their authority over their children, Johnson warned them "to command nothing rashly and unadvisedly, nothing but what is reasonable, fit, and just." Such fairness would teach youngsters to respect lawful authority and eventually become "orderly, obedient and well-behaved members of the community." The Anglican minister also chastised New England parents for spoiling their children. "You must teach them early to deny themselves," he pleaded, because children soon would expect satisfaction of all their desires and "insist on the gratification of their basest appetites and most vicious inclinations when they grow up."[22]

In exhorting parents to keep a "strict eye" on their offspring, Johnson nevertheless insisted upon the importance of parental "tenderness." Such advice, self-evident as it appears in our own times, represented then a significant departure from traditional child rearing. Throughout western Europe parents had usually considered their offspring as unwanted burdens. One indication of this feeling was the widespread evidence of child neglect—of beating, starving, abandonment. By the eighteenth century, however, that attitude was rapidly changing and child abuse, though by no means extinct, was less socially acceptable.[23]

Samuel Johnson's advice to parents needs to be seen in this context. Instead of abusing the young, Johnson insisted that children should not "be treated as trifling foundlings, merely to be played with at first and then neglected as below your notice." "They come into the world [as] strangers to everything, but with an eager curiosity to know things," Johnson observed; "their curiosity is to be indulged, and their little questions should be carefully and distinctly answered."

Johnson also criticized the contemporary phenomenon of teaching children by fright. Warning children of "bogey-men" might curb their juvenile inclinations, but the spiritual costs, Johnson suggested, might be high. As reasonable creatures they should not "be put off with shadows and delusions, but should be plainly and easily indoctrinated with right notions of things." Children, of course, would not always grasp the implications of their lessons, as Johnson discovered when he broke some bad news to one of his young students. But in a strangely modern way he remained optimistic about the advantages of rational appeals and candor.[24]

While stressing the importance of stern discipline, Johnson seldom mentioned corporal punishment and advised parents to reason calmly with misbehaving youngsters. If adults were dissatisfied with the conduct of their offspring, he recommended that they "take them alone and in a serious and dispassionate manner explain to them the mischief of any ill courses they are in danger of." Such strategies, by appealing to a sense of conscience, might reclaim delinquent youngsters before they became addicted to vice.[25] But reason, however calm and sincere, worked only if the children were sufficiently mature to understand the logic of adult discourse. Mere infants could not be corrected solely by rational appeals. It is possible, then, that Samuel Johnson's silence about corporal punishment–a voicelessness he shared with most of his contemporaries–assumed that only older children, youngsters able to reason, should be spared the pain and indignity of physical chastisement. The youngest infants may well have faced the full wrath of their angry parents.[26]

To raise obedient children, Johnson praised not only the efficacy of reason, but also the value of setting virtuous examples for them to imitate. "Teach them the utmost abhorrence of all impurity," he implored, "but also keep a strict watch over all [your] own words and behavior especially in the presence of [your] children." Johnson shared these attitudes with other provincial New Englanders. "The nature of man is very prone to be led by example," pronounced the Connecticut election preacher in 1719, "and especially by the example of superiors that are honored and esteemed." Idealization of these "superiors" moved people to "an imitation of the person admired."[27]

New England parents, by exhibiting the culture's values in their own lives, inspired their offspring to reproduce those preferred ideals. In psychological terms, the children internalized the cultural values as they strove to imitate their parents. Besides transferring the cultural patterns to the next generation, the socialization process sought to reinforce sanctions associated with shame. In imitating their parents, provincial children adopted ideals that they themselves hoped to attain. Later violations of those standards would produce a sense of guilt, but failure to achieve the internalized ideals brought different feelings, those of self-contempt and shame.[28]

In arousing a sensitivity to shame in their children, in emphasizing the importance of achieving ideal patterns of behavior, New England parents defined their expectations for the various roles within the family. Each member of the family–husband, wife, and child–enjoyed particular privileges and assumed specific responsibilities. Family order depended upon a proper balance of these functions. Such attitudes toward family life, particularly the emphasis upon mutual responsibility, not only delineated ideal social roles but also established limits upon personal autonomy. To embrace one's place in the family order involved a renunciation of individualized activity, an acceptance of specific hierarchical limitations, a submission to what Samuel Johnson called "family government."[29]

Parents, according to Johnson, assumed two primary responsibilities to their children: "to be concerned for their bodies and their comfortable subsistence in the world" and, more important, to assure "the welfare of their souls" hereafter. While warning of the dangers of worldliness, the Anglican minister nevertheless agreed that parents should "lay up and provide" material security for their progeny.[30] After selling his share of his Guilford inheritance to his brother in 1730, Samuel Johnson began to invest in real estate in the growing towns of Woodbury and Derby. During the following decade he amassed considerable holdings, while the value of his property increased sixfold.[31] By any accounts Johnson had provided for the comfort and security of his sons in this world. The minister also took pains to assure their spiritual happiness "to all eternity." Before William Samuel Johnson had reached the age of seven, he had read, at his father's request, no less than three catechisms, the New Testament, and the Psalter. Thereafter the lad continued to peruse as many books dealing with religion as with secular matters.[32] Samuel Johnson, the father, took seriously the messages he conveyed to his congregation each Sabbath.

Samuel Johnson's image of the family—his emphasis upon the balance of privileges and duties, the mutuality of trust and love—represented a microcosm of his vision of the universe. As the father presided over the household, providing material support for his family and improving the spiritual welfare of his dependents, so too did God oversee the operations of the universe. "Our heavenly father deals with us," preached the Anglican minister, "as we do with our children."[33] In his own family, Johnson endeavored to live by the rule of justice and reason. While insisting upon the obedience of his children, he recognized their value as human beings and accepted his responsibility for their welfare. He could not doubt but that the father of mankind would treat His own children with similar beneficence, with charity, with mercy, with love.

Stressing the benevolence of the Lord, Johnson described Him as "a most tender and indulgent father." Mere mortals, like the innocent children they raised, could not know their own best interests and consequently must obey the will of God. Yet, in submitting to the Almighty, people did not surrender to "an imperious and spiteful enemy," but to a God of love, "who out of mere friendship and good will" determined the rules of conduct. Like a concerned parent, God watched over His children, "a constant spectator of all our behavior, of all our thoughts and affections of our hearts, as well as all the actions of our lives." It was vain, Johnson assured his congregation, to attempt "to deceive Him or hide ourselves from his all-seeing eye." These paternal images dominated Johnson's explicit theology. Heaven, for example, was a place where people enjoyed "free access to [God] as children to a reconciled, tender and compassionate father." As in the human family, filial deference involved not only the avoidance of known evils, but also the imitation of ideal standards of behavior. "Copy . . . out into [your] own hearts and lives [the] conduct and behavior of our blessed savior," Johnson counseled, and conform your lives "to his divine instruction and his heavenly examples."[34] Happiness in heaven, as on earth, depended upon fulfilling the idealized roles of the cosmic family.

The beneficence of God—His essential goodness, mercy, and charity—convinced Samuel Johnson that the Lord had created an equally perfect and happy universe. "The whole show of nature is a kind of language," he suggested, with which God communicated to His mortal creatures. The Lord offers us "baubles and playthings to divert and amuse us while we are children" on earth, Johnson explained. "But as a wise and good parent contrives the diversity and amusement of his children" to improve their minds and prepare them for things of greater importance, so "our heavenly father gives us . . . the things of the world" to strengthen our reason in preparation "for that more perfect state of being in the life to come." God, the Anglican minister declared, in His infinite wisdom, power, and goodness, had transformed the natural chaos of the universe into a rational system, "a most excellent order," in which everything functioned "to the good, the beauty, strength and advantages of the whole."[35] The order of the natural universe, celebrated by all eighteenth-century writers after Newton, bolstered Samuel Johnson's emotional commitment to cosmic harmony.

Samuel Johnson's view of the universe served as a prototype of his image of proper human relations. As physical nature constituted a balance of forces, as the human body consisted of balanced fluids and solids, so too the mind or soul required a natural harmony. A healthy soul existed, said Johnson, when every mental "faculty, the understanding, affections, will and executive powers" performed its function and contributed "to the tranquility and joy of the whole soul." Above all, the rational faculties had to regulate the boisterous tendencies of the "appetites" and "passions." "It is the highest attainment [of] human nature," the Anglican minister announced, "truly Godlike and divine . . . to feel our passions and resentments under command." In social terms, these psychological virtues emerged as an ability to remain "calm, mild and patient" regardless of the difficulties encountered in life. Self-control, Johnson argued, meant a refusal to be easily provoked, a readiness to forgive, "obsequiousness to superiors, condescension to inferiors, complaisance to equals." Ever fearful of the emotions, he advocated meekness, humility, and deference.[36]

Like most of his contemporaries, Samuel Johnson accepted a hierarchical notion of society and believed that God had distributed human talents and worldly goods according to His inscrutable will. Differences in status, wealth, or intelligence simply reflected the diversity of mankind. Yet social inequalities, under ideal conditions, need not create disorder or disharmony. Each social group—what eighteenth-century people called "estate"—enjoyed particular privileges and accepted specific responsibilities. As Johnson stated it, "all depends upon a perpetual exchange of mutual good offices." Such interaction provided everything "that is easy, comfortable and pleasant in society," Johnson observed, "and the contrary is ever attended with mischief, confusion and every evil work." These attitudes justified the institution of slavery and Johnson, like many of his Connecticut neighbors, felt no reservations about dealing in human chattels.[37] In this manner, the hierarchical cosmology rationalized the existing social order and the growing stratification of social arrangements.

The emphasis upon cooperation also structured Johnson's attitude toward economic relations. "Benevolence is to society what attraction is to nature," he remarked; "as the one preserves order and harmony in the natural world; so the other preserves peace and happiness in the moral world." In the language of the Protestant ethic, the Anglican minister beseeched his parishioners to remain "innocently and virtuously employed; for," he advised, "idleness is a state of perpetual temptation." Though accepting the necessity of personal profit, Johnson nevertheless condemned the search for exorbitant wealth and implored New Englanders to approach the world of business with a spirit of Christian charity.[38]

The notion of the natural harmony of economic interests reinforced Johnson's vision of a spiritual union of mankind. In creating geographical differences throughout the world, God intended to encourage trade between nations, "to promote a general acquaintance, intercourse, faith and friendship among mankind; so that all the inhabitants of the whole globe are obliged to consider themselves . . . as one community." Such ideas appealed to Johnson's belief in a universal Christian society. The Gospel of Jesus Christ, he declared, had been intended to create a "commonwealth or society" that included "all nations and languages" and united them "into one body, and family, under Him their one head and master."[39] Only the perverseness of human nature had prevented the formation of a Christian community on earth.

Johnson's economic ideals, besides repeating traditional homilies, seemed particularly relevant in eighteenth-century Connecticut.[40] Throughout this period people in all social groups, even ministers like Samuel Johnson, engaged in considerable land speculation and often obtained large profits. Preoccupation with investment disturbed conservatives, who worried about the social consequences of economic competition. Such activity, pervasive as it appeared, threatened the traditional image of virtuous behavior. In his own case, Johnson felt sufficiently uneasy about his economic success to deny any business acumen, insisting ingenuously that he lacked "a turn for worldly wisdom." Meanwhile, the concomitant rise in litigation further challenged the social order. Acknowledging the necessity of certain lawsuits, Johnson nevertheless implored his countrymen to approach the law "with a Christian temper." The happy resolution of particular cases, he hoped, might help absorb some of the social tension caused by the expanding economy. Johnson's plea for equity and moderation in economic affairs thus reflected a larger fear of social disintegration, a concern that exploitation and oppression would undermine the Christian ideals of charity and concord.[41]

The desire to preserve the patterns of a traditional social order in New England led Samuel Johnson to draft an elaborate essay on moral philosophy entitled "Raphael: or The Genius of the English America."[42] In this piece he criticized the individualistic tendencies that threatened the welfare of the community and called for a return to a harmonious social system. Nearly everyone viewed himself as the center of the universe, Johnson complained, and consequently neglected the interests of the commonwealth. Such selfishness flowed from a "meanness of soul," a "despicable narrowness of mind," a "contemptible grovelling temper." Johnson argued that the interrelationship of mankind obviated the quest for individual betterment at the expense of others.[43]

The maintenance of the social order required people tosubmit to a due form of government.[44] A firm proponent of vigorous social institutions, Johnson saw the alternative as "a mere chaos and confusion." He recognized, however, that "constitutions, laws and administrations" merely provided the skeleton of a healthy body politic. Political order ultimately depended upon the virtue and integrity of the people. Only if men "in all ranks, orders and conditions" promoted the public weal could government achieve its intended ends. As in economic relations, Johnson conceded that such self-denial required a "truly divine temper." Yet he optimistically hoped that the Christian religion would prevail even among the most selfish people and inspire a happy political community.[45]

Like most of his countrymen, Samuel Johnson glorified the English constitution—the balanced government of King, Lords, and Commons—as the bulwark of liberty and property. No other political system, he insisted, worked so well and he urged colonials to support the transplanted institutions of the mother country. Yet, in evaluating provincial politics, Johnson detected several deficiencies. First, the citizens seldom elected the "wisest and best men to represent them," thereby imperiling the public welfare. Second, the large size of the provincial legislatures meant that many representatives lacked the "skill and integrity . . . of a true statesman or patriot." Finally, American politicians too readily formed factions and parties, which jeopardized the "unity and unanimity" of the commonwealth. In short, Johnson worried about the democratizing tendencies of provincial politics and feared that the rule of the masses would subvert the political order. To remedy the situation he suggested that public-spirited men "indoctrinate the bulk of the people . . . in the right understanding of their true public interest." Political education might yet thwart the evils of majority rule.[46]

Johnson's hostility to democratic politics reflected much more than his elitist assumptions. As a member of a minority group that had suffered at the hands of a powerful majority, he well understood the potential oppressiveness of popular government. " 'Tis not reason or a sense of what is right that generally governs" human affairs, he remarked with chagrin, "but it is education, 'tis custom, 'tis interest, 'tis prejudice, 'tis empty names and sounds, 'tis fondness for a party . . ., 'tis everything besides what it should be that possesses, biases and determines us on all occasions." Nothing less than a change of spirit would save the country from further confusion and disorder.[47]

Although Samuel Johnson remained interested in secular affairs and worried about the social and political order of provincial New England, he never lost sight of a higher purpose to human life—to prepare people for Eternity. Firmly convinced that God had created a heaven to reward saints and a hell to punish sinners, the Anglican minister maintained that the quality of one's life on earth determined whether a person could anticipate eternal joy or everlasting damnation. Johnson did not deny the importance of faith, nor did he doubt that God remained absolutely sovereign throughout the universe. Yet he strongly suggested that a life of holiness and virtue enabled individuals "to look death in the face, to defy even the king of terrors, . . . to resign up our spirits into the hands of God . . . with hopes full of immortality." If we walk in the ways of the Lord, he repeatedly assured his congregation, "we may . . . with cheerfulness and comfort, and without guilt or fear, . . . hold up our faces before [God], and receive that joyful sentence" of eternal bliss.[18] Thus Johnson held human beings morally responsible for all their acts on earth.

These theological premises led the Connecticut clergyman to oppose the predestinarian assumptions of the orthodox Calvinists of New England. Denying that God damned people eternally without regard for their moral activity, Johnson asserted that "such a severe decree" contradicted the "amiable characters" of the Lord, His "goodness, love, kindness, justice and impartiality." He argued that God would receive all people who sincerely had repented their sins and had lived according to the Gospel. Johnson also rejected the idea that humans remained passive in the process of spiritual regeneration. "We are free active creatures," he preached, and therefore we must participate actively in our religious conversions. Such ideas enabled Johnson to reconcile the notion of God's omnipotence with his belief in the essential goodness of the Lord.[49]

Johnson's image of heaven, his vision of the future City of God, represented a logical outgrowth of his commitment to harmony and order. "What a glorious city must that needs be, which is united together in heart and soul under the government and conduct of the almighty," he exclaimed. "A glorious community indeed, where all members are entirely free from everything that can offend or occasion the least uneasiness," a place "where there is not the least . . . envy, malice or ill-will . . ., but every one seeks . . . the interest, weal and happiness of every one as his own." Such spiritual joy, such universal happiness, Johnson repeatedly affirmed, came from that "infinitely tender and fatherly mercy and compassion which God had for his poor fallen creatures."[50]

On May 14, 1727, six days after the death of his father, Samuel Johnson preached from his Stratford pulpit on the text, "For I am a stranger with thee and sojourner as all my fathers were." He spoke slowly and somberly, urging his listeners to wean themselves from the world, imploring them to labor for the more durable gifts of heaven. We should lay up treasure for ourselves in heaven, he concluded, striving to overcome his personal grief, so that "when we come to journey's end, we may be welcome at our father's house."[51] Samuel Johnson's cosmology ended where it began, in the bosom of his family, in the family of mankind.

NOTES

1. Stiles, *Literary Diary,* 1: 206. Not everyone shared Stiles's opinion; Cadwallader Colden, a leading provincial intellectual, described Johnson as "a distinguished character for candor and learning." Cadwallader Colden to John Mitchell, November 7, [1745], *The Letters and Papers of Cadwallader Colden,* 9 vols. (New York, 1918–37), 8: 335.

2. For cogent analyses of this pattern, see Ellis, "Puritan Mind"; Fiering, "President Samuel Johnson" and "Moral Philosophy." For the books read by Johnson, see *SJ Papers,* 1: 497–526.

3. SJ, "Preface," in John Beach, *A Second Vindication of God's Free Grace Indeed* (Boston, 1748), printed in *SJ Papers,* 3: 207.

4. SJ, "Autobiography," pp. 16–17; see, for example, SJ to Edmund Gibson, September 27, 1727, Fulham MSS.

5. Records of the First Congregational Church of Guilford, 1: 7–10, Connecticut State Library, Hartford.

6. Samuel Johnson, Sr., to SJ, October 14, 1725, March 8, 1726, JCU, 1; SJ, "Autobiography," pp. 19–20; "Liber Dierum," p. 68.

7. SJ, "Liber Dierum," p. 67.

8. Ibid., pp. 68–69.

9. Johnson's will is in Guilford Probate Records, Liber 2, Guilford Town Hall. Demographic information appears in Steiner, "Supplementary Notes," p. 298.

10. For a comparative perspective on this phenomenon, see Kenneth Lockridge, "Land, Population and the Evolution of New England Society: 1630–1790," *Past and Present,* 39 (1968): 62–80, and Greven, *Four Generations.* For a larger study of Connecticut society, see Richard L. Bushman, *From Puritan to Yankee: Character and the Social Order in Connecticut, 1690–1765* (Cambridge, Mass., 1967). Four decades later Johnson described this social process to an English correspondent; see SJ to Daniel Burton, September 10, 1764, JHP.

11. William Andrews, *A History of Christ Episcopal Church in Guilford, Connecticut* (Guilford, Conn. 1895), pp. 20–21; Steiner, *History of Guilford,* p. 381. Johnson frequently returned to Guilford to preach to his former neighbors; see Church Wardens of Guilford to SPG, July 8, 1768, SPG MSS, ser. B, 23: 170.

12. SJ to WSJ, July 7, 1747, *SJ Papers,* 1: 128–29.

13. For a clear discussion of the problems of identity and personal intimacy, see Erikson, *Identity: Youth and Crisis,* pp. 135–38.

14. See Laslett, *The World;* SJ, "Liber Dierum," p. 66.

15. Bailey, *Nicoll Family,* pp. 19, 84; Thompson, *History of Long Island,* 1: 443, 2: 431–32; SJ, Catalogue of my library, August 15, 1726, JCU.

16. Petition from the Inhabitants of Suffolk County to SPG, May 8, 1724, SPG MSS, ser. A, vol. 18, p. 172; SJ, "Autobiography," 20; Records of the First Episcopal Church of Stratford, 1: 30, Connecticut State Library.

17. SJ, "Autobiography," p. 20; William Nicoll, Jr. to SJ, May 11, 1765, JCU, 2.

18. SJ, "Liber Dierum," pp. 69–70.

19. Samuel Johnson, Sr., to SJ, October 14, 1725, JCU, 1.

20. SJ, A Sermon of the Eternal Rule of Justice, November 10, 1745, *SJ Papers,* 3: 475, 477–78; Minutes of Sermons on Christ's Sermon on the Mount, August 1741, JCU.

21. Ibid.

22. SJ, Sermon of the Eternal Rule, *SJ Papers,* 3: 475; "Raphael," pp. 555–57; and *A Sermon concerning the Obligation . . . in the Public Worship of God* (Boston, 1746), p. 8. For comparison see *The Educational Writings of John Locke,* ed. James L. Axtell (Cambridge, 1968).

23. See deMause, *History of Childhood,* passim.

24. SJ, "Raphael," pp. 558, 561; SJ to Peter Jay, July 27, 1739, printed in Monaghan, "Letters," pp. 88–89.

25. SJ, "Raphael," pp. 557–58; Sermon: Of the Duty of Feeding the Sheep, JCU.

26. The prevalence of child-beating in contemporary England is strongly suggested by John Locke; see *Educational Writings,* p. 172.

27. Nathaniel Chauncey, *Honouring God the True Way to Honour* (New London, Conn., 1719), pp. 19–20.

28. The psychological dimensions of this process are elaborated in Piers and Singer, *Shame and Guilt,* pp. 11–17, 53–54. Piers makes a significant distinction between shame and guilt: "unconscious guilt is aroused by impulses to transgress the internalized prohibition of punishing parents, and the unconscious threat is mutilation; unconscious shame, on the other hand, is aroused by a failure to live up to the internalized ideals of loving parents, and the unconscious threat is abandonment" (pp. 53–54). Orthodox New England ministers also attempted to maintain cultural standards by encouraging feelings of shame. Daniel Wadsworth, pastor at Hartford, observed: "Mr. [Nathaniel] Ward's advice concerning young people . . . was, whatever you do be sure to maintain shame in them; for if that become gone there is no hope that they'll ever come to good." See *Diary of Rev. Daniel Wadsworth, Seventh Pastor of the First Church of Christ in Hartford, 1737–1747,* ed. George Leon Walker (Hartford, Conn., 1894), p. 18. Ward was an orthodox Puritan of the first generation.

29. SJ, "Raphael," p. 556; Sermon of the Eternal Rule, *SJ Papers,* 3: 478. For an analysis of the relationship between sensitivity to shame and a concern for autonomy, see Erikson, *Identity,* pp. 107–14.

30. SJ, Sermon: Of the Duty of Feeding the Sheep; Ten Sermons on the Lord's Prayer, March 1736, sermon 6, both in JCU.

31. Johnson's land records are in JYU. For the value of Woodbury lands see James Walsh, "The Great Awakening in the First Congregational Church of Woodbury, Connecticut," *William & Mary Quarterly* 28 (1971): 544–45, 555–56.

32. SJ, Sermon: Of the Duty of Feeding the Sheep; "A Catalogue of Books read from Year to Year by [William] Samuel Johnson," both in JCU.

33. SJ, A Sermon Concerning the Intellectual World, December 1747, *SJ Papers,* 3: 503–4.

34. SJ, Ten Sermons on the Lord's Prayer; Sermon: Of the Truth and Faithfulness of Almighty God, November 18, 1739; Six Sermons on Psalm XXXVI, July–August, 1766; Sermon showing the Great Advantage of a Virtuous Course of Life, March 12, 1737; A Christmas Sermon, December 25, 1738; Sermon: Of the Love Due to the Public Worship of God, April 12, 1728, all in JCU.

35. SJ, Sermon of the Truth and Faithfulness, JCU; Sermon concerning the Intellectual World; The Foundation of our Faith in Christ, April 18, 1731; A Sermon of the Blessedness of Giving Beyond that of Receiving, November 18, 1744, *SJ Papers,* 3: 503–4, 390–91, 460–61.

36. SJ, Sermon showing wherein consists the Health and Prosperity of the Soul, January 22, 1737; Ten Sermons on the Lord's Prayer; Minutes of Sermons on Christ's Sermon, all in JCU. For a discussion of the psychological basis of these ideas, see chap. 3 above.

37. SJ, Sermon on the Blessedness, *SJ Papers,* 3: 461–62; Sermon showing . . . the Health and Prosperity, JCU. A list of Johnson's household, including servants, appears in *SJ Papers,* 1: 58.

38. SJ, "Noetica," in *Elementa Philosophica* . . . . (Philadelphia, 1752), printed in *SJ Papers,* 2: 399; Ten Sermons on the Lord's Prayer, and Minutes of Sermons on Christ's Sermon, both in JCU; Sermon on the Eternal Rule, *SJ Papers,* 3: 478–79.

39. SJ, "Raphael," 543; Ten Sermons on the Lord's Prayer, and Economy of Redemption, both in JCU.

40. For two fine studies of Connecticut society in this period, see Bushman, *From Puritan to Yankee* and Charles S. Grant, *Democracy in the Connecticut Frontier Town of Kent* (New York, 1961).

41. SJ to WSJ, January 6, 1757, Smyth MSS; Minutes of Sermons, August 1741, JCU. Johnson also criticized the inflationary effects of paper money; see "Raphael," p. 565.

42. The original title of the piece was "Theocles or the Genius of New England," JCU. It was probably written in the mid-1730s.

43. SJ, "Raphael," pp. 524–28.

44. Johnson's ideas on politics repeated the conventional wisdom of eighteenth-century America. The best synthetic studies of provincial politics are Bernard Bailyn, *The Ideological Origins of the American Revolution* (Cambridge, Mass., 1967) and *The Origins of American Politics* (New York, 1968); Greene, "Political Mimesis."

45. SJ, "Raphael," pp. 545–47, 572.

46. Ibid., pp. 546, 574–76. For a provocative statement about the notion that power belonged in the hands of an educated, rather than a social elite, see Bernard Friedman, "The Shaping of the Radical Consciousness in Provincial New York," *Journal of American History* 56 (1970): 785.

47. SJ, "Raphael," pp. 524–28.

48. SJ, A Sermon: Of the Separate State of the Soul, Easter 1726, *SJ Papers,* 3: 362–64; Ten Sermons on the Lord's Prayer, JCU.

49. SJ, Economy of Redemption, JCU; A Letter to Mr. Samuel Browne . . ., January 1, 1737/38 and Sermon: Of the New Creature, February 17, 1738, both in *SJ Papers,* 3: 149–50, 412, 414, 416–17.

50. SJ, A Sermon on the City of God, November 14, 1737, JYU; A Sermon showing what it is to come to Christ, Christmas 1741, JCU.

51. SJ, Notes for a Sermon, May 14, 1727, JCU. The text is from Psalm 39:14.

8

“SURPRISING CONVULSIONS AND INVOLUNTARY AGITATION”

IN THE late summer of 1740 an evangelical preacher named George Whitefield arrived in Newport, Rhode Island, and commenced a six-week tour through what had been, but a century before, the bastion of orthodox Puritanism. As a minister of the Church of England, Whitefield had earned considerable notoriety for his unusual style of preaching, his ability to “melt” the hearts of his hearers, to awaken in them a sense of their sins and of the need for a spiritual rebirth. “He speaks from a heart all aglow with love, and pours out a torrent of eloquence which is almost irresistible,” reported Sarah Edwards, the wife of America’s foremost evangelical divine. Throughout New England men and women neglected their chores and thronged to their churches to hear the itinerant preacher proclaim the glorious Gospel of Jesus Christ. And when the buildings became dangerously overcrowded, the apostle led his disciples into open fields, where thousands fell prostrate in their search for redemption.

Other inspired preachers followed Whitefield through New England. From New Jersey came the Presbyterian Gilbert Tennent, from Long Island the eccentric James Davenport, who, together with a flock of native exhorters, fanned the fires of religious zeal. “The seeds of enthusiasm” have produced “a prodigious harvest,” wrote a startled observer, and “the fertile genius of our Americans has improved upon his scheme to a degree unknown . . . in any age or part of the world.” This revival of religion, known to contemporaries as the "great and general awakening," intensified passions throughout the region. Men and women attended the churches as never before in search of spiritual perfection, and ministers of all denominations worked arduously to satisfy the demands for religious instruction.[1]

In provincial New England, the Great Awakening represented a return to the piety and zeal of the founding fathers. For generations, Puritan exhorters had denounced the spread of irreligion and summoned the children of New England back to the pristine churches. During this period many seemingly orthodox ministers, people like the apostate Samuel Johnson, had flirted with eighteenth-century rationalism and subtly altered the tenets of Puritanism; in their sermons the austere God of Calvin became less mysterious, less awesome, and less arbitrary. Meanwhile, their parishioners, just as quietly, renounced the zeal of their forebears and concentrated on more worldly affairs. Within a century of colonization, the rationalism of the Enlightenment and the reasonableness of the marketplace had subverted the spiritual piety of the Puritan patriarchs. Religion, to be sure, remained a fundamental aspect of provincial life. But only sporadic revivals shattered the stillness of the New England way, bespeaking the secret depths of religious enthusiasm, hinting at dormant passions within the soul. Then, in 1740, Whitefield penetrated to the roots.

Like their Puritan ancestors, proponents of the Awakening emphasized the absolute sovereignty of God in the cosmic order. They argued that people remained utterly dependent upon God's mercy and could attain salvation only by undergoing a conversion experience whereby the Lord imputed His grace to otherwise helpless sinners. Once saved, however, once reborn, the believer became a new person, sanctified by God, chosen for life everlasting. While acknowledging the social importance of godly behavior, the revivalists denied the spiritual value of what they called mere morality and condemned the religious indifference that had gnawed at the New England conscience for one hundred years. Having acquired the "New Light," converts of the Awakening claimed to be holier than ordinary mortals and readily denounced all skeptics who rejected their theology or questioned the authenticity of the revival.

More traditional New Englanders, accustomed to more orderly expressions of religious piety, responded by challenging the "excesses" of revivalism. Thus the Great Awakening, instead of bringing spiritual peace to the colonies, exacerbated factional antagonism and denominational competition. The Church of England in Connecticut, long a symbol of religious deviation, became a special target of sectarian hatred, and Samuel Johnson, as the leading Anglican in the colony, confronted anew the enmity of his divided neighbors. "My case is not altogether dissimilar to that of the great Apostle," he wrote in frustration, "particularly in being in journeyings often and in peril among false brethren."[2]

By the time Whitefield's arrival in New England raised new storms of religious controversy, Samuel Johnson had already prepared an elaborate defense of the Church of England. During the previous two decades he had confronted the systematic opposition of his orthodox neighbors and had labored untiringly to mitigate their hatred. These conflicts had forced him to articulate his position with vigor and clarity. Indeed, one confrontation with the Congregational minister of Woodbury, a man named John Graham, had produced a series of public letters in which Johnson tried to enlighten his "dear, though mistaken brethren" about the "true principles" of the Anglican church.[3]

Throughout this prolonged controversy with Graham, Samuel Johnson preserved an outward calm. His arguments emphasized the institutional advantages of the Church of England and he repeatedly chastised his opponent for introducing a venemous tone. Johnson's dispassionate exterior, however, concealed a cauldron of animosity and aggression. By scoffing at Johnson's religious beliefs and by ridiculing his ideological commitments, people like Graham challenged the meaning of Johnson's life. At stake was nothing less than the Anglican's identity as an exponent of a spiritually superior denomination. Though profoundly insulted, Johnson carefully controlled his anger and confined himself to the rules of logic. But the thoroughness of his retort, by which he demolished every shred of criticism, revealed the depths of his resentment. Equally significant, the style of argument enabled the Anglican to unleash considerable aggression at the orthodox establishment while maintaining a polite façade.

Johnson's suspicion of emotionalism gave him further grounds for opposing the ministers of the New England way. Puritan religion always had possessed a strong pietistic strain, but by the mid-eighteenth century few New Englanders retained the strident enthusiasm of the first generation. An exception to this pattern, however, was Jonathan Edwards, the minister of the church at Northampton, Massachusetts, and perhaps the most inspired preacher in the colonies. In 1734 a series of powerful sermons by Edwards ignited a religious revival in western Massachusetts that promptly spread through the Connecticut River Valley. Within months the evangelical spirit had reached Stratford, Connecticut, and aggravated tensions between Samuel Johnson and the local congregational clergy. When one female "dissenter," allegedly "crazed with love," accused an Anglican lad of impropriety, Johnson investigated the charges, found the youth innocent, and offered the lady "some serious suggestions and exhortations." According to Timothy Cutler, who described the affair for the Bishop of London, the episode drove the woman toward "this imaginary religion, and set her to crying for she knew not what, and thereby made others cry for they did not know what, especially little girls." Two of these women married "soon after these religious raptures," Cutler reported, "and had each of them a child in six or seven months. Mr. Johnson knoweth nothing of their having been remarkably vicious before or serious since."[4]

However accurate the story, Johnson evidently had some idea of the nature of religious enthusiasm and he should have anticipated what the consequences of Whitefield's revivalism would be five years later. But the itinerant's unique position as an episcopally ordained minister who preached Calvinist doctrines upset Johnson's tendency to classify people according to traditional denominational categories. Looking to London for guidance on the eve of the Awakening, he naively asked the SPG to explain "the general sense of the clergy about Mr. Whitefield and his proceedings."[5]

Before he received a reply, however, the eruption of the revival erased whatever doubts existed in his mind. As scores of people embraced the evangelical message, Johnson swiftly realized that the religious enthusiasm threatened the foundation of his own more rational faith. "We are not to preach to you any schemes of our own," he had declared from his Stratford pulpit on the very day that

Whitefield debarked in Rhode Island, but he felt that he had to describe "the plainness and simplicity of the Gospel just as it lies in the Bible."[6] For the next decade, amidst the turmoil of the Awakening, Samuel Johnson devoted his energies to an explication of that "plainness and simplicity." His labors in defense of the Anglican church reflected not only his religious orthodoxy but also an abiding emotional commitment to order, to harmony, and to unity.

In his diatribe against John Graham, Samuel Johnson warned New Englanders not to forsake "the love of the truth" lest they provoke the Lord "to send [them] strong delusions."[7] The frenetic effects of the Great Awakening convinced Johnson of the accuracy of his prediction. The revivalist preachers shouted "the most frightful things they could think of about the devil, hell and damnation," Johnson recalled, "so as to scare people almost out of their wits, in order to bring them to what they called conversion." Their meetings "looked like a very hell upon earth; some sighing, some groaning, some screeching and wringing their hands, the minister . . . tormenting them, till they would come to Christ." Others, meanwhile, believing themselves to be reborn, moved "in the greatest raptures, and transports, triumphing and singing psalms and hallelujahs and some fell into trances and saw Christ and angels, and who were saved, and who were damned." To Johnson the rationalist, such "hideous doings" revealed the excesses of "a strange, wild enthusiasm."[8]

Evangelical preachers depicted the terrors of hell not, as Johnson suggested, "to scare people almost out of their wits," but rather to demonstrate the helplessness of the human condition. By contrasting the fires of hell with the ecstasies of heaven, the revivalists drove people from the depths of anguish to the glee of salvation. The process involved a spiritual rebirth, a psychological metamorphosis that transformed the emotional life of the convert. Made to feel insecure by thoughts of eternal damnation, the "reborn" believer found spiritual solace in the gospel of love. No wonder Samuel Johnson witnessed people transported "in the greatest raptures" singing praises to the Lord.

The evangelism of George Whitefield and his followers appealed primarily to people who felt insecure about their religious condition, who feared divine retribution for their sins.[9] This spiritual anxiety reflected a more visceral insecurity about life on earth. Indeed, the extensiveness of the Great Awakening suggests the existence of a general cultural crisis in eighteenth-century America. During the 1730s, a throat "distemper"—probably an epidemic of diphtheria, followed by one of scarlet fever—raged through New England, leaving widespread death and suffering in its wake.[10] The outbreak of war between England and Spain, though geographically remote from New England, added to the uncertainty. "We have assuredly much to fear . . . that the war will come nearer to us if not to our own doors," preached Samuel Johnson on a day of public thanksgiving in 1740.[11] These dramatic terrors reinforced more subtle uncertainties caused by the rapidly changing society. As population growth and land speculation encouraged geographic and social mobility, eighteenth-century colonials—particularly those in the expanding areas of provincial Connecticut—perceived and lamented the disruption of the traditional social order.[12] Such worldly concerns prepared people in all status groups—rich or poor, rural or urban, young or old—for the revivalist message. By accepting the Word, by coming to Christ, men and women could achieve a security unknown in this world and a promise of eternal salvation in the next.

Although contemporaries saw the Awakening as "great and general," one social group—adult white males—proved especially receptive to the call for redemption.[13] Church membership soared throughout New England, but the largest group of new communicants were males in their early and mid-twenties, a group of people who, in "normal" times delayed joining a church until their later twenties or beyond. Thus the Great Awakening produced a significant drop in the age of church admission among colonial men. This demographic pattern suggests that the social problems of the era—epidemic, war, and social mobility—affected these men more than other New Englanders and that they were the ones who most needed the emotional ballast of the evangelical churches.

In colonial America young men attained "adulthood" not at the end of puberty, but somewhat later—in their mid- or late twenties, at the age when they established autonomous households.[14] Prior to that time, the sons of New England, though physically mature, often remained unsure of their relationship to adults, uncertain about their place in society. At a time of social crisis, such generational ambiguities, similar to the dilemmas associated with adolescence in the modern world, made these young men susceptible to ideological movements that promised to resolve their confusion and offered to clarify or reinforce their sense of self. By experiencing religious conversion, by identifying with the evangelical movement, young males in New England "found" themselves in the cosmic order. Thus the revival brought New England men not only the assurance of heaven, but also a greater certainty and coherence about life on earth.

Yet, if many young men found in the Great Awakening an answer to their personel anxieties, others perceived the revival as a threat to the traditional order and their place within it. To people who faced no confusion of identity, the evangelical movement often appeared as a dangerous disruption. The opponents of the Awakening—known pejoratively as "Old Lights"—especially resented the spiritual pride of the converts, the enthusiasm that moved the New Lights to condemn religious conservatives as unregenerate people. Moreover, such critics of the revival as Boston's Charles Chauncey insisted that reason, not evangelical passion, represented the proper guide to religious truth. The practice of itinerancy, by which revivalist preachers traveled from pulpit to pulpit, further threatened the established clergy, provoking bitter discord and passionate debate.

Such acrimony "threw the country into the greatest confusion imaginable," remarked Samuel Johnson, "and occasioned endless divisions and separations." Amidst the contention, the Anglican missionaries strove to protect their parishioners from the temptations of enthusiasm. The church has not suffered from the "commotions," Johnson reported, "but it has required great care and pains . . . to prevent the mischief." "We are obliged to be continually riding and preaching," he informed the SPG during the winter of 1741–42, "preaching three times, frequently four times, and sometimes five and six times a week, and this often not only in this town but in divers other parts of the colony."[15]

These missionary labors soon produced visible results. Many orthodox New Englanders, frustrated by the continuing religious debate and anxious for spiritual peace, sought solace within the Church of England, forming new congregations in such towns as Guilford (where Samuel Johnson's brother Nathaniel played a leading role), Norwalk, Reading, and Derby. "The distractions of the times," observed Samuel Johnson, opened "people's eyes and awaken[ed] their attention towards the Church as their only refuge." These converts welcomed the institutional stability of the episcopacy and extolled the structured liturgy that characterized Anglican services. By contrast to "the sad effects of Methodism" and the "endless separations," the episcopal church indeed appeared "as their only ark of safety."[16]

The Anglican cause also provided the proselytes with an ideological alternative to the jeremiad cosmology of both Old Lights and New. By identifying with the Church of England, the official religion of the mother country, Anglican converts in America embraced a world view based upon the provincialism of the colonies. For those who repudiated the New England way for Anglicanism—a movement that grew in strength in the decades before 1776—England, not the Puritan fathers of the seventeenth century, represented the epitome of historical development. Thus, for example, when Samuel Johnson described the new church at Stratford, he emphasized that "it will be more truly English" than similar buildings in Boston and New York.[17] Such attitudes reflected a general sympathy for the culture of the mother country.

For many provincial Americans, the confusions of the Great Awakening demonstrated the superiority of metropolitan institutions—their sophistication, their certainty, their durability. Others—both Old Lights and New—reacted to the crisis by reaffirming the purity and uniqueness of New England society. The revival thereby dramatized a subtle fissure within American culture, a dialogue, as it were, between colonials who denied that they were provincials and provincials who denied that they were colonials. The paradox had existed for generations. But after 1776 these groups faced each other on a different battleground, as Whigs, Loyalists, or trimmers.

Throughout the Great Awakening, revivalist ministers met with their greatest success in areas where the Church of England appeared most vigorous, where it represented a serious threat to the "established" religions, where denominational competition seemed most acute.[18] Thus the expansion of the Anglican church, largely through the conversion of members of other religious groups, aroused the fears, and then the antagonism, of the neighboring ministers. In Stratford, the center of Connecticut Anglicanism, the growth of the Church brought Samuel Johnson into conflict with his ecclesiastical opponents. "I would not for the world censure others as they censure me," he announced in the midst of one controversy, but he nevertheless prepared his parishioners to answer the accusations of the "false teachers" around them.[19]

These debates, full of the rhetorical splendor of the eighteenth century, demonstrated the depths of religious passion in the so-called age of reason. In one episode a congregational minister condemned the holiness of the episcopal church while his New Light parishioners defiled the building "with ordure in several places."[20] In another quarrel the issue focused on the conversion of several prominent Stratford families to the Church of England. Here Johnson was accused, probably with some accuracy, of "fishing in troubled waters."[21] A third contest involved the employment of William Samuel Johnson as a lay reader while the young man was studying law, a coincidental situation that smacked of favoritism, if not corruption.[22] Taken by themselves, each of these cases amounted to little more than sectarian petulance. As a whole, however, they revealed a broad commitment among the masses of people to particular denominational principles. The Great Awakening, for all its emotional intensity, did not produce the gross anti-intellectualism associated with later revivalist movements.

When Samuel Johnson described the Great Awakening, he spoke of an "epidemical frenzy" and he praised God for preserving his own congregation from "this contagion." To the Anglican minister the evangelism of Whitefield and his followers appeared as a noxious infection, no less deadly than the smallpox that God employed to scourge the sinners of the earth. The revivalists, by preaching false doctrines, by plunging the churches into chaos, imperiled the immortal souls of all godly people. Johnson therefore mustered his reserves to combat this dreadful plague. "I have laboriously studied, and wrote, and rid, and preached, and pleaded, and lived all that was in my power," he exclaimed in the midst of the revival, "to promote the growth of the best of Churches."[23]

Samuel Johnson's opposition to the Great Awakening focused on the anti-institutional tendencies of the revivalist religion. The "strolling preachers," Johnson observed with disgust, "broke through all order" and propagated doctrines that undermined "all government both in family, church and state."[24] Johnson replied by defending the "lawful" ministers of Christ. "Do not implicitly resign your faith to every teacher," he advised his parishioners, "however so much he may pretend . . . to inspiration, *or however so surprising effects attend his ministry.*"[25] Johnson also denounced the New lights for regarding the Scriptures as "a dead letter." "This doctrine is indeed a dangerous downfall!" he exclaimed, for it made religious instruction "entirely unmeaning and useless" and consequently subverted "the whole system of Christianity." For Johnson, such reckless assaults threatened the order of the universe.[26]

He also deplored the tendency of the revivalists to depict the attributes of God in the austere language of Calvinism. Johnson acknowledged that God possessed "boundless wisdom, power, goodness, holiness, justice, mercy, truth and faithfulness." Yet the New Lights viewed God as "an arbitrary being" who ignored the "prayers, cries and endeavors of his creatures." To Johnson such "hard thoughts of God" seemed heretically absurd. In conceding God's sovereignty Johnson saw nothing incompatible with His ultimate mercy, His love for mankind, His willingness to forgive sinners. Do not think that "you have committed the unpardonable sin," he implored his congregation, nor believe that "there is no hope." For "the father of our spirits" would never abandon His children on earth.[27]

For Samuel Johnson the true saint not only enjoyed a spiritual rebirth but also enacted a holy existence by following the moral injunctions of the Bible. Godly activity, Johnson admitted, would not in itself bring salvation; but no one could claim to be godly who failed to implement the "temper of the gospel." It was on these grounds that Johnson condemned the predestinarian doctrines of the New Light theology. Where the revivalists emphasized the inevitability of the human condition, Johnson suggested that people, as "free agents," could determine their own fates. Otherwise, he remarked, God became "the author of our sins," a notion that threatened all "moral government." Assuring the revivalists that the Lord would never forsake a truly repentent Christian, Johnson concluded by asking his opponents to embrace the charity and love of the Gospel.[28]

Johnson's statement, though overtly conciliatory, actually challenged the fundamental premise of the Awakening and provoked an immediate response from the evangelical Presbyterian Jonathan Dickinson.[29] The New Light preacher, long a foe of the Church of England, not only expounded the Calvinist doctrine of the absolute sovereignty of God, but also attacked the Anglicans as false Christians. Johnson replied in a public letter by reaffirming his original position. Calling predestination a "mischievous doctrine," he observed that it endangered "all religion and morality, and all civil and family government, and render[ed] them unmeaning ridiculous things." More seriously, Johnson accused the Presbyterian of approaching an atheistic position by reducing all existence to mere fate. Such ideas, he warned, led logically to freethinking and deism, and challenged the essentials of Christianity.[30]

Searching for a middle ground between the predestinarian doctrines of the evangelists and the fatalism of the eighteenth-century deists, Samuel Johnson drafted an extensive essay on moral philosophy, which he called *A New System of Morality.*[31] In this tract the Anglican proposed that the true object of life was "happiness." But he stressed that temporal happiness, to be authentic, could not conflict with the eternal happiness of the soul. Earthly existence simply prepared people for the perfection of "a better state hereafter." What humans did in this world, he insisted, and not some arbitrary decree or mere chance, determined one's future condition.

People could assure their eternal happiness, according to Johnson, by pursuing "the right knowledge" of themselves and by practicing "virtue." Believing that self-knowledge provided the surest guide to morality, he exhorted his readers to exercise their reason "to regulate and discipline [their] will, affections, appetites and passions." Like his famous correspondent Benjamin Franklin, who published a revised edition of this work in Philadelphia, Samuel Johnson emphasized the value of "self-denial and mortification." Slavery to one's appetites was "a most wretched and abject condition," he observed, and self-interest alone justified the pursuit of virtue. Yet Johnson always underscored the social basis of morality. "My true interest," he proclaimed, "depends on the general interest and good order of the community." Such ideas encouraged individuals to perpetuate the existing social institutions even as they prepared for life everlasting. "Every thing that concerneth the weal of mankind," Johnson contended, was "best promoted by social combination," and he summoned his countrymen to "unite together in promoting our happiness." The unity of humanity on earth would inaugurate the universal harmony of heaven.

Johnson's ethical writings brought him into contact with Cadwallader Colden, a member of the provincial elite of New York, who solicited the Anglican's opinion of his own philosophical ruminations.[32] Colden had attempted to reformulate Newtonian physics by explaining the nature of gravitation. According to his elaborate hypothesis, the attraction of physical bodies (which Newton himself could not explain) derived from a self-exerting principle of action that existed within matter itself. When confronted with this complicated theory, much of which hinged upon Colden's understanding of abstruse calculus, Samuel Johnson acknowledged his inability to understand, much less criticize it. The Anglican minister nevertheless perceived that Colden's system, by ascribing activity to matter, threatened the notion of a rational universe thoroughly dependent upon the will of God. "A blind senseless . . . principle of activity appears to me repugnant," he confessed, "and if it were possible, it would be [so] far from being of any use in nature that it would be mischievous without a mind to direct . . . it."

Samuel Johnson worried that a mechanistic philosophy, however accurate mathematically, would encourage the spread of atheism. In his own work, for example, he had employed the contrary argument, "that nothing corporeal can move itself," to prove the existence of God. In his subsequent correspondence with Colden, he defended Bishop Berkeley's conception that all moral activity stemmed from human interaction with the mind of God. Johnson, at last, seemed satisfied that Colden's theories did not radically contradict his own and that their major disagreements were semantic.[33] But he continued to fear that other rational philosophers would prove less pliable than his provincial colleague.

Criticizing "a fashionable sort of philosophy" that endeavored "to keep God as much out of sight" as possible, Johnson insisted that the Lord "very often secretly and insensibly influence[s] the minds of man." Such statements revealed Johnson's persistent attempt to steer a middle course between the enthusiasm of the New Lights and the atheism of the freethinkers.

In arguing these metaphysical points, Johnson employed the verbal distinctions of eighteenth-century discourse. Yet his quibbling over semantics—complicated and obscure as it is—served a more immediate purpose than sophisticated inquiry. It enabled Johnson to conceal the emotional basis of his position. No less than his evangelical enemies, Samuel Johnson remained a child of New England, subject still to the passions of his people.

When George Whitefield preached at Stratford in 1740, Johnson attended the meeting and listened dispassionately to the itinerant's discourse. The following year, while attending the Yale commencement at New Haven, he heard James Davenport preach to "a vast crowd" at night. On two other occasions, "by mere accident," Johnson intruded upon "private houses where these wild meetings were carrying on."[35] In these seemingly innocent encounters the Anglican minister witnessed the inner workings of revivalism; inadvertently, he also confronted the most secret recesses of his heart. It was for profoundly personal reasons that Samuel Johnson dissented from the evangelical movement and raised his voice in opposition to the revival.

One year after Whitefield landed in New England, in the early days of September 1741, ministers throughout Connecticut bade farewell to their families, mounted their horses, and headed for New Haven to observe the annual commencement ceremonies at Yale. Many of the college students had already imbibed the revivalist spirit and two of the scholars had been denied their diplomas for possessing New Light inclinations. Daniel Wadsworth, the Old Light pastor of Hartford's First Church, listened to the evangelical preaching of James Davenport, Joseph Bellamy, and Jedidiah Mills. "Much confusion this day at New Haven," he remarked, "and at night the most strange managements and pretense of religion that ever I saw."[36] Amidst this turmoil, Samuel Johnson, James Wetmore, and a few of their colleagues slipped into the frenzied throng to view the proceedings. We heard Davenport "raving among the people . . . in the dark," Johnson reported, "and stood at the edge of the crowd and heard him rave about [a quarter of an hour], and then went about our business." It was nothing "more than a visit to Bedlam," he maintained, for we heard only "the ravings of a man distracted."[37]

From this experience Samuel Johnson described the Great Awakening to his numerous correspondents in England.[38] "Not only the minds of many people are at once struck with amazing distresses upon their hearing the dismal outcrys of our strolling preachers," he explained, "but even their bodies are in a moment affected with with [*sic*] surprising convulsions and involuntary agitation and cramps, *which also have sometimes happened in those who came as mere spectators and are no friends to their new methods and even without their minds being at all affected*." For all this apparent detachment Samuel Johnson was describing himself; it was he who had been "affected" by the revivalist preacher! Deep in his soul, unbeknownst even to himself, the Anglican minister had retained a sensitivity to the religious instruction of his youth, to the Puritan heritage of his father and grandfather. Betrayed by his bodily "cramps," by "surprising convulsion and involuntary agitation," Samuel Johnson experienced the terror of the revival—the discovery of hidden passions and uncontrollable emotions.

The incident, moreover, did not go undetected. Theodore Morris, the Anglican missionary at West Haven, reported the episode to the commissary at Boston, who, in turn, chided Johnson for attending the "dissenting" meeting. Johnson replied with a strident rebuttal, far more passionate than most of his correspondence, in which he chronicled his extraordinary service on behalf of the Church of England. "If it would not savor of something like vanity," he averred, "I might almost venture to say [that] I have labored more abundantly" than all my brethren. "No, sir, I trust the danger is not from any conduct of mine," exclaimed Johnson with increasing anger, "but from that spirit of indolence and negligence, of bigotry and bitterness, which has called my conduct into question, and let him that is without fault, or has less fault than I, cast the first stone."[39]

This emotional outburst, unique in Johnson's long career of public debate, reflected his abiding sensitivity to shame, his dread of open humiliation. Yet he seemed particularly distraught, not at the reaction of his superiors in Boston or in London, but rather at what he had learned about himself.[40] In describing the situation to his English correspondents, Johnson inadvertently revealed the extent of his embarrassment by repeating the preposition "with" before mentioning the bodily "agitation and cramps." By lingering on that word Johnson demonstrated his unwillingness to proceed with the sentence, his reluctance to confront, even privately, his forbidden feelings.[41] For Samuel Johnson feared, above all, emotions and passions that lay beyond the control of his rational mind, feelings that, to his surprise and horror, evoked the primal religious experiences of his New England childhood.

The expansion of the Church of England during the Great Awakening, besides exciting the fears of the provincial orthodoxy, accentuated the political problems of the minority religious group. In the two decades before the revival, the Connecticut legislature had blatantly discriminated against the colony's Anglicans. "It is the design of this government not only to prevent the growth of the Church in this colony," complained the episcopal clergy to the SPG, "but even utterly to destroy it in its infancy." New Light control of the Assembly failed to alleviate the unhappy situation. And threats of English interference simply fell on deaf ears. "I am apprehensive of the damage to the present constitution," Johnson warned the colony's governor. But the congregational establishment, aware of the lethargy of the British government, continued to disregard the Anglican pleas.[42]

The autonomy of the Connecticut government derived from the colony charter of 1662, which did not require royal approval of provincial legislation. For nearly a century this patent had served as a bastion of "liberty," protecting the colony's inhabitants from royal interference. To Anglicans like Samuel Johnson, however, the charter represented a source of oppression that enabled the political majority to harass deviant groups. "Liberty is here licentiousness," Johnson declared in frustration; "a junto rules and the true anecdote of their policy seems to be a tacit agreement between them and the people that the one shall enjoy their places . . . on condition that the others are allowed to live and act as they please." Determined to effect change, the Stratford missionary transmitted a lengthy proposal to the SPG calling for the revocation of the charter and requesting the introduction of a royal government. Even Johnson realized the extravagance of his suggestion, for he begged his London patrons not to divulge the source of his scheme to the Connecticut authorities.[43]

The colony officials had nevertheless gauged English opinion accurately, and Johnson's appeal went unanswered. And, for all its apparent secrecy, Connecticut politicians learned, and did not soon forget, about the Anglicans' willingness to sacrifice the colony's charter. When in later years episcopalians requested the British government to effect ecclesiastical reform, the provincial establishment rose as one voice to oppose the measure. By linking religious demands to political change, Connecticut churchmen had opened a sore, sensitive, and unhealing wound.[44]

Despite his protests against the Connecticut establishment, however, Samuel Johnson recognized that the absence of an American episcopate represented the greatest obstacle to the growth of the Church of England. To persuade British politicians to remedy this situation, he stressed the political advantages of a colonial diocese. He noted that the dissenters were "generally people of antimonarchial as well as antiepiscopal principles." Citing the conservative influence of episcopal institutions, Johnson advised the Archbishop that the best way to secure the political dependence of the colonies "would be to render our constitution here, both in church and state, as near as possible . . . to that of our mother country" by sending bishops to preside over ecclesiastical affairs and by appointing royal governors to oversee matters of state.[45]

Besides these political advantages, Johnson stressed the pragmatic importance of bishops. An American episcopate would not only facilitate the ordination of native-born ministers, but also attract additional converts among the laity. "There never was so large a tract of earth overspread with Christians," he complained, "without so much as one bishop." That defect had brought grave sorrow to New England. By mid-century, twenty-five candidates had traveled to London for episcopal orders, but only twenty had survived the sea voyage and the smallpox to return to the colonies.[46]

"I have a son preparing for orders of whom I have good hopes . . . [that he] may be of some good use in the cause of religion," Samuel Johnson wrote prophetically to the Bishop of London, "but it is somewhat shocking to me that he must go a thousand leagues [when] . . . it is but five to one whether he ever returns."[47] Lacking episcopal leadership and at the mercy of the "dissenting" majority, Samuel Johnson in his personal impotence symbolized the condition of the Church of England in America. Within five years his hopeful son lay dead in a cold vault in London, another prey of the smallpox, still another victim of English indifference.

NOTES

1. The standard account of the Great Awakening in the northern colonies is Edwin Scott Gaustad, *The Great Awakening in New England* (New York, 1957); an intelligent synthesis of recent scholarship is Cowing, *Great Awakening,* chap. 2. The quotations are from Sarah Pierrepont Edwards to James Pierrepont, October 24, 1740, in Luke Tyerman, *The Life of the Rev. George Whitefield* (New York, 1877), 1: 428–29; Henry Caner to Mr. Gostling, September 25, 1741, Letter Book of Henry Caner, MSS, Wills Memorial Library, University of Bristol.

2. SJ to Cadwallader Colden, June 7 [1747], *SJ Papers,* 2: 298.

3. SJ to John Burton, [ca. September 1736], quoted in Beardsley, *Samuel Johnson,* p. 91. Johnson's description of the pamphlet war appears in his "Autobiography," p. 29. The essays, written in 1733, 1734, and 1736, are reprinted in *SJ Papers,* 3:19–130.

4. Timothy Cutler to Edmund Gibson, May 28, 1739, "An Anglican Critique of the Early Phase of the Great Awakening in New England: A Letter by Timothy Cutler," ed. Douglas C. Stenerson, *William & Mary Quarterly,* 30 (1973): 484–85.

5. SJ to John Berriman, September 10, 1739, *SJ Papers,* 1: 100.

6. SJ, A Sermon: Of Hearing the Word of God, September 14, 1740, JCU.

7. *SJ Papers,* 3: 34.

8. SJ, "Autobiography," p. 28.

9. The psychology of religious conversion remains a much-debated

subject, but the seminal work is William James, *The Varieties of Religious Experience* (New York, 1902).

10. Ernest Caulfield, "A History of the Terrible Epidemic, Vulgarly Called the Throat Distemper, as It Occurred in his Majesty's New England Colonies between 1735 and 1740," *Yale Journal of Biology and Medicine* 11 (1938–39), 219–72, 277–335.

11. SJ, Sermon: On the Great Duty of Thankfulness to God, November 5, 1740, *SJ Papers,* 3: 444.

12. The clearest analysis of this idea is Bushman, *From Puritan.* Johnson himself noted that "migrations are frequent in these countries from older to newer settlements where land is cheaper" and had personally profited from the rise in land values. See SJ to SPG, October 5, 1750, *SJ Papers,* 3: 238 and chap. 7 above.

13. Demographic evidence regarding the Great Awakening remains fragmentary, but recent scholarship suggests that young males were most affected by revivalism. See Cowing, *Great Awakening,* pp. 67–72; J. M. Bumsted, "Religion, Finance, and Democracy in Massachusetts: The Town of Norton as a Case Study," *Journal of American History* 57 (1971): 817–31; Cedric B. Cowing, "Sex and Preaching in the Great Awakening," *American Quarterly* 20 (1968): 624–44; Walsh, "Great Awakening in . . . Woodbury."

14. For a discussion of this problem, see Greven, *Four Generations,* and Philip J. Greven, Jr., "Youth, Maturity, and Religious Conversion: A Note on the Age of Converts in Andover, Massachusetts, 1711–1749," *Essex Institute Historical Collections* 108 (1972): 119–34.

15. SJ, "Autobiography," p. 28; SJ to George Berkeley, October 3, 1741; SJ to SPG, March 25, 1742, *SJ Papers,* 1: 102–3, 3: 230–31.

16. SJ, "Autobiography," pp. 28–29; Smith, *History of Guilford,* p. 108; SJ to SPG, September 29, 1744, SPG MSS, ser. B, v. 13, no. 100; SJ to SPG, March 25, 1742, *SJ Papers,* 3: 230–31; SJ to SPG, September 29, 1748, *HP,* 1: 244.

17. SJ to SPG, September 29, 1744, SPG MSS, ser. B. v. 13, no. 100.

18. See William Howland Kenney, 3d, "George Whitefield, Dissenter Priest of the Great Awakening, 1739–1741," *William & Mary Quarterly* 26 (1969): 75–93; Gerald J. Goodwin, "The Anglican Reaction to the Great Awakening," *Historical Magazine of the Protestant Episcopal Church* 35 (1966): 343–71.

19. SJ, A Sermon: Of the Trial of the Spirits, July 12, 1741, JCU.

20. *George Whitefield's Journals* (London, 1960), p. 480; SJ to Jedediah Mills, November 23, 1741, *SJ Papers,* 3: 145–48; SJ to SPG, September 30, 1743, *HP,* 1: 197–98.

21. The correspondence is printed in *SJ Papers,* 3: 133–44.

22. SJ to SPG, October 14, 1751, *SJ Papers,* 3: 243; SJ, "Preface," in John Beach, *A Calm and Dispassionate Vindication of the Professors of the Church of England* (Boston, 1749); *A Sermon on the Beauty of Holiness in the Worship of the Church of England* (New York, 1761), printed in *SJ*

Papers, 3: 521–22, 536 (Johnson first drafted this sermon in 1749); S.J. to the Publisher of the *Boston Post-Boy,* June 5, 1751, in *Boston Post-Boy,* June 24, 1751; S.J. to the *Post-Boy* August 2 [1751], printed in John Beach, *A Continuation of the Calm and Dispassionate Vindication of the Church of England* (Boston, 1751), appendix; see also Robert Sklar, "The Great Awakening and Colonial Politics: Connecticut's Revolution in the Minds of Men," *Connecticut Historical Society Bulletin* 28 (1963): 81–95.

23. SJ to SPG, March 25, 1742, *SJ Papers,* 3: 230–31; SJ to SPG, October 3, 1741, SPG MSS, ser. B, v. 9, no. 13; idem to Roger Price, July 5, 1742, *SJ Papers,* 1: 107. For a more general analysis see Goodwin, "Anglican Reaction."

24. SJ, "Autobiography," p. 28; SJ to Mr. Tomlinson, December 1, 1742, *SJ Papers,* 1: 112.

25. SJ, Sermon: Of the Trial, JCU; Johnson added the italicized words May 23, 1742, after James Davenport preached in Stratford.

26. SJ, A Sermon: Showing what it is to come to Christ, Christmas, 1741; A Sermon: On the New Creature, May 31, 1741, both in JCU.

27. SJ, A Sermon: On the Spiritual Discerning of Spiritual Things, March 4, 1742, *SJ Papers,* 3: 452; Ten Sermons on the Lord's Prayer, JCU (postscript added during the Great Awakening).

28. SJ, Sermon on the New Creature; [SJ], *A Letter From Aristocles to Authades, Concerning the Sovereignty of God* . . . . (Boston, 1745), printed in *SJ Papers,* 3: 166–67, 170, 176–77, 182.

29. Jonathan Dickinson, *A Vindication of God's Sovereign free Grace* (Boston, 1746).

30. SJ, *A Letter to Mr. Jonathan Dickinson, In Defense of Aristocles to Authades* . . . . (Boston, 1747), printed in *SJ Papers,* 3: 191–92, 200.

31. The best analysis of this essay is Fiering, "Moral Philosophy." Also helpful is James W. Woeful, "William Wollaston's Religion of Nature and Samuel Johnson's System of Morality,"*Historical Magazine of the Protestant Episcopal Church* 34 (1965): 239–64. Johnson's essay was printed in 1746; quotations are from the second edition of 1752, printed in *SJ Papers,* 2: 442–515.

32. The philosophical writings of Cadwallader Colden remain virtually unexplored. The best starting point is Brooke Hindle, "Cadwallader Colden's Extension of the Newtonian Principles," *William & Mary Quarterly* 13 (1956): 459–75.

33. Cadwallader Colden to SJ, June 2, 1746; SJ to Cadwallader Colden, June 23, 1746, April 15 [1747], and June 7, 1747, all in *SJ Papers,* 2: 290–92, 294–96, 298–99; SJ to Cadwallader Colden, October 31, 1746, MSS, Historical Society of Pennsylvania; "Ethica," in *Elementa Philosophica,* in *SJ Papers,* 2: 466.

34. SJ, A Sermon: On The Entire Dependence of the Creature Upon God, August 20, 1749, *SJ Papers,* 3: 544–45; A Sermon: Another of our Salvation by Grace Through Faith, May 1753, JCU.

35. SJ to SPG, January 10, 1743–44, *HP,* 1: 203–204.

36. *Diary of Rev. Daniel Wadsworth,* p. 72.

37. SJ to Roger Price, July 5, 1742, *SJ Papers,* 1: 106; SJ to SPG, January 10, 1743–44, *HP,* 1: 203–4. In the letter to Price, Johnson claimed to have heard Davenport preach for only "about five minutes." The circumstances of the letter, and the contrary statement in the letter to the SPG, suggest that he deliberately minimized the time period.

38. SJ to George Berkeley, October 3, 1741, *SJ Papers,* 1: 102–3; SJ to SPG, October 3, 1741, SPG MSS, ser. B, v. 9, no. 13 (italics added). These letters are nearly identical, except that the latter missive contains a significant slip of the pen.

39. Roger Price to SJ, June 18, 1742; SJ to Roger Price, July 5, 1742; S.J. to Theodore Morris, July 14, 1742, *SJ Papers,* 1: 105–8.

40. Helen Lynd writes: "[T]he deepest shame is exposure to oneself even though no one else may pay any attention or even know of it." "[S]hame is the outcome not only of exposing oneself to another person but of the exposure to oneself of parts of the self that one has not recognized and whose existence one is reluctant to admit." *On Shame,* p. 31.

41. Sigmund Freud offers a slightly different, but compatible, interpretation of this phenomenon: "If the writer repeats a word he has already written, this is probably an indication that it was not so easy for him to get away from it: that he could have said more at that point but had omitted to do so." *The Psychopathology of Everyday Life,* trans. Alan Tyson (New York, 1960), p. 129.

42. The Episcopal Clergy of Connecticut to SPG, November 15, 1738; SJ to Governor Jonathan Law, February 20, 1744, May 14, 1750, *SJ Papers,* 1: 94–98, 116, 140.

43. SJ to SPG, April 14, 1751; [SJ], "Proposals Regarding the Government of this Colony" [ca. June 1751], *SJ Papers,* 1: 146–50.

44. For a fuller discussion of this problem, see Bridenbaugh, *Mitre,* passim, and below, chap. 9, 10.

45. SJ to the Archbishop of Canterbury, May 3, 1737, *SJ Papers,* 1: 88.

46. SJ to Mr. Tomlinson, December 1, 1742; SJ to the Bishop of London, September 17, 1750, *SJ Papers,* 1: 113, 144; SJ's Draft of a Statement . . . about Sending Bishops, Autumn 1750, *SJ Papers,* 3: 242; SJ to the Archbishop of Canterbury, May 22, 1743; SJ to SPG, March 30, 1750, *HP,* 1: 195, 259–60.

47. SJ to the Bishop of London, September 25, 1751, *SJ Papers,* 1: 151.

9

"CULTIVATING THE RISING GENERATION"

IN OCTOBER 1746 Samuel Johnson celebrated his fiftieth birthday, having devoted half his life to the episcopal cause in Connecticut. For twenty-five years he had "studied, and wrote, and rid, and preached, and pleaded, and lived" to proclaim the Church of England. Now, amidst his quarrels with the New Light religion, the Stratford minister urged the SPG to appoint additional missionaries to ease his burden. "As things now stand," he solemnly announced, "either the Church or I, or both, must soon come to an end," thereby eradicating the labor of a lifetime. "And the case both of these people and me is the more piteous," Johnson continued, because "I am now arrived to that time of life, when, instead of having such an increase to my burden, I much need to be rather released from a position of what I had before." At the age of fifty, then, Samuel Johnson prepared for the end of his life. The following year a sudden fall on the ice immobilized him with a broken leg, accentuating his sense of declining vigor.[1]

As he approached old age, Samuel Johnson searched for evidence of coherence and continuity in his long career, for aspects of permanence among his creative achievements, for symbols of personal immortality that would transcend his death.[2] By mid-century, both his sons, heirs to his worldly estate and reputation, seemed safely headed toward professional careers and he found great satisfaction in their early accomplishments. He would live in their loins as he himself had perpetuated the memory and spirit of his own ancestors. Such organic continuities pleased Johnson immensely. He eagerly awaited the birth of grandchildren, particularly the arrival of male progeny who would bear not only the family's Christian names but the surname as well.[3]

For all his pride in his descendants, however, Samuel Johnson wished to contribute to the larger community in which he lived and yearned for the lasting recognition of his countrymen. "The great governing principle of every good man in the conduct of his life," he declared, should be "to do the greatest possible good to mankind." As a missionary and a pedagogue, Johnson could enlighten the children of America and assure the spread of "wisdom and virtue" throughout the colonies. Such activity, he believed, would provide continuity beyond his lifetime. "Though the culture bestowed on youth be successful only with a few," Benjamin Franklin had assured him, "yet the influence of those few . . . may be very great." Seeking to consolidate his personal accomplishments, Samuel Johnson dedicated his last years of creativity to the rising generation.[4]

The Stratford minister's desire to extend his influence often conflicted with the need to preserve his past achievements. Thus when "more easy, honorable and profitable pulpits" fell vacant at Boston and New York, he preferred to remain in Connecticut "lest what I have been so many years laboring for here might suffer and decay." For similar reasons Johnson declined an invitation from Trinity Church at Newport, Rhode Island, to fill the vacancy left by the death of their pastor in 1750. "My years and the difficulty of leaving these parts," he explained, convinced him that he should stay where he was.[5]

That same summer, however, Johnson received an even more prestigious opportunity. The trustees of the Philadelphia Academy, led by the resourceful Benjamin Franklin, invited him to assume the presidency of the new institution, destined to become the University of Pennsylvania. "As the view of being useful has most weight with generous and benevolent minds," Franklin wrote to Johnson, "you may do great service not only to the present but to future generations." Johnson replied cautiously, expressing fear of dividing the Anglicans of Pennsylvania, pointing to his advanced age, his inappropriateness both for urban life and for the particular position, his physical infirmities, especially his dread of the smallpox. Franklin strove to overcome the New Englander's objections. Observing that the erection of a new Anglican church would promote the expansion of the Church of England, the Philadelphia printer dismissed the minister's age as a reason for declining, advised him of the advantages of inoculation, and tried to assuage his self-doubts. "Your objection about the politeness of Philadelphia, and your imagined rusticity, is mere compliment," the apostle of the self-made man declared, "and your diffidence of yourself absolutely groundless."[6]

The academic appointment was very tempting to Johnson, especially considering his lifetime commitment to American education. But his lengthy objections also revealed a more fundamental ambivalence gnawing at his soul. The problem clarified greatly, however, when Johnson learned of a smallpox epidemic in Philadelphia. By arousing Johnson's most profound fears, it virtually eliminated whatever interest he had in the academic position. Though he still wavered for a while, he at last refused the post. "I am now plainly in the decline of life," he notified Franklin, "and must, therefore, consider myself as being an *emeritus,* and unfit for any new situation in the world."[7] Fearful of exposure, whether to the pox or to metropolitan society, the Stratford minister decided to promote the welfare of mankind in his native New England.

One reason for declining the presidency of the Philadelphia Academy was Johnson's desire to reside near his family, particularly in the neighborhood of his oldest son, William Samuel Johnson. As a parent he had established a remarkable rapport with his maturing children that he was now unwilling to jeopardize by a removal from the colony. These feelings revealed more than paternal pride in his offspring. More fundamentally, he possessed genuine respect for the young men, a love based as much upon his need for them as theirs for him. This mutual dependence—a sincere dialogue between the generations—derived from the parent's earlier ability to implement the gentle caveats on child rearing that he had professed in his pulpit oratory.

As William Samuel Johnson passed through his teens, his father continued to supervise his moral development, suggesting "the great danger of bad company," and warning him to avoid the ethical pitfalls of "free thinking."[8] The youth assured his father of his welfare.

"My conduct [is] not unworthy [of] such a father," he wrote in describing the high regard that Johnson commanded among the Anglicans of Boston. The clergyman also offered his son advice on the "human frailty which is called *Love.*" Writing to the youth to avoid the embarrassment of direct contact, Johnson explained that most people possessed "some tincture of distraction," of which love was one type, and reminded him of "the apostle's aphorism, 'Let him that thinketh he standeth take heed lest he fall.' " He praised the youth for his fear of "making a woman unhappy" and cautioned him to be "tender" toward members of that "unwary sex." Finally, the clergyman assured his son that he could provide an adequate estate to enable him to marry. "I am glad you have opened the way" for a "free correspondence and conversation upon these subjects," Johnson acknowledged, "and would wish you always to converse with me in the . . . most unreserved manner. . . . For," he concluded, "there is nothing [that] pleases me better than a decent, open, and unreserved freedom."[9]

Samuel Johnson's sensitivity to his oldest son emerged even more clearly when the young man began to search for a suitable career. "It is the greatest desire of my soul to be useful to mankind," William Samuel declared, echoing the sentiments of his father, "but the difficulty is to determine in what way."[10] At the brink of adulthood, uncertain about his future, William Samuel Johnson's predicament reflected a more general cultural phenomenon. As colonial society became more complicated, offering young people various occupational opportunities, the transition from childhood to adulthood also became more complex. Instead of simply inheriting the "calling" of one's parent, young people, particularly college-educated men, confronted alternative career choices. Such personal dilemmas, difficult as they appeared, probably explain why young males seemed to be particularly sensitive to the evangelical appeal of the Great Awakening.[11]

In William Samuel Johnson's case, the choice of "a course of life" focused on one of three professions: the clergy, the bar, or the military. The proximity of the armies during King George's War (1744–48) made the last occupation temporarily alluring, but both father and son soon concurred that it was "out of the question." Both men also agreed that of the remaining choices, divinity, in itself, constituted "the best profession." The problem, however, was that the young man, like many of his contemporaries, found himself more attracted to the study of the law.[12] The burgeoning interest in legal careers among provincial intellectuals reflected, in part, the increased complexity within American society, a tendency that required more lawyers to settle disputes between people. The expansion of the legal profession also revealed a growing secularism in the colonies, a shift typified by William Samuel Johnson's occupational dilemma.[13]

In determining a career the young Johnson surmised that "every man ought to choose that which is most agreeable to his dispositions and abilities, for in that he is most likely to succeed." "We cannot unmake ourselves," he remarked. "We may correct but can never eradicate the first principles of our constitution." That statement reflected a subtle, but fundamental transformation within Western culture. In earlier societies, people accepted social roles befitting their social group or class. Here, however, William Samuel Johnson appealed to his individual talents, his personal qualities. By the eighteenth century these expressions had become fairly typical—at least among the educated elite in the colonies. The appeal to individualism, moreover, had vast implications for other aspects of life. William Samuel Johnson, of course, did not write the Declaration of Independence (though he did sign a petition from the Stamp Act Congress in 1765); nor did he advocate the implementation of a laissez-faire society (though he made many brilliant business investments). Both of those movements—the development of political and economic individualism—emerged in the late colonial period. Both were manifestations of a wider cultural movement that stressed the autonomy of individuals. At the age of twenty, then, William Samuel Johnson spoke for his emerging generation, a group that would assume political leadership in America in the last decade before independence.

There is a powerful irony, therefore, to the discourse between William Samuel and his father. The older man had long stressed the importance of communal interaction and warned of the dangers of pursuing self-interest. Yet that ideology, self-conscious as it was, belied the course of his entire life. As a young man he had taken a brave, independent step in converting to the Church of England. Now, he listened sympathetically to his son's plea for autonomy and agreed to let the young man attend the courts to make "a trial of the study of the law." In the end William Samuel Johnson became one of Connecticut's most prominent lawyers, a credit to his family, the pride of his father, Samuel Johnson's paternal "tenderness" had enabled the youth to develop his talents to the full.[14] The juxtaposition of overt ideology and covert commitments thus revealed a basic trend within American culture. The appeals to social organicism notwithstanding, colonial parents prepared their children for independence.

The success of those lessons, of course, depended as much on the pupils as on their teachers. Thus Samuel Johnson's relationship with his youngest son, Billy, pointed in a significantly different direction. As with William Samuel, Johnson attempted to shape the youth's character by setting ideal models for imitation. "Let the world see that you are *my son*," he admonished, "worthy of me, and answerable to their expectations and my hopes." This pattern, unconsciously designed to invoke a sensitivity to shame and public exposure, also influenced the boy's more formal education.[15]

Like his older brother, Billy Johnson discovered that his father's reputation had preceded him in influential Anglican circles. "I am greatly pleased to find Daddy's character so universally esteemed," he wrote from London. But where William Samuel Johnson's attempt to emulate his famed parent had reinforced his self-confidence and enabled him to embark on a career in the law, Billy found himself unable to diverge from the paternal path. The younger son not only decided to become a clergyman like his father, but also slavishly copied the older man's sermons. "His only fault was too great self-diffidence," Samuel Johnson commented in explaining Billy's lack of originality, "which made it very difficult [for] him to make compositions nearly his own." This lack of self-confidence troubled the father and he begged his older son "to be always as helpful to [Billy] as you can."[16] The younger son, perhaps overwhelmed by his superior brother, had chosen the surest, but most conservative course. Of such stuff were Loyalists and Tories made.

In preparing his sons for their professional careers, Samuel Johnson overcame the difficulties of a provincial education by instructing them himself. To assist them in "methodizing their thoughts" and to elucidate "the whole circle of learning," the Anglican philosopher resumed his work on encyclopedias and composed a "small manual" of the sciences. Benjamin Franklin, searching for a suitable synopsis for the students of the Philadelphia Academy, read the manuscript and promptly agreed to print it in 1752. *Elementa Philosophica,* as the piece was called, embraced a revised edition of *A New System of Morality* and contained "Noetica," Samuel Johnson's latest effort at intellectual synthesis. Used by college students in Pennsylvania and New York, it became the first philosophy textbook in American history.[17] The work introduced colonial students to an overview of all parts of learning, enabling them to see the relationship of each particular "science" to the entire body of knowledge. Following the ideas of Bishop Berkeley, to whom the book was dedicated, Johnson suggested that all learning separated into two distinct categories: "philology, or the study of words and other signs, and philosophy, or the study of things signified by them." Mastery of these subjects, he declared, would provide "the knowledge of every thing useful to our well-being and true happiness."[18]

Johnson's theological attitudes, his belief in an amiable, omnipresent God, underlay his entire philosophical position. All mental activity, he said, depended upon "a perpetual intercourse with the great parent mind." Physical nature, the Newtonian universe of mathematical order, similarly bespoke the presence of the deity, and the Anglican philosopher exhorted his students to examine the world for "the plain signatures of design and contrivance." Johnson's analysis of ethics reaffirmed the importance of imitating God by conforming to Him "as our great original and pattern." To obtain happiness people had to control their irrational impulses. For Johnson, then, education and what he called "culture" became a primary means "to discipline and moderate the passions, . . . to inure them to a ready submission to the dictates of reason and conscience." The rationality of the soul thereby corresponded to the harmony of God's creation.[19]

Elementa Philosophica concluded with an extended chapter on "the progress of the mind," in which Johnson analyzed the development of thought in children and suggested appropriate forms of education. With his characteristic sympathy for the young, he emphasized the "prodigious" mental activity that occurred during the formative years of life. "We ought to think little children to be persons of much more importance than we usually apprehend them to be," he contended, and we should indulge "their inquisitive curiosity." Arguing that juvenile ignorance merely reflected the "want of experience," Johnson urged American parents to develop the natural intelligence of the young. "They should be led on to a sense of order and public virtue, and the love of their country," the pedagogue advised, "and finally of the whole human kind."[20]

The concern for future generations moved Johnson to denounce the spread of philosophical skepticism and "free thinking," which seemed to imperil the cause of Christianity. "Popery itself, as bad as it is, does nothing so near the mischief towards destroying the virtue and morals of mankind," he exclaimed, "as scepticism, and the loose notions that are so much in vogue . . . in these degenerate and apostasizing days." Those words, full of frustration and hostility, became a familiar refrain in Johnson's letters, the complaints of an old man losing touch with his society.

Then in 1751 Johnson discovered the writings of John Hutchinson, a contemporary British writer, who attacked the eighteenth-century rationalists by demonstrating the "scientific" value of the Bible. Hutchinson's interpretation hinged on his ability to retranslate the Hebrew of the Old Testament, an intellectual performance that earned Johnson's complete approval. Calling Hutchinson "a prodigious genius," the Anglican extolled the works as "the only right system of philosophy" and became an untiring advocate of the study of Hebrew. "I have heretofore been long wandering after the wisdom of this world, and eagerly pursued the philosophy so much in vogue," the minister confessed, "but of late . . . I have been almost entirely devoted to the study of the Holy Scriptures, and especially in the pure and noble original." By bolstering orthodox Christianity, the Hutchinsonians offered Johnson a philosophical alternative to what he regarded as "the reasoning humor . . . in matters of religion."[21]

As a stepfather Samuel Johnson had guided the education of Charity Johnson's children and had prepared both her sons for admission to Yale College. When Benjamin Nicoll, the younger stepson, expressed interest in the law, the Stratford minister wrote on his behalf to several prominent lawyers in New York City to arrange for his professional training. Family contacts and business acumen enabled Nicoll to prosper in the bustling environment of the port city, then inhabited by about 10,000 persons, free and slave. By mid-century he had achieved considerable respect and popularity; in his stepfather's words, he had become "the darling of the city." Ben Nicoll had imbibed Samuel Johnson's passion for education and he appreciated the importance of establishing institutions of learning. When several of the prominent merchants and lawyers of New York, led by the resourceful Presbyterian William Livingston, proposed the creation of a local college, Ben Nicoll emerged as one of its leading advocates.[22]

In 1746 the Assembly of New York agreed to promote the academic institution. "I heartily wish success to it," Samuel Johnson informed Cadwallader Colden, and offered to do "anything in my little power that may tend to promote it." The denominational competition that followed the Great Awakening had produced considerable interest in colleges throughout the American provinces. Evangelicals had recently founded the College of New Jersey, an institution that Samuel Johnson viewed as "a fountain of nonsense" since "the most virulent Methodists" supervised its curriculum. Episcopalians in the northern colonies therefore hoped that the New York college would become an Anglican institution, an antidote to religious enthusiasm, a sectarian academy that would serve as a bastion of orthodoxy between the "dissenting" schools of Connecticut and New Jersey. Such denominational affiliation, typical of all institutions of higher learning in America prior to the American Revolution, would enable Anglican parents to provide a liberal, yet religiously sound education for their children.[23]

The idea of a denominational college reflected the conventional wisdom of colonial society. In a culture that viewed the universe as an organic whole—that, in other words, did not separate the sacred from the secular—the notion of distinguishing religious facts from scientific truths was literally unthinkable. It was this sense of the indivisibility of learning—not some moral conservativism—that motivated the college founders of the eighteenth century. Only much later in American history would the reverse become true.

These intellectual imperatives—self-evident though they appeared to people like Samuel Johnson—nevertheless encountered the massive opposition of William Livingston and his "dissenting" allies. When it became apparent that the Anglicans would dominate the Board of Trustees of the new college, Livingston launched a weekly newspaper, *The Independent Reflector,* to protest the thrust of the institution. "Let us . . . strive to have the college founded on an ample, a generous, an universal plan," he cried. "Let not the seat of literature, the abode of the muses, and the nurse of science; be transformed into a cloister of bigots, an habitation of superstition, a nursery of ghostly tyranny, a school of rabbinical jargon."[24]

Livingston's position, modern as it now appears, symbolized the growing secularization of western values. In calling for a separation of religion and education, Livingston was denying the organic wholeness of the universe, demystifying the visible world, segregating human consciousness into tidy categories of civil and spiritual. Though still a minority view in eighteenth-century America, this rationalistic impulse would eventually dominate American culture. In time people would be separated from the natural world with the same precision that Livingston now proposed to separate the mind from the soul.

In 1752, however, these were radical ideas, extremely threatening to the established values. To Samuel Johnson the notions seemed incredible, awful symptoms of the moral degeneracy of the age. As for the Reflectors, as he called his opponents, he could only condemn them as exponents of evil. It was necessary, therefore, to launch a counterattack to vindicate not alone the Church of England but the very principles of Christianity. Soon Johnson was joining his colleagues in the columns of the *New-York Mercury,* denouncing the atheistic ideas of his critics.

Livingston's polemics soon offended the political leaders of the province–headed by the loyal Anglican James DeLancey–and he was forced to suspend publication of the *Independent Reflector.* But Livingston had not yet surrendered. As a member of the Board of Trustees he now tried an alternative strategy. He would nominate the Anglican Samuel Johnson to become president of the college in hopes that the gesture would demonstrate his commitment to the college. Perhaps then he might influence the new curriculum. In a curious reversal, Samuel Johnson found himself summoned to New York by his philosophical enemy.[25]

The invitation to assume the leadership of the new institution offered Johnson a unique opportunity to extend his influence over his countrymen. "There is nothing I should more rejoice in," he declared, than in "cultivating the rising generation." Johnson had always "loved learning and colleges." As a young man he had introduced significant changes into the Yale curriculum; later he had supported Bishop Berkeley's project for an American college, which, he indicated subsequently, "probably would have been [in] New York"; more recently, he had counseled the trustees of the Philadelphia Academy. Now at the age of fifty-seven, Samuel, "the founder of the school of prophets," confronted an exciting enterprise that opened the prospect of being even more serviceable to the future of mankind.[26]

Such possibilities, instead of arousing Johnson's enthusiasm, alerted his cautious instincts. Where a man like Benjamin Franklin might have rushed to New York City, Johnson remained at Stratford contemplating his choices. To his friends he suggested that he was too old for the job. But that excuse, contrived as it was, made no headway. Closely related to the question of age, however, was Johnson's search for psychological continuity. Throughout his life he had invested enormous emotional energy in his self-image as an intellectually superior person, as perhaps the most learned man of his country. Now the trustees were asking him to display and, in consequence, to risk, that sense of self. I am "extremely fearful whether I shall be able to answer your expectations," he wrote cautiously to the college planners of New York, "as they seem . . . to have gone far beyond any notion I can have of myself and especially at these years."[27]

This fear of exposure or, more profoundly, self-exposure, structured the remainder of Samuel Johnson's objections to assuming the direction of the college. Like most of his contemporaries in England and America, he regarded urban centers with distrust and dislike. The high cost of living "in the great towns," he believed, reflected the pervasive immorality popularly associated with cities. Writing from New York he lamented the temptations of "luxury, with which I am obliged to live in continual warfare." The city, in Johnson's mind, represented an evil habitation, a snare to be avoided, a real contrast to the country life with which he was familiar. By living in New York the minister chanced exposure to the worst vices of the age.[28]

A removal to New York City also threatened to expose Samuel Johnson to a more deadly peril: the virulence of the smallpox. The Anglican explained to the trustees that he had never contracted the disease "and that it will not be safe in this time of life to run the hazard of it." Dating from his earliest years, Johnson's fear of the infection had been reinforced by the death of Daniel Browne in London. He now realized that New York, no less than Franklin's Philadelphia, remained dangerously exposed to the pestilence. To allay his anxieties, the college planners agreed that the president could depart from the town whenever the smallpox "prevailed."[29]

Johnson weighed these "discouragements" against the beneficent contributions he could make to his young countrymen. The balance shifted considerably when Ben Nicoll and some of the other Anglican promoters indicated that they would abandon the scheme if he refused to accept the presidency. For Johnson, this consideration clinched the argument. Nothing "could have induced me" to accept the position "but the hopes of rendering the little remainder of my life more useful to mankind," he declared sincerely to his son, "especially in laying a foundation for sound learning and true religion in the rising and future generations that might stem the torrent of irreligion and vice." By February 1754 Johnson consented to "make a trial" as president, but delayed a binding agreement until the institution obtained a formal charter "and he should see what sort of college it was to be."[30]

Johnson's inability to act at this crucial time soon placed him on the horns of an insoluble dilemma. Under the leadership of William Livingston, the opponents of the episcopal college successfully bottled the proposal in the New York Assembly. Though Johnson advertised the opening of the college and commenced instruction during the summer of 1754, the educational enterprise still lacked official sanction from the royal government. Despite assurances from influential New Yorkers, Johnson remained extremely anxious about the success of the project.

Meanwhile the Anglican congregation in Stratford, abandoned by their minister, "had begun to have hard thoughts" about his absence. This tension illuminated a general trend among lay Anglicans in the colonies to assume control of ecclesiastical affairs. In England, where the episcopal church was established by law, the laity accepted the leadership of their ministers and allowed the prelates to control the church. But in America the absence of an episcopate and the tradition of congregational autonomy encouraged the independence of the laity. Throughout the colonies the vestries retained considerable power regarding such basic matters as the appointment of ministers. When one European-born missionary encountered opposition from his parishioners, Samuel Johnson explained "their want of good manners." "The spirit of liberty beats high in their veins," he remarked, and they expect to regulate parish business.[31] Johnson himself usually enjoyed peaceful relations with his congregation. But his contemplated departure now aroused deep resentments.

Besides the criticism from his own people, Johnson also found himself exposed to the bitter sarcasm of his congregational neighbors. "Now they say, ay, all Dr. Johnson's schemes for the Church are now like to come to nothing, both here and there," he reported, "and my own church into the bargain." Such humiliation, coming from friend and foe alike, disturbed Johnson immensely, destroying his equilibrium. "I am almost crazy and know not what to do," he confessed. Fortunately for Johnson, Governor DeLancey resolved the problem in late 1754 by endorsing the charter of King's College, the institutional predecessor of Columbia College. After thirty-two years of service, Samuel Johnson surrendered his position as pastor of Christ's Church in Stratford and moved to New York.[32]

Johnson's anxieties revealed a curious interaction of cultural, social, and psychological forces. First, there was his fear of metropolitan life, the possibility of exposing his talents to more sophisticated observers. Second, there was his involvement in his life's work, his strong commitment to the Anglican cause in Connecticut. Finally, there was his anxiety about separation from his family. "It looks more unnatural for parents to leave their children than vice versa," he confessed to William Samuel Johnson. "But I beg you will think as favorably of me as you can, and believe that it has been the greatest shock to my mind to leave you, that I ever met with."[33] Such statements, sincere expressions of pain, illuminated

Johnson's ambivalence about leaving Stratford. As a father and grandfather, he needed his progeny far more than they needed him.

For the Anglican minister, the direction of King's College represented an alternative mode of fatherhood, a form of paternity that transcended the biological limitations of ordinary parenthood, which, as he explained, promised to "secure a fame more honorable and lasting than that of sons and daughters." It was this paternalism that enabled Samuel Johnson to leave his son's family and it was with this fatherly perspective that he assumed the leadership of the college.[34]

When Samuel Johnson designed the official seal of King's College, he portrayed the college as "a lady sitting on a throne . . ., with several children at her knees, representing her pupils." This family metaphor, stylized perhaps in the eighteenth century, symbolized the pattern of collegiate education during Johnson's tenure as president. During the first decade of tuition, about three-fifths of the student body were relatives of Johnson himself or of members of the board of trustees. It was entirely characteristic therefore for one interested parent to request the president to accept his son not into the college but "into his family."[35]

The gentleness of Johnson's paternalism, typical of his relations with his own sons, extended to the young men who studied under him. Indeed, his "tenderness and lenity in discipline" brought the president the rebuke of the trustees, who complained about a lack of severity. These paternal traits emerged in Johnson's "Exhortation" to one graduating class, a ceremonial address in which he interchanged the phrases "my dear pupils" and "my dear sons." "Fear God, and keep his commandments," Johnson advised, "for this is the whole–the whole duty, and the whole happiness of man."[36]

Johnson's valedictory address represented the culmination of an education designed to produce true gentlemen and true Christians, "creditable to their families and friends, ornaments to their country, and useful to the public weal."[37] He himself instructed the youngest classes, perfecting their Latin, teaching them the New

Testament "in its Greek original," and, true to his Hutchinsonian predilections, encouraging them at every opportunity to study the Hebrew of the Old Testament, "the mother of all language and eloquence, as well as the fountain of all knowledge and true wisdom . . ., the first oracles of God." Johnson also lectured to the senior classes on moral philosophy, leading the scholars through his *Elementa Philosophica,* the capstone of his own intellectual achievement. Regardless of subject matter, however, Samuel Johnson always underscored the value of public service and urged his students to make themselves "amiable in the eyes of all mankind." Those who "have had greater advantages than others," he charged one graduating class, must fulfill "higher expectations" and consequently must "be as exemplary as possible in all piety and virtue; in humility, meekness, justice, truth and universal benevolence." With such guiding principles, the men of King's College left the bosom of the academy and confronted what Johnson called "the business of life."[38]

Throughout Samuel Johnson's tenure as president, the fortunes of the college closely paralleled the circumstances of his personal life. Having settled his family in New York, he devoted his energies to establishing a curriculum, drafting a collection of prayers for the students, instituting a body of laws governing collegiate activities, and designing a plan for the college buildings. Benefiting from the patronage of the royal governor, the college prospered, despite the opposition of the Livingston faction and despite the strains of the French and Indian War. In August 1756 the college celebrated the laying of the cornerstone, a ceremony highlighted by a short presidential speech in which Johnson prayed for "the advancement of . . . true religion and good literature."[39]

During the earliest months of operation, the presence of Billy Johnson as assistant tutor eased the burdens of the college president. Working near his father, the younger man pursued his studies in divinity and, in the autumn of 1755, determined to sail to London for episcopal ordination. For Samuel Johnson the preparations for Billy's voyage evoked strong memories of his own exploration of the British metropolis thirty-three years before. He recalled the splendor of the capital city, the amazing monuments, palaces, libraries, and curiosities. Thinking of the wonders of the mother country also reminded Johnson of the inadequacies of a provincial education. In letters of introduction to his English correspondents, he apologized for Billy's intellectual limitations and begged them to "make much allowance for him as he hath been bred up in this raw uncultivated country."[40] In Johnson's mind, England remained the center of civilization, the bulwark of true religion, the seat of learning and culture.

Yet the Anglican divine also remembered that London, for all its advantages, possessed the worst sins of the age, the seductive glitter of luxury, prostitution, and vice. Sympathizing with William Samuel's inability to leave Stratford, the churchman suggested that England might not be worth visiting after all. Closely related to Johnson's distrust of the mother country was his dread of the smallpox, the hidden pestilence that pervaded the capital. To his English correspondents, the worried parent explained that Billy had not yet contracted the disease and begged them to protect the young man from needless exposure. Johnson even requested the secretary of the SPG to obtain a good physician for his son should the traveler require one.[41]

These precautions, while thoroughly reasonable in an age of early and sudden death, nevertheless revealed Samuel Johnson's ambivalence about the mother country—his admiration of things English paired with his abiding insecurity about metropolitan sophistication. In a fundamental way these paradoxical feelings constituted a dialogue within the provincial mind, its simultaneous attraction and repulsion to Great Britain, its love and its hate for the English superiors who wielded power and determined the fate of men and women in the distant American colonies. Not until the war for independence would Americans attempt to resolve that ambivalence, untangle the paradox, reassess their loyalties. In 1776 many Anglicans in the northern colonies, colleagues and disciples of ministers like Samuel Johnson, chose to support the British authority. To their shock and dismay these "Loyalists" found themselves thrust beyond the pale of American society, treated as pariahs of the body politic. Only twenty years before, at a time when men like Billy Johnson ventured to London, these provincials had stood in the mainstream of American culture.

Though Billy's welfare remained uppermost in his father's mind, the president's anxiety also revealed a subtle interaction within the Johnson family. To his older son in Stratford the aging parent expressed frustration at the feeling of childlessness and requested William Samuel to visit him in New York.[42] Bereft of his children, he yearned for a sense of fatherhood, for a visible reinforcement of his paternal identity. For Samuel Johnson, the departure of the youngest child had awakened a fear of isolation, a dread of old age.

Billy's approaching maturity coincided with Johnson's sense of aging. As both men anticipated important psychological changes, they each found comfort in the numerous similarities in their lives. Thus the older man took special pride that his son had followed him into the service of the SPG. Billy too noticed significant parallels. "My fortune in this voyage has been something similar to yours," he wrote from England, having "escaped seasickness, the small pox and all other evils, and am esteemed, honored and kindly treated, by all that know me here." The thought that Billy would continue his father's work comforted the churchman as he approached old age.

These dreams quickly vanished when Samuel Johnson learned that Billy had died of smallpox in London shortly after obtaining episcopal ordination. "This was indeed a dismal shock," the bereaved parent declared, and profound remorse shook the old man's soul to its foundations. "Paroxysms of grief will now and then occur which no considerations will wholly assuage, and [which] time alone can abate," the father reported to his surviving child, "and it is fit it should be so, lest we should too soon forget the wormwood and the gall."[43] The trauma of Billy's death remained to haunt the rest of Samuel Johnson's days, reawakening memories of earlier survivals, reinstilling a sense of guilt for sending his son to his death.

For the grieving father, the coincidences between the two voyages augmented feelings of survivor guilt, a sense that Samuel Johnson had been spared by God but only at the expense of his son's life. Johnson revealed these unconscious sentiments in a letter that analyzed the mysteries of heaven. When God bestowed life upon children, Johnson observed, He provided them with "tender parents and other friends" to guide their development on earth. "Can we then doubt," he asked, "but that the same great and good father of our spirits hath provided some good guardian friends," to facilitate our transition to eternal life in heaven. For the corporeal Johnsons, then, for Samuel and Charity and William Samuel, the ethereal Billy would become a guardian angel; Billy, in other words, would become the surrogate parent of his father and mother. The youngest had died that the others might live.[44]

The reversal of generations appeared more ironic shortly after Johnson learned of his son's death, when an outbreak of smallpox in New York forced the college president to abandon the city for Westchester. "Being desirous to administer to the poor people who were deprived of his dear son," Johnson preached to the Westchester congregation for over a year, waiting for the epidemic to subside. The president and his wife passed a peaceful year in the country, but in the spring of 1758 Charity Johnson sickened and, "to the inexpressible grief" of her husband, died at the age of sixty-six. "You are now my all," Johnson told his son in conveying the news.[45]

The president returned to New York shortly thereafter to attend the first commencement of King's College. Seeking to forget his loss, he plunged into his academic duties and resumed direction of the college. But he longed for companionship and in mid-winter, barely six months after Charity Johnson's death, he proposed a marriage to Anne Watts, the widow of a prominent New York merchant. "I blush . . . that one of my sacerdotal character and advanced years should think of taking such a step," the suitor confessed, but his situation required the assistance of someone skilled in "economic affairs." Johnson frankly acknowledged several "objections" to marrying him, including his age and his "public station." He assured his friend, however, that he desired nothing but herself and promised not to be "deficient" in forming "the most entire, tender, intimate and endearing friendship." The widow Watts remained unimpressed by Johnson's honesty and politely declined the invitation. The formality of the Anglican's proposal suggests that Johnson himself did not suffer much heartbreak by the rebuff.[46]

In the autumn another outbreak of smallpox forced the president to seek refuge at his son's house in Stratford. This perennial problem, together with Johnson's advanced age, led him to think increasingly about retirement. While at Stratford, Johnson and the college suffered yet another setback when Ben Nicoll, the president's primary link with the trustees, died suddenly. In May 1760 Johnson returned to New York, but, as he stated, the metropolis "was now so stripped that it seemed almost a wilderness to him," barren of his relatives and infested with the smallpox. The president resumed his academic duties but found it increasingly difficult to win the cooperation of the trustees. His fear of the smallpox continued to limit his activities—"a wretched embarrassment" he called it—and he resolved to retire permanently if another epidemic erupted. In November the smallpox claimed James Wetmore, his former Yale classmate and lifelong friend, thereby aggravating Johnson's dread.[47]

During the winter of 1760–61 a new outbreak of the disease confined the president to his rooms at the college, "a prisoner," he complained, to the caprice of providence. Isolated and lonely, the Anglican again contemplated marriage, this time with Sarah Beach, the widow of one of his Connecticut friends and the mother of William Samuel Johnson's wife. "It seems very ridiculous, and I am really ashamed of the thoughts of matrimony at this time of day," he confessed to his solicitous son; "but in truth it seems so doleful in old age to be destitute of a contemporary companion, that I am almost apt to think a man never wants one more, and," he continued, "if he has a good one in his younger years, there is nothing in life he needs more earnestly to pray for than her continuance to the last." These feelings, certainly an appropriate epitaph for Charity Johnson, persuaded the Anglican to consummate the marriage in June 1761.[48]

Samuel Johnson brought his second wife with him to New York and, after the "wretched drudgery" of social visits, renewed his instruction at the college. Having obtained a "well-qualified" professor to assist the aging president, the college flourished during this period. Meanwhile, Johnson's personal spirits soared. With Sarah Beach, he took great pleasure with the grandchildren who came to visit them. "I never was happier in my life than now," he stated confidently. In October 1761 William Samuel's spouse, Anne Beach Johnson, after having delivered four still-born sons, gave birth to a boy "that seems likely to stand," an event that brought endless gratification to the grandfather. "I give you joy of having seen your 34th year, and bless God that I . . . begin my 66th," he wrote to the boy's father. "It seems this little youth stands between us," he observed with pride, and "may be [will] excel us both."[49]

Johnson's happiness quickly faded when his second wife contracted the smallpox and died suddenly. Shocked by her death, he submitted his resignation to the trustees and, at the age of sixty-six, returned to Stratford. That decision, though hastened by Sarah Johnson's death, had been long in coming. Relations between Johnson and his superiors had deteriorated, particularly because his enforced exiles from the college left the institution in a vulnerable position. In November 1762, just four months before he resigned, the president had applied, unsuccessfully, for a pension. The refusal infuriated William Samuel Johnson, who drafted an angry defense of his father. "He has seen his family ruined and experienced nothing but distress and trouble," the lawyer exclaimed, "since he quitted a peaceful and secure retreat . . . to enter the service of an ungrateful people." Such protests, together with the influence of Johnson's friends, persuaded the trustees to reconsider their decision and, in the end, they voted to grant their first president fifty pounds per year.[50] The sum assured Johnson's financial independence for the remainder of his life.

Upon his return to Stratford, Samuel Johnson moved into his son's house, residing in "an elegant apartment" built for that purpose. After nearly nine arduous years at King's College, he eagerly anticipated the joys of retirement, the pleasure of his grandchildren, the peace of country life. "I am glad you have a prospect of relief from an employment inconvenient to the decline of life," his old friend Henry Caner declared. "I wish you all imaginable happiness and comfort in your retirement."[51] The old minister, white with age, could only nod, and breathe amen.

Samuel Johnson easily ascribed his difficulties at King's College to the perversity of the trustees, to the peculiar combinations within New York politics, and to the providence of the smallpox. As always, he denied the possibility of personal failure by projecting his deficiencies onto other people. Yet his fortunes in New York closely paralleled his earlier experience as a tutor at Yale College, a coincidence that suggests that Johnson's problems derived less from circumstances than from himself.

Throughout his long and turbulent career, Johnson demonstrated a remarkable optimism about his work, a vision so positive as to suggest a lack of touch with reality. It was in such spirits that the Anglican drafted encyclopedias, planned colleges, and promoted an American episcopate. Those schemes, brilliant as they appeared on paper, seldom related to the actual conditions in the colonies. Johnson's creativity, in other words, revealed his personal isolation from his culture, a psychological estrangement that, it should be remembered, stemmed from his earlier decision to reject his cultural heritage. Alone, his imagination knew no bounds.

Johnson's grandiose dreams nevertheless concealed a basic sense of inadequacy, a psychological fear, which explains his contorted efforts to avoid exposure. This instinct not only interfered with his acceptance of prestigious positions, but also undermined his efforts once installed in important offices. Johnson's dislike of social visits, for example, betrayed his fear. Lacking personal confidence, Johnson escaped from the maelstrom of metropolitan life at every opportunity. Thus the dissatisfaction of the King's College trustees, like that of the Yale rebels in 1718, may well have demonstrated Johnson's incompetence in positions of authority.

These shortcomings, personal though they were, found reinforcement in cultural values of provincial America. In a society that accepted the intellectual preeminence of Great Britain, provincial minds, even when well educated, could never attain the distinction of European scholars. That is why Johnson was always so apologetic about his learning. Yet provincials, like Johnson personally, also believed in their moral superiority over the natives of the metropolis. In the purity of the provinces, free from the responsibility of leadership, they might dream of better worlds to come. It was in this paradoxical illusion, then, that Samuel Johnson retreated to his Stratford domicile.

NOTES

1. SJ to Roger Price, July 5, 1742, *SJ Papers,* 1: 107; SJ to SPG, March 7, 1747, January 12, 1747/8, SPG MSS, ser. B, v. 15, pp. 52, 38.

2. The concept of "generativity," upon which this discussion is based, appears in Erikson, *Childhood and Society,* pp. 266–68.

3. SJ to WSJ, December 15, 1760, JCU, 2; SJ to WSJ, October 26, 1761, *SJ Papers,* 1: 315.

4. SJ to East Apthorp, December 1, 1759, *SJ Papers,* 4: 54; Benjamin Franklin to SJ, August 23, 1750, in Beardsley, *Samuel Johnson,* p. 162.

5. SJ to SPG, March 27, 1747, SPG MSS, ser. B, v. 15, p. 52; Church Wardens at Newport to SJ, July 17, 1750, SJ to Church Wardens at Newport, July 25, 1750, JHP; James Macsparran to SPG, "The State of Trinity Church in Newport, R.I.," [October] 1750, SPG MSS, ser. B, v. 18, p. 66; SJ to Walter Cranston, August 1750, JCU.

6. Benjamin Franklin to SJ, August 9, 1750, *SJ Papers,* 1: 141; Benjamin Franklin to SJ, August 23, 1750, in Beardsley, *Samuel Johnson,* pp. 163–64; see also editor's note in *The Papers of Benjamin Franklin,* ed. Leonard Labaree et al., 15 vols. (New Haven, Conn., 1959–), 4: 37.

7. Benjamin Franklin to SJ, October 25, 1750, SJ to Benjamin Franklin [November 1750], Benjamin Franklin to SJ, November 22, 1750, SJ to Benjamin Franklin, December 14?, 1750, *Franklin Papers,* 4: 71–72, 74–76, 79; Benjamin Franklin to SJ, September 13, 1750, SJ to Benjamin Franklin, January 1752, *SJ Papers,* 1: 143, 155.

8. SJ to WSJ, December 21, 1741, Stokes MSS, Yale University.

9. WSJ to SJ, July [1743], JCU, 1; SJ to WSJ, June 23, 1747, July 7, 1747, *SJ Papers,* 1: 125–29; WSJ to SJ, June 13, 1747, in Beardsley, *Samuel Johnson,* p. 146; WSJ to SJ, July 6, 1747, WSJ MSS.

10. WSJ to SJ, June 13, 1747, in Beardsley, *Samuel Johnson,* p. 146.

11. See chap. 8 above.

12. SJ to WSJ, June 23, 1747, *SJ Papers,* 1: 125–26.

13. A suggestive essay is Edmund S. Morgan, "The American Revolution Considered as an Intellectual Movement," in Arthur M. Schlesinger, Jr. and Morton White, eds., *Paths of American Thought* (Boston, 1963).

14. WSJ to SJ, June 13, 1747, in Beardsley, *Samuel Johnson,* pp. 146–47; SJ to WSJ, June 23, 1747, July 7, 1747; SJ to Edward Antill [1762?], *SJ Papers,* 1: 125–28, 332. The best biography of Johnson's son is George C. Groce, Jr., *William Samuel Johnson: A Maker of the Constitution* (New York, 1937).

15. SJ to William Johnson, January 5, 1749/50, JCU, 1; William Johnson to SJ, June 14, 1754, SJ to William Johnson, June 17, 1754, *SJ Papers,* 1: 186–88.

16. William Johnson to WSJ, February 13, 1756, WSJ MSS; SJ to WSJ, January 6, 1757, Smyth MSS; SJ to WSJ, October 12, 1755, *SJ Papers,* 1: 223.

17. SJ to Benjamin Franklin, May 10, 1750, SJ to Bishop Berkeley, August 12, 1752, *SJ Papers,* 2: 327–29. *Elementa Philosophica: Containing chiefly, Noetica, Or Things relating to the Mind or Understanding: And Ethica, or Things relating to the Moral Behavior* (Philadelphia, 1752) is printed in *SJ Papers,* 2: 359–518. The best analysis of Johnson's philosophy is Fiering, "President Samuel Johnson" and "Moral Philosophy." A decade earlier, Johnson had published anonymously *An Introduction to the Study of Philosophy,* 2d ed. (New London, Conn. 1743). "What I aim to do in this small tract," he noted in the preface, "is, to be a little useful to young gentlemen that are to be introduced into the knowledge of the sciences . . . by setting before them a general view of the whole system of learning, as it were in miniature."

18. *SJ Papers,* 2: 359–68.

19. Ibid., 2: 374, 386, 420–22.

20. Ibid., 2: 422–35. The failure of the book to sell well in America "vexed" Johnson considerably; see Benjamin Franklin to SJ, April 15, 1754, *SJ Papers,* 1: 183.

21. SJ, "A Letter to a Friend," January 15, 1758, in SJ, *A Demonstration of the Reasonableness, Usefulness, and Great Duty of Prayers* (New York, 1760), p. 3; "Autobiography," pp. 30-31. SJ to WSJ, January 30, 1757, and SJ to Anne Watts, February 24, 1757, *SJ Papers,* 1: 270, 273; Johnson's interest in Hutchinson is discussed in Herbert Wallace Schneider, "The Mind of Samuel Johnson," *SJ Papers,* 2: 19-22 and Theodore Hornberger, "Samuel Johnson of Yale and King's College: A Note on the Relation of Science and Religion in Provincial America," *New England Quarterly* 8 (1935): 378-97. The psychological origins of Johnson's interest in Hebrew are discussed above, chap. 3.

22. SJ to Mr. DeLancey, to Mr. Orem, and to Mr. Murray, all dated February 24, 1740, JCU; SJ, "Autobiography," pp. 38-39.

23. SJ to Cadwallader Colden, April 15 [1747], *SJ Papers,* 2: 296; SJ to the Bishop of London, April 28, 1747, *HP,* 1: 236-37. For the general movement of education in this period, see Beverly McAnear, "College Founding in the American Colonies, 1745-1775," *Mississippi Valley Historical Review* 42 (1955): 24-44 and Bernard Bailyn, *Education in the Forming of American Society* (Chapel Hill, N.C., 1960). The best analysis of the founding of the New York college is David Churchill Humphrey, "King's College in the City of New York, 1754-1776," Ph.D. diss., Northwestern University, 1968.

24. The debate is discussed in Bridenbaugh, *Mitre*, chap. 6. *The Independent Reflector*, ed. Milton M. Klein (Cambridge, Mass., 1963), no. 22, April 26, 1753, p. 214.

25. SJ, "Notes in Reply to Henry Barclay's Letter," April 1753, JHP; William Smith to SJ, July 1753, *SJ Papers,* 4: 4; SJ, "Autobiography," pp. 33–34. Writing to his father, William Samuel recommended that he abstain from public debate. "If they whose business it is, form a college you can accept the presidentship with cheerfullness. If they do not you can retreat with honor." WSJ to SJ, June 13, 1753, JCU, 1.

26. SJ to William Livingston and the Trustees, January 17, 1754, *SJ Papers,* 4: 8–9; "Autobiography," pp. 25, 32–33.

27. SJ, "Autobiography," pp. 32–33; SJ to William Vassall, April 5, 1752, HU; SJ to William Livingston and the Trustees, January 17, 1754, *SJ Papers,* 4: 8–9.

28. SJ to the Bishop of Oxford, to John Berriman, October 30, 1752, and to WSJ, May 6, 1754; WSJ to SJ, June 22, 1747, SJ to SPG, December 1762, *SJ Papers,* 1: 162, 159, 184, 124, 326. Peter Jay, a correspondent of Johnson, removed his blind children to a country house because of "the dangers and confusions of the city life"; see Laura Jay Wells, *The Jay Family* (New York, 1938), p. 13.

29. SJ, "Autobiography," pp. 32–34; SJ to William Livingston and the

Trustees, January 17, 1754; "A True and Just State of the Case . . . [with] the Governor's of King's College," January 31 [?], 1763, *SJ Papers,* 4: 8-9, 94.

30. SJ, "Autobiography," pp. 32-34; SJ to WSJ, January 20, 1755, SJ to the Bishop of London, July 6, 1754; "A True and Just State of the Case," *SJ Papers,* 1: 208-9, 4: 20, 93.

31. SJ to Benjamin Nicoll, October 25, 1754, King's College MSS, CU; "Autobiography," p. 33; SJ to Matthew Graves, June 27, 1748, *SJ Papers,* 1: 132-33. For further discussion of this pattern, see Ellis, "Anglicans," pp. 78-80.

32. SJ to Benjamin Nicoll, October 25, 1754, and November 1, 1754; also Minutes of a meeting of the SPG, March 1, 1755, photostat, all in King's College MSS; SJ, "Autobiography," p. 34.

33. SJ to WSJ, April 20, 1755, JCU, 1; WSJ to SJ, May 19, 1755, WSJ MSS; SJ to WSJ, May 14, 1755, *SJ Papers,* 4: 35.

34. SJ to Dr. Bristow, January 5, 1758, *SJ Papers,* 4: 45.

35. SJ, "The Meaning of the Device for the Seal" [1754?], *SJ Papers,* 4: 224-25; Humphrey, "King's College," p. 140; Henry Lloyd II to Henry Lloyd, February 21, 1759, "Papers of the Lloyd Family of the Manor of Queens Village," 2 vols., *New-York Historical Society Collections* (1927), 2: 565.

36. SJ, "A True and Just State of the Case," [SJ], "An Exhortation to the Graduates" [1762], *SJ Papers,* 4: 95, 278, 280.

37. SJ, "Advertisements," *SJ Papers,* 4: 223. Johnson's attitude toward higher education revealed his approval of the work of David Fordyce, *Dialogues Concerning Education;* see SJ to Cadwallader Colden, June 7 [1747], *SJ Papers,* 2: 299. For a full discussion of the intellectual origins of Johnson's theories of education, see Humphrey, "King's College," pp. 399-408.

38. SJ, "Advertisements"; "A Paper which I desire may be read . . . after my decease . . .," [September 1759]; SJ to East Apthorp, December 1, 1759; and "Exhortation," [1762], all in *SJ Papers,* 4: 223-24, 115-16, 56, 278-79.

39. SJ, "Autobiography," pp. 35-36; SJ to the Bishop of London, October 27, 1755, "The Account of the Laying of the Cornerstone of King's College, prepared for the *Gazette* by Samuel Johnson," August 23, 1756, *SJ Papers,* 4: 36, 230.

40. SJ, "Autobiography," p. 36; SJ to WSJ, October 12, 1755, and to SPG, October 27, 1755, *SJ Papers,* 1: 224-25; SJ to George Berkeley, Jr., October 27, 1755, JCU.

41. SJ to WSJ, October 12, 1755, *SJ Papers,* 1: 224; SJ to SPG and to George Berkeley, Jr., October 27, 1755, both JCU.

42. SJ to WSJ, December 12, 1755, *SJ Papers,* 4: 37.

43. SJ to SPG, October 27, 1755, December 21, 1757, *SJ Papers,* 1: 225, 4: 42; William Johnson to WSJ, May 5, 1756, in Beardsley, *Samuel Johnson,* p. 219; William Johnson to SJ [ca. March 1756], JCU, 2; SJ, "Autobiography," p. 36; SJ to WSJ, November 8, 1756, *SJ Papers,* 1: 266. Even

in planning a memorial to Billy, Samuel Johnson revealed his acceptance of England's cultural superiority. Sending an elegy to be inscribed on the tomb, he asked that "a gentleman of better capacity for such purposes" be obtained to perfect the wording, SJ to James Rivington, January 1, 1758, JCU, 2.

44. SJ to WSJ, November 8, 1756, *SJ Papers,* 1: 267.

45. SJ, "Autobiography," p. 37; SJ to WSJ, May 29, 1758, *SJ Papers,* 1: 277.

46. SJ, "Autobiography," 38; SJ to Anne Watts, January 15, 1759, *SJ Papers,* 1: 280–81.

47. SJ, "Autobiography," pp. 38–39; SJ to the Archbishop of Canterbury, October 20, 1759, SJ to East Apthorp, December 1, 1759, SJ to SPG, November 25, 1760, *SJ Papers,* 4: 51, 54, 75; SJ to WSJ, June 16, 1760, JCU, 2; SJ to WSJ, November 17, 1760, *SJ Papers,* 1: 303.

48. SJ, "Autobiography," pp. 39–40; SJ to WSJ, January 11, 1761, February 16, 1761, *SJ Papers,* 1: 305, 306.

49. SJ, "Autobiography," pp. 40–41; SJ to WSJ, December 15, 1760, July 27, 1761, both JCU, 2; SJ to WSJ, October 12, 1761, October 26, 1761, November 22, 1762, *SJ Papers,* 1: 314, 315, 4: 88.

50. SJ, "Autobiography," p. 43; WSJ to Daniel Horsmanden, November 18, 1762, SJ to Daniel Horsmanden, March 11, 1763, *SJ Papers,* 4: 86–87, 97–98.

51. SJ, "Autobiography," p. 42; Henry Caner to SJ, December 23, 1762, *SJ Papers,* 1: 329.

10

"THIS DECAYING BODY"

AS SAMUEL Johnson basked in the "sweet retirement" of the Connecticut countryside, England and France at last consented to the terms of the Treaty of Paris, ending the overt hostilities known in America as the French and Indian War. That diplomatic agreement promised a new era of peace and prosperity in the colonies, a political tranquillity that mirrored the ease of Johnson's new life. "No man could be happier," reported the Anglican, "only as I have never for almost 50 years been without some public charge . . ., it seems strange now to be without one."[1]

While enjoying his freedom, Samuel Johnson nevertheless desired to remain serviceable to humanity, longed, as he put it, to feel "yet further useful." Old age, he prayed, would not destroy the coherence and continuity of his past life. "I hope I may live here to [do] some good," he averred, "by directing [ministerial] candidates . . . [in] their studies" and by "preaching frequently" for Edward Winslow, his successor in the Stratford pulpit. He also hoped "to be of some use to the college." In this manner the retired minister strove to preserve a feeling of autonomy and a sense of personal worth. It was at this time too that he commenced his autobiography, the "Memoirs of the Life of the Rev. Dr. Johnson, and Several Things Relating to the State Both of Religion and Learning in His Times."[2] For Johnson, retirement was a time of psychological consolidation, a period of recapitulation.

The old minister, like his own grandfather seven decades earlier, now devoted considerable time to his grandchildren, enjoying their "endearments and caresses" and supervising their education. Samuel William (so named at Johnson's request and called, at his suggestion, Billy) and Robert Charles, while still toddlers, came under the old man's scrutiny. To assist their development, he composed a brief grammar, which he published in 1765, and revised his catechism for young children. These efforts speeded the youngsters' education and, by the time Billy reached his sixth birthday, his grandfather was introducing him to the mysteries of Hebrew.[3] These boys, obedient and promising, would perpetuate Johnson's own being.

To protect his sense of continuity, Johnson also devoted himself to the Anglican cause in America. To a convocation of ministers he again proclaimed the importance of education, "because we that are just going off the stage are extremely solicitous that we may leave those behind us that shall be able well to support and defend the great and important cause that we have pleaded."[4] He also initiated a tutorial program designed to assist young ministers preparing for ordination.[5] Finally, the old man drafted one last defense of "the true nature of Christianity," a long tract that attempted to "preclude any further disputing about it."[6] Such labors, genuinely ambitious for a man of Johnson's years, revealed his continued commitment to the principles of his youth.

Johnson's search for spiritual coherence ultimately depended not only on his personal efforts, but also on his relationship to the provincial culture. As a child of New England, he had imbibed the jeremiad tradition, a series of ideas that suggested the uniqueness of the American colonies. But in converting to the Church of England, he had self-consciously rejected many of those notions. For the mature Johnson, therefore, the concept of the English "nation" embraced all members of the British Empire, regardless of their geographic residence. Moreover, he now believed that the English "nation," not just the children of Puritanism, enjoyed the special favor of God.

These attitudes governed Samuel Johnson's understanding of the French and Indian War, which erupted in 1754, shortly before he moved to New York City. Early in the war, when French victories struck terror through the colonies, Johnson explained the defeats as a divine scourge for the sins of the people. What else could be expected, he asked in a fast-day sermon, "but that God would . . . [interpose] his providence [to] chastise and awaken this stupid age." As the fortunes of war improved, Johnson again pointed to the providential hand of God. By 1763, then, when the British had effectively removed the French together with the Roman Catholic religion from the Canadian wilderness, Samuel Johnson, like other loyal Protestants, anticipated a reinvigoration of Christian godliness.[7]

The conclusion of the Great War for Empire also promised to stabilize relations between Great Britain and her American colonies. For Samuel Johnson such harmony might facilitate major revisions of the British Empire, including the appointment of an American episcopate. Like his friend Benjamin Franklin—whose Albany "Plan of Union" had been rejected by the colonies in 1754—Johnson had long condemned the autonomy of the colonial legislatures, a political situation that had enabled Connecticut authorities to discriminate against provincial Anglicans. In 1760, therefore, Johnson drafted an imperial scheme, based on Franklin's earlier plan, and transmitted it for publication in England. Stressing the close relationship between "our ancient mother country" and her colonial "daughters," the Anglican prelate recommended the royalization of all the charter governments and suggested a curtailment of popular participation in provincial politics. "The people are nearly rampant in their high notions of liberty," he objected, "and thence perpetually running into intrigue and faction."[8] Johnson's call for constitutional changes reflected forty years of political impotence, four decades of discrimination at the hands of the congregational establishment. But by linking the episcopal cause to imperial reform, he inadvertently destroyed the likelihood of success.

The episcopal authorities in England had advised Johnson to work for an American bishop quietly, by soothing the fears of dissenters, by reaffirming the Church's commitment to religious toleration, by avoiding direct confrontation. Colonial Anglicans chafed at the restraint. If our opponents have achieved "this pitch of influence," declared Henry Caner ominously, "poor England cannot be far from some sad revolution."[9] The issue climaxed in a vitriolic pamphlet war between the SPG's missionary at Cambridge, Massachusetts, and a prominent Congregational preacher of Boston,

Jonathan Mayhew.[10] From his retirement in Stratford, Samuel Johnson entered the debate, writing a lengthy appendix to Caner's brief against Mayhew. "We are neither French, nor Indians, nor Serpents, nor Dragons," Johnson assured his opponent. "Is this not our country . . . as well as yours? . . . Have we not all one common interest . . . being embarked in the same bottom?"[11] Despite such logic, the Congregationalists remained unimpressed. In the public mind, the dispute underscored the intimate relationship between political liberty and the appointment of bishops.

The persistent sniping at the Church of England troubled Johnson greatly, and the failure of the royal government to support the besieged minority in New England aggravated his frustration. "I am afraid that both the Bible and the episcopate . . . are both very fast sinking together in this apostatizing age," he asserted, intertwining these two very personal concerns. The nation "has almost lost all thoughts of another world," he complained, "and considers religion itself only a mere worldly thing." A reinvigoration of the episcopacy, however, might yet preserve the Christian cause in the face of this widespread indifference.[12] Such imperatives persuaded Johnson to devote his largest efforts to the establishment of an American diocese.

In this decision Johnson seriously miscalculated the temper of the country. For the conclusion of the French and Indian War had also convinced royal authorities that they should reform the imperial administration. Seeking to raise revenue to finance the expanded Empire, the British Parliament had passed what Samuel Johnson called "two very ill judged acts." The first, the Sugar Act of 1764, sought, in Johnson's words, "to raise unreasonable duties on our trade," while the Stamp Act of 1765 enforced a "severe stamp duty upon us." As these statements indicate, Johnson clearly dissented from the parliamentary legislation. So too did many of his Connecticut neighbors, who initiated mass protests, mob violence, and widespread "tumults." Meanwhile, Johnson's son, now an eminent lawyer in the province, drafted a petition for the Connecticut Assembly and represented the colony in the Stamp Act Congress held in New York City.[13]

Samuel Johnson's opposition, however, flowed from different motives from those of his revolutionary contemporaries. What upset him most about the legislation was not its violation of American rights—he had, after all, made even more extravagant constitutional proposals himself—but rather its impact upon provincial politics. The spontaneous dissent—which eventually forced Parliament to repeal the law—aimed at all British interference in the colonies. The episcopal cause no less than the revenue legislation became suspect because American protesters linked both issues to the same tyrannical rulers. By raising a "clamor," therefore, the American patriots imperiled Johnson's deepest commitments.

A more prudent man might have suffered in silence. But Johnson, now approaching the end of his life, could not afford to wait. Thus while the repeal of the Stamp Act in 1766 was filling the colonies with jubilation, Johnson was seizing the opportunity to reapply for a bishop. "Will our dear mother country have no bowels of compassion for her poor depressed, destitute children," he pleaded. Certainly, now, when "all America [is] over-flowing with joy," he cried, it was time to act.[14] Johnson's alacrity, besides betraying his personal impatience, also reflected an altered tone among other colonial Anglicans, a movement stimulated by the emergence of such aggressive young Churchmen as Johnson's protégé from New Jersey, Thomas Bradbury Chandler. These vigorous clergymen, convinced of the equity of their appeals, now hoped to obtain a bishop by loudly advocating their point.[15]

These efforts, however, proved disastrous for the episcopal cause. Instead of convincing "dissenting" Americans of the reasonableness of their requests, the Anglicans raised the specter of further English interference in colonial affairs. Such perceptions, distorted though they may have been, nevertheless alarmed Americans everywhere. "Our religious privileges and civil liberties are inseparably connected," declared one Connecticut minister.[16] Thus the Anglican proposal fanned the flames of colonial discord, virtually eliminating the possibility of an episcopal appointment.

These protests were extremely influential in English political circles. But the real problem, as the American churchmen soon discovered, was the religious apathy of the mother country. William Samuel Johnson, representing Connecticut in a complex legal dispute in England, reported how factional controversy within the government precluded the possibility of obtaining an American bishop. When Chandler published a strenuous plea for a bishop, William Samuel merely remarked that it would "have no effect in this country." Instead, he urged American Anglicans "to stand upon their own ground," and he advised his aging parent to be "satisfied that you have done all you can." British politicians, the colonial agent realized, had little time and less interest in American affairs.[17]

William Samuel Johnson's denunciation of the spiritual climate of the mother country confirmed his father's worst fears about "the miserable condition of the times." "The truth is," he asserted sadly, "I [would] rather now leave a family in America than in England."[18] For Samuel Johnson, the apparent decline of Christian virtue helped to explain the course of political events in England. William Samuel's descriptions of the machinations within the adminstration first perplexed the old man and then convinced him of the futility of reform. Even William Pitt, the hero of America, could not surmount "the rage of avarice, ambition, and lust."

From Connecticut Johnson looked with chagrin at the passage of such legislation as the Townshend Acts, which attempted to raise revenue by taxing certain commodities, and he prayed that a change in the English ministry would "be advantageous to America." Meanwhile, affairs in the colonies excited his fears about the future of the Empire. Parliamentary interference in the New York Assembly, the stationing of redcoats in Boston and, finally, the Boston Massacre in 1770 horrified the old man. As his son in London predicted "the destruction of all our harmony and happiness," the aged minister warned that "Old England and New will fall together, and both [will] become a prey to the House of Bourbon."[19]

The situation, desperate as it was, demanded one more action. And so the old minister, with his last energy, launched a final appeal to England. Stressing the intimate connection between "republicanism and antiepiscopal principles," Johnson beseeched the crown to provide "a uniform scheme of government for America, including . . . an episcopate." Otherwise, he declared ominously, "their principles all lead toward republicanism and independence of the mother country."[20]

Throughout his life, Samuel Johnson had extolled the grandeur of England—"that dear island," he had called it when his son first touched the European shores—and acknowledged the superiority of British institutions in church and state.[21] In his mind the colonies appeared as mere "children" or "daughters" of that older and finer "mother country." During his retirement, however, Johnson, like so many of his contemporaries, began to doubt the superiority of English culture. Infidelity and immorality seemed to pervade the capital, crippling any opportunity for reform. Worse still, England appeared unconcerned about the welfare of her colonial offspring; the parent was rejecting her children.

Johnson remained apprehensive about independence as his warnings to royal officials attest, and he preferred to preserve the bonds of Empire. Yet his anxiety about a political separation, perhaps awakening unconscious dreads of more primal separations, revealed a genuine ambivalence about the mother land. The unwillingness of English officials to support the American church, besides dashing Johnson's fondest dreams, radically affected the old man's understanding of his life's work. As his historical context changed—as, in other words, the imperial relationship began to collapse—Johnson's lifelong labors seemed to lose coherence. What would it mean, after all, to champion a Church of England in the colonies if America emerged as an independent nation?

Mercifully for Johnson, he never had to confront that question directly, for he died in 1772. Though the American Revolution had deep historical roots in provincial culture, there was, in Johnson's lifetime, nothing inevitable about a separation from England. Samuel Johnson lived in revolutionary times. But he himself never accepted the logic of colonial protest nor understood the future of his people. That clouded vision makes his dire forecasts even more poignant today.

But William Samuel Johnson, like other provincial sons, inherited the same dilemma, a paradoxical situation that the Stratford lawyer could not resolve either. With twisted loyalties and an ambivalent heart, Samuel Johnson's heir simply "retired" from politics in 1776, allowing more certain men to determine the future of his land. As he explained to a friend, he could not bring himself to separate from the "parent" state.[22]

When William Samuel Johnson sailed to England in 1765 to represent the Connecticut Assembly, he had already undergone inoculation for the smallpox and consequently he anticipated a pleasant, though brief, stay in the metropolis. Like provincial travelers before him, he raved about the wonders of the mother country, writing amusing descriptions of his encounters with English sophistication. Samuel Johnson advised the young man to retain "a just sense of the vanity of grandeur" and prayed that he soon would grow "weary of show." Yet the older man continued to encourage his son's explorations of the countryside, particularly William Samuel's visit to Yorkshire where he located some of the family's English relatives. Meanwhile, the intrigues of British politics delayed a resolution of the lawyer's business, permitting him to travel on the Continent–to France, Holland, and Flanders. "You are now grown so wonted to the grandeur and delicacies" of Europe, the parent chided his son, that "home, when you see it, will look mean and despicable. . . . However," he added, "I believe you will be glad to see it."[23]

Johnson's statement, undoubtedly the wishful thinking of an aging father, revealed his growing concern about the absence of his only son. Each season, just as William Samuel contemplated a return to Connecticut, a recess in London prolonged the affair. Reflecting about his child, the old minister doodled idly on the back of letters, unconsciously scrawling "London" across the addresses, in effect, readdressing the missives "to the Rev. Dr. Samuel Johnson at London," perhaps the place where he desired to be.[24] As months passed into years, Johnson's longings became more vocal and, in a "pathetic" message, he appealed to the governor of the colony to recall his son. Little could be done to expedite the matter, however, and it was not until October 1771, after nearly five years' absence, that William Samuel Johnson returned to Stratford. The reunion brought "unspeakable comfort and satisfaction" to his father, easing immeasurably the loneliness of old age. From Boston, Henry Caner congratulated his colleague on William Samuel's return and prayed for their mutual well-being. "God preserve you, my good brother," he wrote to his comrade, "and prepare both you and me for his good pleasure."[25]

Samuel Johnson passed his seventy-fifth birthday shortly after his son's return and seemed to enjoy a "comfortable state of health." The running sores on his legs, which had forced him to hire a ministerial assistant, had abated somewhat. But an arthritic hand interfered with his writing, forcing him to dictate his letters. Yet the old man retained his intellectual vigor, following the course of current events, pursuing his scholarly activities, and even drafting a short defense of the Church of England against the diatribes of one of his Congregational foes. The ravages of time nevertheless cramped his activity, slowly narrowing his circle of interests to the family that surrounded him.[26]

As he approached the end of his life, the aged minister spoke often of his death, mentioning his wish to die peacefully in the manner of his mentor, Bishop Berkeley. On the morning of the Epiphany, January 6, 1772, he repeated this desire while speaking with his family. Then he lit his pipe, enjoying the smoky aroma, and "conversed cheerfully" for a while. Ten minutes later, "without a struggle or a groan," the old man expired in his chair. Mourning the loss of "*so good* a father and so good a friend," William Samuel Johnson found reason "to rejoice in the noble manner in which he finished his course and triumphed over the King of Terrors. . . . His exit," the bereaved son acknowledged, "was precisely such as a wise and good man could wish for."[27]

Three days later, friends and family crowded into Christ's Church in Stratford to bid farewell to the clergyman. Jeremiah Leaming, a young pastor whom Johnson had assisted, preached the eulogy. "He was well known and approved in the learned world; was regarded and honored in our mother country, and revered and beloved in his native land," Leaming intoned, praising Samuel Johnson's achievements. "His true character may be [comprised] in three words, he was the gentleman, the scholar, and the Christian." Several weeks later John Beach, one of Samuel Johnson's closest colleagues, presented another encomium to the senior episcopalian of the province. Stressing the dead man's intellectual achievement, he praised his learning, his dedication to education, and particularly his love of Hebrew studies. "The sum is this," Beach concluded, "he was the most excellent scholar, and most accomplished divine that this colony ever had to glory in; and what is infinitely more excellent, he was an eminent Christian."[28]

And Samuel Johnson, the wise and the virtuous, was laid to rest.

In the autumn of 1721 Governor Gurdon Saltonstall, Deputy Governor Joseph Talcott, and the other members of the Connecticut General Assembly—the most eminent leaders of their communities, men full of years and experience—had listened respectfully to a twenty-five-year-old pastor from nearby West Haven preach on the subject of aging. With irony in their minds, the seasoned politicians heard the young minister depict the despair and disappointment of old age, the disgust at "our hot youth's folly," the disillusionment with the other stages of life. Old age, the lecturer affirmed, "is dissatisfied with almost everything it meets with," filled as it is "with uneasy reflections upon what is past and out of its reach," overwhelmed "with anxious fears about what is to come."[29] The older men sat quietly, wondering inevitably about themselves, their pasts, their futures.

Forty-two years later—a veritable lifetime of experience—Samuel Johnson rested in the peace of "sweet retirement" and contemplated these questions anew. Scanning a piece called "Osian's Address to the Sun," he paused to copy some "Reflections on Old Age and Death."[30] "But it is only this decaying body that can fade and die," he noted; "my soul which only is myself shall continue to live, to think and act, and flourish in immortal youth." Then, turning his paper over, the old minister added, "as for me, O my God, my continuance here can be but short. I must soon put off this earthly tabernacle." These words—not of despair and disappointment, not the result of "uneasy reflections" nor feelings of "anxious fears"—bespoke satisfaction, fulfillment, optimism. They invoked the spirit of a life well lived and the joyful expectation of a life to come, a future when the soul of this man would dwell forever "in unfading bliss, with the universal father of spirits" and "forever drink of the river of his pleasure."

NOTES

1. Myles Cooper to the Archbishop of Canterbury, June 23, 1763, SJ to the Archbishop of Canterbury, August 10, 1763, *SJ Papers,* 4: 99, 3: 274; SJ to WSJ, January 11, 1763, January 24, 1763, both in JCU, 2: SJ, "Autobiography," pp. 42, 45.

2. SJ, "Autobiography," p. 42; SJ to the Archbishop of Canterbury, August 10, 1763, *SJ Papers,* 3: 274. Johnson wrote the autobiography between ca. 1768 and 1771, probably at the request of Thomas Bradbury Chandler, who used it as the basis of his biography of the Connecticut churchman. See Thomas Bradbury Chandler to SJ, February 1, 1766, in *Historical Magazine of the Protestant Episcopal Church* 32 (1963): 375.

3. SJ "Autobiography," pp. 42, 45–46; "Samuel Johnson's Will," January 1, 1767, in *SJ Papers,* 1: 57–58; [SJ], *The First Easy Rudiments of Grammar, Applied to the English Tongue* (New York, 1765), title page and preface; SJ to Edward Nicoll, February 2, 1762, and to Stephen Sewall, March 1, 1768, JCU, 2, 3. Johnson's grammar also contained an appendix (pp. 29–36) embracing "A Synopsis of all the Parts of Learning," yet another of his attempts to reduce all knowledge to brief, orderly formulae.

4. SJ to the Archbishop of Canterbury, October 10, 1763, JCU, 2; SJ to SPG, April 5, 1771, SPG MSS, ser. B, v. 23, no. 204; SJ, Concio ad Clerum: A Sermon, JCU, pp. 9–10 (notes added after 1763). The growth of the Church of England is described in Frederick V. Mills, "Anglican Expansion in Colonial America, 1761–1775," *Historical Magazine of the Protestant Episcopal Church* 39 (1970): 315–24. Johnson himself explained the Church's growth on the basis of the quarrels among the dissenting churches; see SJ to the Bishop of London, July 15, 1765, *SJ Papers,* 1: 353.

5. WSJ to SJ, April 2, 1764, in E. Edwards Beardsley, *Life and Times of William Samuel Johnson, LL.D.* (New York, 1876), pp. 29–30; Joshua Bloom to SJ, February 11, 1768, SJ to WSJ, November 12, 1768, JCU, 3; SJ to SPG, June 11, 1770, *HP,* 2: 136; SJ to SPG, April 5, 1771, SPG MSS, ser. B, v. 23, no 204.

6. SJ, *The Christian Indeed; Explained, in Two Sermons* (New Haven, Conn., 1768), p. 7; Six Sermons on Psalm XXXVI, July-August 1766, *SJ Papers,* 3: 576–77, 585–86.

7. SJ, A Sermon: On the Fast to Implore God's Blessing on the Expedition against Niagara, May 21, 1756; *A Demonstration . . ., SJ Papers,* 3: 549, 551–52, 565–66, 571; Sermon Concerning Keeping the Heart, postscript dated September 5, 1756, JCU; "Two Collects" [May 1756]; "A Prayer for the Church and Kingdom" [1756], *SJ Papers,* 3: 640, 641. The following prayer is also relevant: "Bless Great Britain and all the dependencies and these her colonies on this continent in particular. Let religion and literature, wisdom and piety, peace and plenty, harmony and quiet, public virtue and private integrity flourish and increase among us, —Make us a peculiar people . . ., a people whom the Lord will delight to bless. . . ." Collection of Prayers, undated, JCU.

8. SJ to Archbishop of Canterbury, July 12, 1760, and "Questions Relating to the Union and Government of the Plantations" [July 1760], *SJ Papers,* 1: 295, 298–301. The Albany Plan is printed in Franklin, *Papers,* 5: 374–92.

9. Archbishop of Canterbury to SJ, September 27, 1758, *SJ Papers,* 3: 260; Henry Caner to SJ, April 24, 1759, Henry Caner Letter Book.

10. The controversy is explained in Charles W. Akers, *Called unto Liberty: a Life of Jonathan Mayhew, 1720–1766* (Cambridge, Mass., 1964).

11. [Henry Caner], *A Candid Examination of Dr. Mayhew's Observations* (Boston, 1763) included SJ, "A Letter to a Friend," pp. 79–80, 89–90.

12. SJ to Archbishop of Canterbury, September 5, 1765, *SJ Papers,* 1: 355.

13. SJ, "Autobiography," pp. 44–45; SJ to Archbishop of Canterbury, September 5, 1765, *SJ Papers,* 1: 355. The Anglican minister shared many of the political values of the protesters. Thus in his English grammar, written during 1765, he remarked, "a *King* should be not the *Tyrant,* but the Father of his People"; *First Easy Rudiments,* p. 5. William Samuel Johnson's revolutionary position is described in Groce, *William Samuel Johnson* and William Allen Benton, *Whig-Loyalism: An Aspect of Political Ideology in the American Revolutionary Era* (Rutherford, N.J., 1969).

14. SJ, "Autobiography," p. 47; SJ to Archbishop of Canterbury, May 2, 1766, *SJ Papers* 1: 361; Morgan Dix, *A History of the Parish of Trinity Church in the City of New York* (New York, 1898), p. 314; SJ to the Bishop of London, July 15, 1766, *HP,* 2: 94; Clergy of Connecticut to Bishop of London, October 8, 1766, Fulham MSS.

15. Publications by Anglicans brought counterpublications from their opponents, producing a large literature on the subject of the bishopric. The controversy is described in Cross, *Anglican Episcopate;* for a bibliography, see William Nelson, *The Controversy over the Proposition for an American Episcopate, 1767–1774. A Bibliography of the Subject* (Paterson, N.J., 1909).

16. Joseph Perry, quoted in Peter N. Carroll, ed., *Religion and the Coming of the American Revolution* (Waltham, Mass., 1970), p. 124.

17. SJ, "Autobiography," p. 48; SJ to Sir William Johnson, November 1, 1766, Peter Force MSS; WSJ to SJ, April 4, 1767, January 9, 1768, September 12, 1769 in Beardsley, *William Samuel Johnson,* pp. 39, 52–53, 66–67; WSJ to SJ, August 12, 1768 in Beardsley, *Samuel Johnson,* pp. 322–23.

18. SJ to WSJ, October 7, 1768, JCU, 3; SJ to WSJ, October 5, 1767, April 22, 1768, *SJ Papers,* 1: 420–21, 439.

19. SJ to WSJ, June 8, 1767, September 22, 1767, March 7, 1769, *SJ Papers,* 1: 404, 418, 452–53; WSJ to SJ, August 12, 1768, [April 1769], in Beardsley, *Samuel Johnson,* pp. 322–23, 338; WSJ to SJ, April 4, 1767, in Beardsley, *William Samuel Johnson,* p. 39; SJ to WSJ, March 14, 1768, JCU, 3; Henry Caner to SJ, April 23, 1770, Henry Caner Letter Book.

20. Charles Inglis to SJ, December 4, 1770, JHP; SJ to Myles Cooper, [1771], JCU, 3.

21. SJ to WSJ, February 11, 1767, *SJ Papers,* 1: 392.

22. See Benton, *Whig-Loyalism.*

23. SJ, "Autobiography," pp. 48–49; SJ to WSJ, April 24, 1767, October 17, 1767, September 5, 1769, *SJ Papers,* 1: 400, 423–24, 459–60; SJ to WSJ, January 18, 1768, March 14, 1768, JCU, 3.

24. The doodles appear repeatedly; see, e.g., Charles Inglis to SJ, March 22, 1768, February 5, 1771, June 17, 1771, JHP. On one letter the clergyman wrote "York" as well as "London"; on others, the letter "L" spreads across the page. See also chap. 5.

25. Jonathan Trumbull to SJ, January 22, 1770, Trumbull MSS, Connecticut Historical Society; SJ, "Autobiography," p. 49; Henry Caner to SJ, November 1, 1771, Henry Caner Letter Book.

26. Henry Caner to SJ, November 1, 1771, Henry Caner Letter Book; SJ to WSJ, January 25, 1770, JCU; S.J. to SPG, November 7, 1768, SPG MSS, ser. B, v. 23, no. 198; Charles Inglis to SJ, December 14, 1771, JHP.

27. WSJ to George Berkeley, January 13, 1772, JYU; WSJ to Bishop Lowth, January 13, 1772, *SJ Papers,* 1: 486; WSJ to James Duane, March 16, 1772, in Beardsley, *William Samuel Johnson,* pp. 206–7.

28. Jeremiah Leaming, *The True Christian's Support under Affliction* (New Haven, Conn., 1772), p. 15; John Beach, *A Funeral Sermon. . . .* (New Haven, Conn., [1772]), pp. 14–15, 17.

29. See above, chap. 1 n. 5.

30. Johnson's notes are in *SJ Papers,* 2: 602–3. It was probably written in 1763; see SJ to Peter Jay, October 27, 1763, in Monaghan, "Letters."

BIBLIOGRAPHY

Bibliographical Note: Samuel Johnson's passion for organization led him to accumulate and preserve a vast store of personal manuscripts. Some of his letters—particularly his correspondence to his wife—have been lost, perhaps during the war for independence. However, a large body of material remains in various archives, especially in the Samuel Johnson Manuscripts held by Columbia University. Many of Johnson's papers have been published in Herbert and Carol Schneider, eds., *Samuel Johnson: President of King's College: His Career and Writings,* 4 vols. (New York, 1929). The last volume of this edition also contains a calendar of the Johnson papers that unfortunately has numerous inaccuracies and omissions. I have deposited an annotated revision of this calendar in Butler Library, Columbia University. The following bibliography comprises those sources which have been most helpful in preparing this study.

Manuscripts

Church Historical Society, Austin, Texas
- Samuel Johnson MSS, Hawks Papers (microfilm)
- William Smith MSS, Hawks Papers (microfilm)

Columbia University
- Samuel Johnson MSS
- King's College MSS

Connecticut Historical Society, Hartford, Connecticut
- Trumbull MSS
- William Samuel Johnson MSS

Connecticut State Library, Hartford, Connecticut
- Guilford. First Congregational Church Records, 1
- Guilford. Probate Records
- New Haven. Probate Records
- Stratford. Records of the First Episcopal Church

Guilford Town Hall, Guilford, Connecticut
Guilford Town Records
Historical Society of Pennsylvania, Philadelphia, Pa.
Miscellaneous MSS
Houghton Library, Harvard University
Miscellaneous MSS
Lambeth Palace, London, England
Fulham MSS
Library of Congress
Peter Force MSS
Society for the Propagation of the Gospel MSS (microfilm)
New Haven Colony Historical Society
"Copies from the Papers of Rev. Samuel Johnson D. D.,"
Smyth MSS
New-York Historical Society
Nicholas Bayard MSS
"Copies of Letters of Timothy Cutler and Others to Dr. Zachary Grey"
New York Public Library
"Correspondence of Samuel and W. Samuel Johnson," Bancroft Transcriptions
Wills Memorial Library, University of Bristol, Bristol, England
Letter Book of Henry Caner, 1728–1778
Yale University
Samuel Johnson MSS

Printed Primary Sources

Adams, Eliphalet. *A Funeral Discourse Occasioned by the much Lamented Death of the Honourable Gurdon Saltonstall.* New London, Conn., 1724.

Beach, John. *A Calm and Dispassionate Vindication of the Professors of the Church of England.* Boston, 1749.

———. *A Continuation of the Calm and Dispassionate Vindication of the Church of England.* Boston, 1751.

———. *A Funeral Sermon, upon the Decease of the Reverend Doct. Samuel Johnson.* New Haven, Conn., [1772].

Beardsley, E. Edwards. *Life and Correspondence of Samuel Johnson, D.D.* New York, 1874.

Berkeley, George. *The Works of George Berkeley, Bishop of Cloyne.* Edited by A. A. Luce and T. E. Jessop. 9 vols. London, 1948–57.

Buckingham, Stephen. *The Unreasonableness and Danger of a Peoples renouncing their Subjection to God.* New London, Conn., 1711.

[Caner, Henry.] *A Candid Examination of Dr. Mayhew's Observations on the Charter and Conduct of the Society for the Propagation of the Gospel.* Boston, 1763.

Carroll, Peter N., ed. *Religion and the Coming of the American Revolution.* Waltham, Mass., 1970.

[Chandler, Thomas Bradbury.] "Documentary History of the American Church: Six Letters of Thomas Bradbury Chandler." *Historical Magazine of the Protestant Episcopal Church* 32 (1963): 371–91.

Chauncey, Nathaniel. *Honouring God the True Way to Honour.* New London, Conn., 1719.

Colden, Cadwallader. *The Letters and Papers of Cadwallader Colden.* 9 vols. New York, 1918–37.

Cotton, John. "Gods Promise to His Plantations." [London, 1630.] *Old South Leaflets* 3. Boston, n.d.

Cutler, Timothy. *The Firm Union of a People Represented.* New London, Conn., 1717.

———. "An Anglican Critique of the Early phase of the Great Awakening in New England: A Letter by Timothy Cutler" Edited by Douglas C. Stenerson. *William & Mary Quarterly* 30 (1973): 475–88.

Dexter, Franklin Bowditch, ed. *Documentary History of Yale University.* New Haven, Conn., 1916.

———. *New Haven Town Records.* 2 vols. New Haven, Conn., 1917–19.

Dickinson, Jonathan. *A Vindication of God's Sovereign Free Grace.* Boston, 1746.

Douglass, William. *A Summary, Historical and Political of the First Planting, Progressive Improvements, and Present State of the British Settlements in North America.* 2 vols. Boston, 1755.

Eliot, Jared. *Essays Upon Field Husbandry in New England.* Edited by Harry J. Carman and Rexford G. Tugwell. New York, 1934.

"A Faithful Relation of a Late Occurrence in the Churches of New-England," *Collections of the Massachusetts Historical Society,* 2d ser., 2 (1814): 137–38.

Fiske, Phineas. *The Good Subjects' Wish, or, The Desireableness of the Divine Presence with Civil Rulers.* New London, Conn., 1726.

Fordyce, David. *Dialogues Concerning Education.* 2 vols. 2d ed. London, 1745–48.

Franklin, Benjamin. *The Autobiography of Benjamin Franklin.* Edited by Jesse Lemisch. New York, 1961.

———. *The Papers of Benjamin Franklin.* Edited by Leonard Labaree et al. 15 vols. New Haven, Conn., 1959–.

[Graham, John.] *Some Remarks upon a late Pamphlet entitled, A Letter From a Minister of the Church of England.* [Boston], 1733.

———. *Some Remarks upon a Second Letter From the Church of England Minister to His Dissenting Parishioners.* Boston, 1736.

Greven, Philip J., ed. *Child-Rearing Concepts, 1628–1861: Historical Sources.* Itasca, Ill., 1973.

Hale, John. *A Modest Enquiry Into the Nature of Witchcraft.* [Boston, 1702.] In *Narratives of the Witchcraft Cases: 1648–1706,* edited by George Lincoln Burr, New York, 1914.

Hawks, Francis L., and Perry, William Stevens, eds. *Documentary History of the Protestant Episcopal Church in Connecticut.* 2 vols. New York, 1863–64. Facsimile ed. Hartford, Conn., 1959.

Hubbard, William. *The Happiness of a People.* Boston, 1676.

Johnson, Samuel. *Samuel Johnson: President of King's College: His Career and Writings.* Edited by Herbert and Carol Schneider. 4 vols. New York, 1929.

———. *The Christian Indeed; Explained in Two Sermons, of Humility and Charity.* New-Haven, Conn., 1768.

———. *An English and Hebrew Grammar, Being The first short Rudiments of those Two Languages Taught Together.* [London], 1765.

———. *A Demonstration of the Reasonableness, Usefulness, and Great Duty of Prayers.* New York, 1760.

———. *The First Easy Rudiments of Grammar, Applied to the English Tongue.* New York, 1765.

———. *An Introduction to the Study of Philosophy.* 2d ed. New London, Conn., 1743.

———. *A Sermon concerning the Obligations We are under to Love and Delight in the Public Worship of God.* Boston, 1746.

Knight, Sarah. *The Journal of Madame Knight.* New York, 1935.

Leaming, Jeremiah. *The True Christian's Support Under Affliction, a Sermon Preached . . . at the Funeral of the Rev. Samuel Johnson, D.D.* New Haven, Conn., 1772.

[Livingston, William, et al.] *The Independent Reflector.* Edited by Milton M. Klein. Cambridge, Mass., 1959.

[Lloyd Family.] *Papers of the Lloyd Family of the Manor of Queens Village.* 2 vols. New York, 1927.

Locke, John. *The Educational Writings of John Locke.* Edited by James L. Axtell. Cambridge, 1968.

Manwaring, Charles William, ed. *A Digest of the Early Connecticut Probate Records.* 3 vols. Hartford, Conn., 1904.

Mather, Azariah. *Good Rulers a Choice Blessing.* New London, Conn., 1725.

Mather, Cotton, *Magnalia Christi Americana; Or, The Ecclesiastical History of New-England.* 2 vols. Hartford, Conn., 1855.

Mather, Increase. *A Discourse Concerning the Danger of Apostasy.* Printed with *A Call From Heaven to the Present and Succeeding Generations.* Boston, 1679.

———. *The Order of the Gospel.* Boston, 1700.

———. "The Testimony Finished." Printed with *Elijah's Mantle: A Faithful Testimony to the Cause and Work of God in the Churches of New-England.* Boston, 1722.

Monaghan, Frank, ed. "Dr. Samuel Johnson's Letters to Peter Jay." *Columbia University Quarterly,* 25 (1933): 85–94.

Morgan, Edmund S., ed. *Puritan Political Ideas: 1558–1794.* Indianapolis, 1965.

Moss, Joseph. *An Election Sermon.* New London, Conn., 1715.

Prince, Thomas. *A Chronological History of New England In the form of Annals.* Boston, 1736.

Records [*of the*] *Town of Brookhaven* [*L.I.*], *up to 1800.* Patchogue, N.Y., 1880.

"Records of the Town of Newark [N.J.]." *Collections of the New Jersey Historical Society* 6 (1866).

[Ruggles, Thomas, Jr.] "Extract of a Letter," *Collections of the Massachusetts Historical Society,* 1st ser., 10 (1809): 90–101.

———. "A Sketch of a History of Guilford, in Connecticut." *Collections of the Massachusetts Historical Society,* 1st ser., 4 (1795): 182–88.

Saltonstall, Gurdon, *A Sermon Preached Before the General Assembly.* Boston, 1697.

Sewall, Samuel. "Diary of Samuel Sewall, 1674–1729." *Collections of the Massachusetts Historical Society,* 5th ser., 5–7 (1878–82).

[Smith, William.] *Some Thoughts on Education: With Reasons for Erecting a College.* New York, 1752.

"Some original papers respecting the Episcopal Controversy in Connecticut: 1722," *Collections of the Massachusetts Historical Society,* 2d ser., 2 (1814): 128–40.

[Stiles, Ezra.] *Extracts from the Itineraries and other Miscellanies.* Edited by Franklin Bowditch Dexter. New Haven, Conn., 1916.

———. *The Literary Diary of Ezra Stiles.* Edited by Franklin Bowditch Dexter. 3 vols. New York, 1901.

Stoddard, Solomon. "An Examination of the Power of the Fraternity." Printed with *The Presence of Christ with the Ministers of the Gospel.* Boston, 1718.

———. *The Way for a People to Live Long in the Land that God hath Given Them.* Boston, 1703.

"Talcott Papers." *Connecticut Historical Society Collections* 4–5 (1892–96).

Thomas, Milton Halsey, ed. "The Bible Record of William Samuel Johnson . . . and His Descendants." *New York Genealogical and Biographical Record* 70 (1939): 217–22.

Trumbull, J. Hammond, and Hoadley, Charles J., eds. *Public Records of the Colony of Connecticut.* 15 vols. Hartford, Conn., 1850–90.

[Wadsworth, Daniel.] *Diary of Rev. Daniel Wadsworth, Seventh Pastor of the First Church of Christ in Hartford, 1737–1747.* Edited by George Leon Walker. Hartford, Conn., 1894.

Wakeman, Samuel. *Sound Repentance. The Right Way to Escape Deserved Ruine.* Boston, 1685.

Walker, Williston, ed. *The Creeds and Platforms of Congregationalism.* New York, 1893.

[Wetmore, James, and Johnson, Samuel.] *Eleutherus Enervatus; Or an Answer to a Pamphlet, Intituled, The Divine Right of Presbyterian Ordination.* New York, 1733.

Whitefield, George. *George Whitefield's Journals.* London, 1960.

Whiting, John. *The Way of Israels Welfare.* Boston, 1686.

Whitman, Samuel. *Practical Godliness the Way to Prosperity.* New London, Conn., 1714.

Wigglesworth, Michael. "Autobiography." *New England Historical and Genealogical Register* 17 (1863); 137–38.

Williams, Eleazer. *An Essay to Prove that When God Once enters upon a Controversie with his professing People; He will manage and Issue it.* New London, Conn., 1723.

Winthrop, John. *Winthrop's Journal, "History of New England": 1630–1649.* Edited by James Kendall Hosmer. 2 vols. New York, 1908.

———. "A Modell of Christian Charity." In *Puritan Political Ideas: 1558–1794,* edited by Edmund S. Morgan. Indianapolis, Ind., 1965.

"Winthrop Papers." *Collections of the Massachusetts Historical Society*, 6th ser., 3 (1889).

Newspapers

Boston Gazette
Boston News-Letter
Boston Post-Boy
New-England Courant
New-York Gazette

Secondary Works

Abraham, Karl. "Some Remarks on the Role of Grandparents in the Psychology of Neurosis." In *Clinical Papers and Essays on Psycho-analysis,* edited and translated by Hilda C. Abraham. London, 1955.

Akers, Charles W. *Called unto Liberty: a Life of Jonathan Mayhew, 1720–1766.* Cambridge, Mass., 1964.

Alexander, Franz. "Remarks about the Relation of Inferiority Feelings to Guilt Feelings." *International Journal of Psychoanalysis* 19 (1938): 41–49.

Andrews, William. *A History of Christ Episcopal Church in Guilford, Connecticut.* Guilford, Conn., 1895.

Bailey, Rosalie Fellows. *The Nicoll Family and Islip Grange.* Order of Colonial Lords of Manors in America, Publications, no. 29. New York, 1940.

Bailyn, Bernard. *Education in the Forming of American Society.* Chapel Hill, N.C., 1960.

———. *The Ideological Origins of the American Revolution.* Cambridge, Mass., 1967.

———. *The New England Merchants in the Seventeenth Century.* Cambridge, Mass., 1955.

———. *The Origins of American Politics.* New York, 1968.

Barnett. H. G. *Innovation: The Basis of Cultural Change.* New York, 1953.

Beardsley, E. Edwards. *The History of the Episcopal Church in Connecticut.* 2 vols. New York, 1865–68.

———. *Life and Times of William Samuel Johnson, LL.D.* New York, 1876.

Benton, William Allen. *Whig-Loyalism: An Aspect of Political Ideology in the American Revolutionary Era.* Rutherford, N.J., 1969.

Blake, S. L. "Gurdon Saltonstall, Scholar, Preacher, Statesman." *Records and Papers of the New London County Historical Society* 1, pt. 5 (1894): 3–28.

Blos, Peter. *On Adolescence: A Psychoanalytic Interpretation.* New York, 1962.

Bolton, Robert. *History of the Protestant Episcopal Church in the County of Westchester.* New York, 1855.

Bowlby, John. "Separation Anxiety." *International Journal of Psychoanalysis* 41 (1960): 89–113.

Breen, T. H. *The Character of the Good Ruler: A Study of Puritan Political Ideas in New England, 1630–1730.* New Haven, Conn., 1970.

Bridenbaugh, Carl. *Mitre and Sceptre: Transatlantic Faiths, Ideas, Personalities, and Politics, 1689–1775.* New York, 1962.

Broxap, Henry. *The Later Non-Jurors.* Cambridge, 1924.

Bumsted, J. M. "Religion, Finance, and Democracy in Massachusetts: The Town of Norton as a Case Study." *Journal of American History* 57 (1971): 817–31.

Bushman, Richard L. *From Puritan to Yankee: Character and the Social Order in Connecticut, 1690–1765.* Cambridge, Mass., 1967.

Bushnell, George Eleazer. *Bushnell Family Genealogy.* Nashville, Tenn., 1945.

Calam, John. *Parsons and Pedagogues: The S.P.G. Adventure in American Education.* New York, 1971.

Calder, Isabel MacBeath *The New Haven Colony.* New Haven, Conn., 1934.

Carroll, Peter N. *Puritanism and the Wilderness: The Intellectual Significance of the New England Frontier, 1629–1700.* New York, 1969.

Caulfield, Ernest. "A History of the Terrible Epidemic, Vulgarly Called the Throat Distemper, as It Occurred in his Majesty's New England Colonies between 1735 and 1740." *Yale Journal of Biology and Medicine"* 11 (1938–39): 219–72, 277–335.

Chandler, Thomas B. *The Life of Samuel Johnson, the First President of King's College in New York.* New York, 1805.

Collinson, Patrick. *The Elizabethan Puritan Movement.* Berkeley, Calif., 1967.

Cowing, Cedric B. *The Great Awakening and the American Revolution: Colonial Thought in the 18th Century.* Chicago, 1971.

———. "Sex and Preaching in the Great Awakening." *American Quarterly* 20 (1968): 624–44.

Cremin, Lawrence A. *American Education: The Colonial Experience, 1607–1783.* New York, 1970.

Cross, Arthur Lyon. *The Anglican Episcopate and the American Colonies.* New York, 1902.

Davis, Kingsley. "The Sociology of Parent-Youth Conflict," *American Sociological Review* 5 (1940): 525–35.

DeMause, Lloyd, ed. *The History of Childhood.* New York, 1974.

Demos, John. "Developmental Perspectives on the History of Childhood." *Journal of Interdisciplinary History* 2 (1971): 315–27.

———. *A Little Commonwealth: Family Life in Plymouth Colony.* New York, 1970.

———. "Underlying Themes in the Witchcraft of Seventeenth-Century New England." *American Historical Review* 75 (1970): 1311–26.

———, and Demos, Virginia. "Adolescence in Historical Perspective." *Journal of Marriage and the Family* 31 (1969): 632–38.

Dexter, Franklin Bowditch. *Biographical Sketches of the Graduates of Yale College.* 6 vols. New York, 1885–1911.

Dickens, Arthur G. *The English Reformation.* London, 1964.

Dix, Morgan. *A History of the Parish of Trinity Church in the City of New York.* New York, 1898.

Dunn, Richard S. *Puritans and Yankees: The Winthrop Dynasty of New England, 1630–1717.* Princeton, N.J., 1962.

Eliade, Mircea. *Cosmos and History: The Myth of the Eternal Return.* Translated by Willard R. Trask, New York, 1959.

———. *Rites and Symbols of Initiation: The Mysteries of Birth and Rebirth.* New York, 1958.

Ellis, Joseph J., III. "Anglicans in Connecticut, 1725–1750: The Conversion of the Missionaries." *New England Quarterly* 44 (1971): 66–81.

———. "The Puritan Mind in Transition: The American Samuel Johnson (1696–1772)." Ph. D dissertation, Yale University, 1969. Since published as *The New England Mind in Transition.* New Haven, Conn., 1973.

———. "The Puritan Mind in Transition: The Philosophy of Samuel Johnson." *William & Mary Quarterly* 28 (1971): 26–45.

Erikson, Erik H. "Autobiographic Notes on the Identity Crisis." *Daedelus* 99 (1970): 730–59.

———. *Childhood and Society,* rev. ed. New York, 1963.

———. "Identity and the Life Cycle." *Psychological Issues* 1 (1959).

———. *Identity: Youth and Crisis.* New York, 1968.

———. *Young Man Luther: A Study in Psychoanalysis and History.* New York, 1958.

———. ed. *The Challenge of Youth.* Garden City, N.Y., 1965.

Erikson, Kai T. *Wayward Puritans: A Study in the Sociology of Deviance.* New York, 1966.

Every, George. *The High Church Party: 1688–1718.* London, 1956.

Feuer, Lewis S. *The Conflict of Generations: The Character and Significance of Student Movements.* New York, 1969.

Fiering, Norman S. "Moral Philosophy in America, 1700–1750, and Its British Context." Ph.D. dissertation, Columbia University, 1969.

———. "President Samuel Johnson and the Circle of Knowledge." *William & Mary Quarterly* 28 (1971): 199–236.

Foster, George M. "Peasant Society and the Image of Limited Good." *American Anthropologist* 67 (1965): 293–315.

Foster, Stephen. *Their Solitary Way: The Puritan Social Ethic in the First Century of Settlement in New England.* New Haven, Conn., 1971.

Fox, Dixon Ryan. *Caleb Heathcote: Gentleman Colonist; The Story of a Career in the Province of New York.* New York, 1926.

Freud, Anna. "The Ego and the Mechanisms of Defense." *The Writings of Anna Freud.* rev. ed. New York, 1966.

Freud, Sigmund. *The Future of an Illusion.* Translated by W. D. Robson-Scott. New York, 1955.

———. *The Psychopathology of Everyday Life.* Translated by Alan Tyson. New York, 1960.

Friedman, Bernard. "The Shaping of the Radical Consciousness in Provincial New York." *Jounal of American History* 56 (1970): 781–801.

Garfinkel, Harold. "Successful Degradation Ceremonies." *American Journal of Sociology* 61 (1956): 420–24.

Gaustad, Edwin Scott. *The Great Awakening in New England.* New York, 1957.

"Genealogical Notes" [Newark, N.J.]. *Collections of the New Jersey Historical Society* 6 (1866).

George, Charles H., and George, Katherine. *The Protestant Mind of the English Reformation, 1570–1640.* Princeton, N.J., 1961.

Goodwin, Gerald J. "The Anglican Reaction to the Great Awakening." *Historical Magazine of the Protestant Episcopal Church* 35 (1966): 343–71.

Grant, Charles S. *Democracy in the Connecticut Frontier Town of Kent.* New York, 1961.

Greene, Jack P. "Political Mimesis: A Consideration of the Historical and Cultural Roots of Legislative Behavior in the British Colonies in the Eighteenth Century." *American Historical Review* 75 (1969): 337–67.

———. "Search for Identity: An Interpretation of the Meaning of Selected Patterns of Social Response in Eighteenth-Century America." *Journal of Social History* 3 (1969–70): 189–224.

Greene, Maria L. *The Development of Religious Liberty in Connecticut.* Boston, 1905.

Greven, Philip J., Jr. *Four Generations: Population, Land, and Family in Colonial Andover, Massachusetts.* Ithaca, N.Y., 1970.

———. "Youth, Maturity, and Religious Conversion: A Note on the Age of Converts in Andover, Massachusetts, 1711–1749." *Essex Institute Historical Collections* 108 (1972): 119–34.

Groce, George C., Jr. *William Samuel Johnson: A Maker of the Constitution.* New York, 1937.

Hall, David D. "Understanding the Puritans." In *The State of American History,* Edited by Herbert Bass. Chicago, 1970.

Hall, Michael Garibaldi. *Edward Randolph and the American Colonies: 1676–1703.* Chapel Hill, N.C., 1960.

Haller, William. *The Rise of Puritanism.* New York, 1938.

Heath, Peter. *The English Parish Clergy on the Eve of the Reformation.* London, 1969.

Hindle, Brooke. "Cadwallader Colden's Extension of the Newtonian Principles." *William & Mary Quarterly* 13 (1956): 459–75.

Hornberger, Theodore. "Samuel Johnson of Yale and King's College: A Note on the Relation of Science and Religion in Provincial America." *New England Quarterly* 8 (1935): 378–97.

Humphrey, David Churchill. "King's College in the City of New York, 1754–1775." Ph.D. dissertation, Northwestern University, 1968.

James, William. *The Varieties of Religious Experience.* New York, 1902.

Jantz, Harold S. "The Factor of Generation in German Literary History." *Modern Language Notes* 52 (1937): 324–30.

Jones, Ernest. *Papers on Psychoanalysis.* rev. ed. New York, 1919.

Kardiner, Abram. *The Individual and His Society.* New York, 1939.

Keniston, Kenneth. "Psychological Development and Historical Change." *Journal of Interdisciplinary History* 2 (1971): 329–45.

Kenney, William Howland, 3d. "George Whitefield, Dissenter Priest of the Great Awakening. 1739–1741." *William & Mary Quarterly* 26 (1969): 75–93.

Kett, Joseph F. "Adolescence and Youth in Nineteenth-Century America." *Journal of Interdisciplinary History* 2 (1971): 283–98.

Kuhn, Thomas S. *The Structure of Scientific Revolutions.* rev. ed. Chicago, 1970.

Laing, R. D. *The Politics of the Family and Other Essays.* New York, 1971.

Laslett, Peter, *The World We Have Lost.* New York, 1965.

Lifton, Robert Jay. *Death in Life: Survivors of Hiroshima.* New York, 1967.

———. *History and Human Survival.* New York, 1971.

Lockridge, Kenneth A. "Land, Population and the Evolution of New England Society." *Past and Present* 39 (1968): 62–80.

———. *A New England Town. The First Hundred Years: Dedham, Massachusetts, 1636–1736.* New York, 1970.

Lucas, Paul Robert. "Valley of Discord: The Struggle for Power in the Puritan Churches of the Connecticut Valley, 1636–1720." Ph.D. dissertation, University of Minnesota, 1970.

Luce, A. A. *The Life of George Berkeley, Bishop of Cloyne.* London, 1949.

Lynd, Helen L. *On Shame and the Search for Identity.* New York, 1958.

McAnear, Beverly. "College Founding in the American Colonies, 1745–1775." *Mississippi Valley Historical Review* 42 (1955): 24–44.

MacDonald, Robert H. "The Frightful Consequences of Onanism: Notes on the History of a Delusion." *Journal of the History of Ideas* 28 (1967): 423–31.

Macfarlane, Alan. *The Family Life of Ralph Josselin: A Seventeenth-Century Clergyman. An Essay in Historical Anthropology.* Cambridge, 1970.

Mannheim, Karl. *Ideology and Utopia.* London, 1936.

———. "The Problem of Generations." *Essays on the Sociology of Knowledge,* edited by Paul Kecskemeti. London, 1952.

Mazlish, Bruce, ed. *Psychoanalysis and History.* Englewood Cliffs, N.J., 1963.

Mead, Margaret. "The Implications of Culture Change for Personality Development." *American Journal of Orthopsychiatry* 17 (1947): 633–46.

Mentré, François. *Les Générations sociales.* Paris, 1920.

Meyerhoff, Hans. "On Psychoanalysis as History." *Psychoanalysis and the Psychoanalytic Review* 49 (1962): 3–20.

Middlekauff, Robert. *The Mathers: Three Generations of Puritan Intellectuals, 1596–1728.* New York, 1971.

Miller, Perry. *Errand Into the Wilderness.* Cambridge, Mass., 1956.

———. *The New England Mind: From Colony to Province.* Cambridge, Mass., 1953.

———. *The New England Mind: The Seventeenth Century.* New York, 1939.

———. *Orthodoxy in Massachusetts, 1630–1650.* Cambridge, Mass., 1933.

Mills, Frederick V. "Anglican Expansion in Colonial America, 1761–1775." *Historical Magazine of the Protestant Episcopal Church* 39 (1970): 315–24.

Morgan, Edmund S. "The American Revolution Considered as an Intellectual Movement." In *Paths of American Thought,* edited by Arthur M. Schlesinger and Morton White. Boston, 1963.

———. *The Puritan Dilemma: The Story of John Winthrop.* Boston, 1958.

———. *The Puritan Family: Essays on Religion and Domestic Relations in Seventeenth-Century New England.* rev. ed. New York, 1966.

———. *Visible Saints: The History of a Puritan Idea.* New York, 1963.

Nelson, William. *The Controversy over the Proposition for an American Episcopate, 1767–1774. A Bibliography of the Subject.* Paterson, N.J. 1909.

New, John F. H. *Anglican and Puritan: The Basis of Their Opposition, 1558–1640.* Stanford, Calif., 1964.

Nisbet, Robert A. *Social Change and History: Aspects of the Western Theory of Development.* New York, 1969.

Ortega y Gasset, Jose. *What is Philosophy*? Translated by Mildred Adams. New York, 1960.

Pearson, Gerald H. J. *Adolescence and the Conflict of Generations: An Introduction to Some of the Psychoanalytic Contributions to the Understanding of Adolescence.* New York, 1958.

[Peters, Samuel.] *A General History of Connecticut.* London, 1781. Reprint. New Haven, Conn., 1829.

Piers, Gerhart, and Singer, Milton B. *Shame and Guilt: A Psychoanalytic and a Cultural Study.* Springfield, Ill., 1953.

Pope, Robert G. *The Half-Way Covenant: Church Membership in Puritan New England.* Princeton, N.J., 1969.

Powell, Sumner Chilton. *Puritan Village: The Formation of a New England Town.* Middletown, Conn., 1963.

Pyle, Kenneth B. *The New Generation in Meiji Japan: Problems of Cultural Identity, 1885–1895.* Stanford, Calif., 1969.

Rank, Otto. *The Myth of the Birth of the Hero: A Psychoanalytic Interpretation of Mythology.* Translated by F. Robbins and Smith Ely Jelliffe. New York, 1914.

Rapaport, David. "A Historical Survey of Psychoanalytic Ego Psychology." *Psychological Issues* 1 (1959): 5–17.

Renouard, Yves. "La Notion de génération en histoire." *Revue historique* 209 (1953): 1–23.

Robbins, Caroline. *The Eighteenth-Century Commonwealthman: Studies in the Transmission, Development and Circumstance of English Liberal Thought.* Cambridge, Mass., 1959.

Sachse, William L. *The Colonial American in Britain.* Madison, Wis., 1956.

Santayana, George. *The Life of Reason or the Phases of Human Progress.* New York, 1906.

Schumann, Detler W. "Cultural Age-Groups in German Thought." *Publications of the Modern Language Association* 51 (1936): 1180–1207.

Shepard, James. "The New Haven and Wallingford (Conn.) Johnsons." *New England Historical and Genealogical Register* 56 (1902): 132–40.

Sklar, Robert. "The Great Awakening and Colonial Politics: Connecticut's Revolution in the Minds of Men." *Connecticut Historical Society Bulletin* 28 (1963): 81–95.

Smith, R. D. *The History of Guilford, Connecticut, from Its First Settlement in 1639.* Albany, N.Y., 1877.

Steiner, Bernard Christian. *A History of the Plantation of Menunkatuck and of the Original Town of Guilford, Connecticut.* Baltimore, Md., 1897.

———. "Supplementary Notes on the Johnson Family." *New England Historical and Genealogical Register* 56 (1902): 297–98.

Steiner, Bruce E. "New England Anglicanism: A Genteel Faith?" *William & Mary Quarterly* 27 (1970): 122–35.

———. "Samuel Seabury and the Forging of the High Church Tradition: A Study in the Evolution of New England Churchmanship, 1722–1796." Ph.D. dissertation, University of Virginia, 1962.

Sykes, Norman. *Edmund Gibson, Bishop of London, 1669–1748: A Study in Politics & Religion in the Eighteenth Century.* Oxford, 1926.

———. *From Sheldon to Secker: Aspects of English Church History, 1660–1768.* Cambridge, 1959.

Talcott, Alvan. *Chittenden Family: William Chittenden of Guilford, Conn. and His Descendants.* New Haven, Conn., 1882.

Thompson, Benjamin F. *The History of Long Island from its Discovery and Settlement.* 2 vols. 2d ed. New York, 1843.

Trumbull, Benjamin. *A Complete History of Connecticut, Civil and Ecclesiastical.* 2 vols. Hartford, Conn., 1797; New Haven, Conn., 1818.

Tucker, Louis Leonard. *Puritan Protagonist: President Thomas Clap of Yale College.* Chapel Hill, N.C., 1962.

Tyerman, Luke. *The Life of the Rev. George Whitefield.* 2 vols. New York, 1877.

van den Berg, J. H. *The Changing Nature of Man: Introduction to a Historical Psychology.* New York, 1964.

Ver Steeg, Clarence L. *The Formative Years.* New York, 1964.

Walsh, James. "The Great Awakening in the First Congregational Church of Woodbury, Connecticut." *William & Mary Quarterly* 28 (1971): 543–62.

Walzer, Michael. "Puritanism as a Revolutionary Ideology." *History and Theory* 3 (1963): 59–90.

Warch, Richard. "Yale College: 1701–1740." Ph.D. dissertation, Yale University, 1968. Since published as *School of the Prophets.* New Haven, 1973.

Weinstein, Fred, and Platt, Gerald M. *The Wish to be Free: Society, Psyche, and Value Change.* Berkeley, Calif., 1969.

Wells, Laura Jay. *The Jay Family.* Order of Colonial Lords of Manors in America, Publications, no. 28. New York, 1938.

Wheelis, Allen. *The Quest for Identity.* New York, 1958.

White, Elizabeth Wade. *Anne Bradstreet: "The Tenth Muse."* New York, 1971.

Wilcoxson, William Howard. *History of Stratford, Connecticut, 1639–1939.* Stratford, Conn., 1939.

Wild, John. *George Berkeley: A Study of His Life and Philosophy.* Cambridge, Mass., 1936.

Woeful, James W. "William Wollaston's Religion of Nature and Samuel Johnson's System of Morality." *Historical Magazine of the Protestant Episcopal Church* 34 (1965): 239–64.

Index